Managing Microsoft Hybrid Clouds

Benefit from hybrid cloud scenarios through this detailed guide to Microsoft Azure Infrastructure Services (IaaS)

Marcel van den Berg

[PACKT] enterprise 88
PUBLISHING professional expertise distilled

BIRMINGHAM - MUMBAI

Managing Microsoft Hybrid Clouds

First published: March 2015

Production reference: 1260315

Published by Packt Publishing Ltd.
Livery Place
35 Livery Street
Birmingham B3 2PB, UK.

ISBN 978-1-78217-716-6

www.packtpub.com

Cover image by Pratyush Mohanta (tysoncinematics@gmail.com)

Credits

Author
Marcel van den Berg

Reviewers
V. K. Cody Bumgardner
Xander Oortgiesen
Dr. Rajeev Papneja
Bert Wolters
David Xie

Commissioning Editor
Antony Lowe

Acquisition Editor
James Jones

Content Development Editor
Anand Singh

Technical Editor
Faisal Siddiqui

Copy Editors
Roshni Banerjee
Pranjali Churi

Project Coordinator
Rashi Khivansara

Proofreaders
Simran Bhogal
Maria Gould
Paul Hindle

Indexer
Hemangini Bari

Production Coordinator
Manu Joseph

Cover Work
Manu Joseph

About the Author

Marcel van den Berg is an experienced IT professional with 25 years of experience. He is well known in both the VMware and Hyper-V community for his sharing of knowledge, mainly via his blog. He currently works as a consultant for PQR in the Netherlands, deploying many Microsoft solutions such as Microsoft Azure, Windows Server, Hyper-V, System Center, and StorSimple.

His career started in 1990 as a system administrator for Unix systems. As his career progressed, he was later responsible for managing Windows NT to infrastructures based on Windows Server 2008. About 6 years ago, Marcel focused on server virtualization and moved to the role of a consultant. Marcel designed and built numerous infrastructures based on VMware and Hyper-V for midsized and large organizations. He has experience in working with numerous VDI, SBC, backup, and disaster recovery solutions.

Cloud computing is one of the most exciting shifts we have ever seen in how we use IT. Marcel is really keen to understand new developments in cloud computing, especially on Infrastructure as a Service. In his current job, he has designed several infrastructures hosted on Microsoft Azure. By reading this book, you will learn from his experiences and save hours of work by preventing common mistakes.

He shares a lot of his knowledge on his website, `http://up2v.nl`. Marcel was awarded VMware vExpert for the help he has been giving the community since 2011.

You can follow Marcel on Twitter at `@marcelvandenber`.

I'd like to thank my family for allowing me to spend so much time on writing this book and being away from them. They have been a great help to make my dream come true. Writing a book is a true challenge and it took me many many hours to write and adjust this book to keep it up to date. Thanks Katja, I love you!

Also, I am grateful to the reviewers of this book. Without them, this book would not have been so good.

About the Reviewers

V. K. Cody Bumgardner has been in the IT industry for over 20 years. In this time, he has worked in technical, managerial, and sales roles in the areas of IT architecture, software development, networking, research, systems, and security.

Over the last several years, he has focused on researching, implementing, and speaking about cloud computing and computational economics. He is also currently pursuing a PhD in computer science at the University of Kentucky (UK), focusing on computational economics of cloud computing.

He currently serves as the Chief Technology Architect (CTA) and research computing service owner of a large public land-grant university. He is responsible for technology architectures supporting over 40,000 users in academic, research, and health care (academic) divisions.

He is also the author of *OpenStack in Action, Manning Publishing*.

Xander Oortgiesen has been working in different roles and functions and is currently working for Switch IT Solutions (www.switch.nl) in the Netherlands. Xander also works for his own IT consultancy company called Lorlon (www.lorlon.nl). Before working as a business consultant, he was active in the field as a technical consultant specialized in Microsoft Server, Cloud/Office 365, System Center Technologies, Storage, Virtualization Technologies (Hyper-V, VMware, XenServer), and Citrix.

Xander is a Citrix CCEE, RES RCP, VMware VCP/VCDA, MCSE NT4 — 2012 R2, and several Microsoft Specialties (Exchange, Hyper-V, System Center, and so on).

You can follow him on his blog (www.vWorld.nl) or contact him via Twitter (@vworlddotnl) or e-mail (xoo@vworld.nl).

Vision, purpose, relentless passion for technology, and life of spirituality — that's what **Dr. Rajeev Papneja** brings to the table, combined with over 18 years of extensive systems and software experience on an international scale, including more than 9 years of senior management experience in the United States. Prior to affiliating with bodHOST, in collaboration with his global partners, he founded a firm called Artilligence Inc., a well-respected name in Northeast America as a one-stop service center for all IT services ranging from turnkey software development to supplemental staffing. Employees sometimes refer to him as "a COO with a heart", because in the cut-throat war zone of corporate America, he refuses to compromise his humility, simplicity, sincerity, truthfulness, and loyalty to his co-workers. Dr. Papneja also serves as a COO at ESDS Software Solution Pvt. Ltd, a leading organization in the space of managed hosting and data center services.

A believer in a borderless new economy, his business focus is truly global, and that is what he achieved his doctorate in. His longest tenure was with Pfizer Pharmaceuticals, the largest drug manufacturer in the world with its current headquarters in New York, where he spent more than 7 years providing enterprise-class technology solutions and setting up financial processes.

Inspite of obtaining a master's degree in computer science at the age of 20, his zeal for education did not stop. Along with his professional career in the United States, he pursued his PhD in business administration, the highest honors he achieved at the age of 27. He has worked as a senior consultant at major corporations such as United Parcel Services, Ernst & Young, Dun & Bradstreet to name a few, before becoming an entrepreneur.

When he is not at work, he is usually serving the community and seeking spirituality. He believes in the future, loves his extended family of colleagues and associates, and has faith in his organization's ability to be a Fortune 100 company in his lifetime.

I would like to thank Mr. Probal Dasgupta (CEO, bodHOST) and Mr. Piyush Somani (CEO, ESDS Software Solutions Pvt Ltd) for giving me a perfect platform to use my skills to the best of my abilities and always being there for me as mentors and friends. I would like to thank my colleagues who encouraged me to go ahead with the initiative of reviewing and last but not least, my family and friends who sacrificed my daily association with them, many a time, for this project to get completed on time.

Bert Wolters is a Dutch senior technical consultant on Microsoft on-premises and cloud infrastructures. He started his professional life in the Dutch military, but around 1999, found his talents in IT, helping out the platoon and unit leaders with small IT issues in the field. By the time he started on his first Microsoft certification in 2005, he had found his new vocation in life.

His ability to look at all sides of a story (an issue, problem, and implementation) was formed by the wide variety of jobs he had. Having a background in the business side of IT as well as an incident and change manager, and in the field as an engineer and consultant, helps him deliver the most comprehensive solutions driven by businesses, technology, or business case.

Since 2010, he has specialized further in system management for Microsoft infrastructures and is still riding Microsoft's wave of innovation, looking forward to and experimenting with every single new feature of Microsoft Azure. Because of this focus, he decided to resign from the Dutch Powershell User Group (DuPSUg) when asked to take part in the System Center User Group in the Netherlands (SCUG_NL).

He currently advises companies on how to get the most out of System Center Suite and shares his knowledge on Microsoft's hybrid cloud, Hyper-V, Microsoft Azure, and StorSimple.

I would like to thank my girlfriend and daughters for putting up with all of my efforts to gain and share knowledge. I also thank Marcel van den Berg for accepting me in his team of reviewers.

I would also like to thank all of the people who inspired me over the years; people such as Marco Timmermans, Ernst Rijk, and Alex de Jong who were the first MCTs I encountered and are gravely responsible for my Microsoft addiction. My fellow members of the SCUG_NL community for accepting me in their midst; and Aidan Finn and Marc van Eijk for providing me with their seemingly unending knowledge and passion for technology. Someone who I can't thank enough for giving me insights into myself is Monique Kerssens, who trained me to become an MCT. Without learning from these people, in technology and socially, there is not a chance I could be doing what I'm doing today. It's because of them and others that I may not have listed here that every single day I get out of bed feeling compelled to give my best in my work.

David Xie spent 6 years as a software developer working mainly with Python and PHP, and he's familiar with OpenStack, Linux and web development.

He has worked at IBM for 3 years as a Python developer for OpenStack and currently works at ThoughtWorks bridging operations and software development.

www.PacktPub.com

Support files, eBooks, discount offers, and more

For support files and downloads related to your book, please visit www.PacktPub.com.

Did you know that Packt offers eBook versions of every book published, with PDF and ePub files available? You can upgrade to the eBook version at www.PacktPub.com and as a print book customer, you are entitled to a discount on the eBook copy. Get in touch with us at service@packtpub.com for more details.

At www.PacktPub.com, you can also read a collection of free technical articles, sign up for a range of free newsletters and receive exclusive discounts and offers on Packt books and eBooks.

![PACKTLIB logo]

https://www2.packtpub.com/books/subscription/packtlib

Do you need instant solutions to your IT questions? PacktLib is Packt's online digital book library. Here, you can search, access, and read Packt's entire library of books.

Why subscribe?

- Fully searchable across every book published by Packt
- Copy and paste, print, and bookmark content
- On demand and accessible via a web browser

Free access for Packt account holders

If you have an account with Packt at www.PacktPub.com, you can use this to access PacktLib today and view 9 entirely free books. Simply use your login credentials for immediate access.

Instant updates on new Packt books

Get notified! Find out when new books are published by following @PacktEnterprise on Twitter or the *Packt Enterprise* Facebook page.

Table of Contents

Preface

Microsoft Azure offers many new scenarios for providing applications, data, and infrastructure services. In this book, you will learn how to manage the infrastructure services offered by Azure and how to extend your on-premises infrastructure to the cloud.

What this book covers

Chapter 1, An Introduction to Cloud Computing, introduces the concepts of cloud computing and compares cloud to the usage of electricity as a utility.

Chapter 2, An Introduction to Microsoft Cloud Solutions, provides an overview of the Microsoft solutions that are used to build a hybrid cloud.

Chapter 3, Understanding the Microsoft Azure Architecture, explains the Azure components that are used to offer the Azure services. This chapter provides a look under the hood of Azure to understand how things work.

Chapter 4, Building an Infrastructure on Microsoft Azure, explains how to create storage and networking required to build your first virtual machine on Azure.

Chapter 5, Connecting to Microsoft Azure, deals with establishing connections with the Azure datacenter.

Chapter 6, Managing the Microsoft Hybrid Cloud, shows you how to manage the Azure Active Directory and carry out efficient management. This chapter will explain how PowerShell can be used to automate tasks.

Chapter 7, High Availability, Protection, and Recovery using Microsoft Azure, explains how Azure can be used to both protect on-premises servers and servers running on Azure.

Chapter 8, Migrating to Microsoft Azure, explains the tools that are available for the migration of servers to Azure.

Chapter 9, Summary and a Look into the Near Future, concludes this book and provides a look into the future of Azure.

Appendix, Configuration Maximums, provides an overview of the configuration maximums of Microsoft Azure.

What you need for this book

To be able to perform the procedures described in this book yourself, you need a Microsoft Azure account to start with. Such an account can easily be created. Also, you need at least a Hyper-V host with enough resources to run System Center Virtual Machine Manager and some additional virtual machines.

Who this book is for

This book is great for IT pros, IT managers, consultants and architects who want to learn about hybrid cloud computing using Microsoft Azure, System Center, and Windows Server. It will explain the benefits of a hybrid cloud, how to connect to it, and how to manage it.

Conventions

In this book, you will find a number of text styles that distinguish between different kinds of information. Here are some examples of these styles and an explanation of their meaning.

Code words in text, database table names, folder names, filenames, file extensions, pathnames, dummy URLs, user input, and Twitter handles are shown as follows: "We can include other contexts through the use of the `include` directive."

A block of code is set as follows:

```
[default]
exten => s,1,Dial(Zap/1|30)
exten => s,2,Voicemail(u100)
exten => s,102,Voicemail(b100)
exten => i,1,Voicemail(s0)
```

When we wish to draw your attention to a particular part of a code block, the relevant lines or items are set in bold:

```
[default]
exten => s,1,Dial(Zap/1|30)
exten => s,2,Voicemail(u100)
exten => s,102,Voicemail(b100)
exten => i,1,Voicemail(s0)
```

Any command-line input or output is written as follows:

```
# cp /usr/src/asterisk-addons/configs/cdr_mysql.conf.sample
   /etc/asterisk/cdr_mysql.conf
```

New terms and **important words** are shown in bold. Words that you see on the screen, for example, in menus or dialog boxes, appear in the text like this: "Clicking the **Next** button moves you to the next screen."

> Warnings or important notes appear in a box like this.

> Tips and tricks appear like this.

Reader feedback

Feedback from our readers is always welcome. Let us know what you think about this book—what you liked or disliked. Reader feedback is important for us as it helps us develop titles that you will really get the most out of.

To send us general feedback, simply e-mail feedback@packtpub.com, and mention the book's title in the subject of your message.

If there is a topic that you have expertise in and you are interested in either writing or contributing to a book, see our author guide at www.packtpub.com/authors.

Customer support

Now that you are the proud owner of a Packt book, we have a number of things to help you to get the most from your purchase.

Errata

Although we have taken every care to ensure the accuracy of our content, mistakes do happen. If you find a mistake in one of our books—maybe a mistake in the text or the code—we would be grateful if you could report this to us. By doing so, you can save other readers from frustration and help us improve subsequent versions of this book. If you find any errata, please report them by visiting http://www.packtpub.com/submit-errata, selecting your book, clicking on the **Errata Submission Form** link, and entering the details of your errata. Once your errata are verified, your submission will be accepted and the errata will be uploaded to our website or added to any list of existing errata under the Errata section of that title.

To view the previously submitted errata, go to https://www.packtpub.com/books/content/support and enter the name of the book in the search field. The required information will appear under the **Errata** section.

Piracy

Piracy of copyrighted material on the Internet is an ongoing problem across all media. At Packt, we take the protection of our copyright and licenses very seriously. If you come across any illegal copies of our works in any form on the Internet, please provide us with the location address or website name immediately so that we can pursue a remedy.

Please contact us at copyright@packtpub.com with a link to the suspected pirated material.

We appreciate your help in protecting our authors and our ability to bring you valuable content.

Questions

If you have a problem with any aspect of this book, you can contact us at
questions@packtpub.com, and we will do our best to address the problem.

1
An Introduction to Cloud Computing

In this chapter, we will learn about what cloud actually is, what services are available, what benefits are delivered, and the concerns and barriers for adoption.

We will focus on the benefits and barriers of hybrid cloud and provide a high-level overview of cloud computing.

We will then dive into the features and technologies of Microsoft System Center, Windows Server, and Microsoft Azure in the following chapters.

Here are some of the topics that will be discussed in this chapter:

- How electricity became a utility and how cloud could evolve
- The essential characteristics of cloud
- Service delivery models
- Benefits of cloud and barriers for adoption
- An introduction to Microsoft Cloud OS

The way electricity became a utility

Let's first start with a look at another technology that developed over the years and enabled efficiency, agility, and many other benefits namely electricity.

In the early days of the industry in U.S.A., at the end of the 18th century, each factory had its own power plant. Factories were located close to rivers so electricity could be generated from the flowing water. A waterwheel converted the power of moving water to a rotation, which drove a power generator. This worked but it was a fragile system of cables running everywhere and it was hardly scalable.

Thomas Edison decided to start Edison Illuminating Company and build an electricity generation station in New York City. That was realized in 1882. His thoughts were based on the principle that if enough factories used electricity generated by his power plant, the costs of electricity would be much lower than on-premises, self-made electricity. Also, the available capacity would be unlimited. There was however one issue to solve. At that time, electricity was only available as direct current. The problem with direct current was that it could be economically transported only within one and a half miles (about 2.4 km) from the generating station. Nikola Tesla, a brilliant scientist who was working for Edison, got into an argument with him. Tesla eventually developed a way to generate **alternate current (AC)**. AC could be transported over very long distances using thinner cables. Tesla later sold his patent on AC to George Westinghouse. Soon, a war of currents started in the United States between Edison and Westinghouse. In the end AC won, which finally resulted in a victory for AC and enabled a widespread usage of power plants. Electricity became a utility. Westinghouse is currently one of world's largest companies in the electrotechnical business. General Electric Company started in 1892 as a merger between Thomson-Houston and Edison General Electric.

The development of generating and consuming electricity is very similar to the way we consume computing services now. Before the Internet, each company had its own IT infrastructure and locally installed applications. In the first half of the 90s, more and more personal computers were used and the first Internet browser was launched. I will never forget the place and time when I first saw the browser Netscape being demonstrated by a co-worker. In July 1996, Microsoft launched Hotmail—the first free, web-based e-mail service. This could be considered the first-ever cloud service.

So, here we are in 2015—but what is cloud? Nowadays, cloud is used by about every vendor in IT. They all offer cloud services, if we have to believe the sales pitches. However, what is the cloud or cloud computing?

I remember the first time I heard about the cloud was during VMworld in Cannes. That was in 2009. VMware was looking for a way to make IT services more consumable for businesses. However, a couple of years before 2009, the cloud was already available.

The original provider of large-scale cloud computing targeted at organizations was Amazon. Amazon started as a book-selling company. Selling of books is very much driven by peaks. The highest peak in number of book sales is in the weeks before Christmas and New Year. To be able to cope with the demand, Amazon had to invest in large computing capacity just to cover the peaks of a couple of weeks. The rest of the year, a major part of the IT infrastructure was not used. Then, someone working at Amazon had a smart idea: *let's rent out our excess capacity to others*. This is how **Amazon Web Services (AWS)** started in 2006.

Nowadays, each and every IT vendor lets their customers believe that they sell some sort of cloud-compatible solution. Pretending something is the cloud while in fact it is not is called **cloud washing**.

A virtual infrastructure where an IT professional needs to manually provision a new virtual machine is not a cloud. A hosted, single-tenant Exchange Server infrastructure running in a remote data center with fixed costs per month is also not cloud.

Many definitions of cloud computing are available. The definition given by **National Institute of Standards and Technology (NIST)** is one of the best:

> *"Cloud computing is a model for enabling convenient, on-demand network access to a shared pool of configurable computing resources (e.g., networks, servers, storage, applications, and services) that can be rapidly provisioned and released with minimal management effort or service provider interaction."*

While this describes the characteristics of the cloud, it does not describe the value. What is the driving force for organizations to use cloud computing?

For me, the cloud is not a new technology, but a service. It enables a much more efficient consumption of IT services than using traditional IT, which still has a lot of human intervention, limited resources, strictly IT control, slow delivery, and focus on delivering a platform (keeping the lights on) instead of delivering services that enable the businesses to reach their goals.

Cloud is for IT consumption what electricity is for a household appliance. Just plug it in and you can use it. There is no need to call the electrician to have a new wall outlet built into the house when you buy a new appliance.

The essential characteristics of cloud

The definition of NIST mentions a couple of the essential characteristics of cloud. If a service does not have all of those characteristics, it cannot be called *cloud*. The essential characteristics are:

- **On-demand self-service**: The consumer has to be able to provision the service themselves without any human intervention. The service is provisioned almost instantly. So, an infrastructure using server virtualization that needs an administrator to manually provision a new virtual machine is not cloud. Having to wait days to make a service available to the requester is not cloud.

- **Resource pooling**: The resources of the cloud provider are pooled and can be consumed by multiple customers. The subset of the pool that consists of storage, processing, and networking is assigned to the consumer and can be configured when needed/requested.

- **Rapid elasticity**: The capacity delivered by the cloud service must easily and quickly be scaled up or scaled down to meet the changes in demand.

- **Measured Service (with pay-per-use characteristics)**: The usage of the cloud services must be measured and reported on so that the customer and the cloud provider have insight into the usage. It must provide reports that can be used for billing. The pay-per-use characteristic is not a NIST characteristic but seen by Microsoft as essential. In practice, not all cloud providers have a pay-per-use model.

- **Broad network access**: The cloud service must be accessible over the network (Internet) and can be accessed using different types of clients (like PC, smartphone, or tablet).

Service delivery models

Now that we know the essential characteristics of cloud computing, let's take a look at what kind of services are offered by cloud computing and how they are delivered.

Cloud computing services can be categorized into three service delivery models:

- **Software as a service (SaaS)**
- **Platform as a Service (PaaS)**
- **Infrastructure as a Service (IaaS)**

SaaS allows the consumer of the service to use a specific functionality delivered by an application running in the cloud. Basically, this means consumption of cloud with no management involved. The consumer is not aware of and is not able to manage and adjust any of the components of application and infrastructure. There are many vendors offering SaaS solutions, for example Microsoft Office 365, Salesforce, and Google Apps.

PaaS offers the consumer a set of software tools to develop and publish applications over the Internet. The consumer, mostly software developers, do not have or need control over the infrastructure (networking, storage, and compute) but are able to manage at the application and data level.

IaaS gives the consumer the most amount of control of the three cloud computing delivery models. The provider offers a physical infrastructure that consists of compute, storage, and networking. The provider also manages the virtualization layer. The consumer can than manage workloads (operating system and applications) over which the consumer has full control. Microsoft Azure and Amazon EC2 are just two examples of many cloud IaaS services.

The following figure shows the three delivery models and their responsibilities:

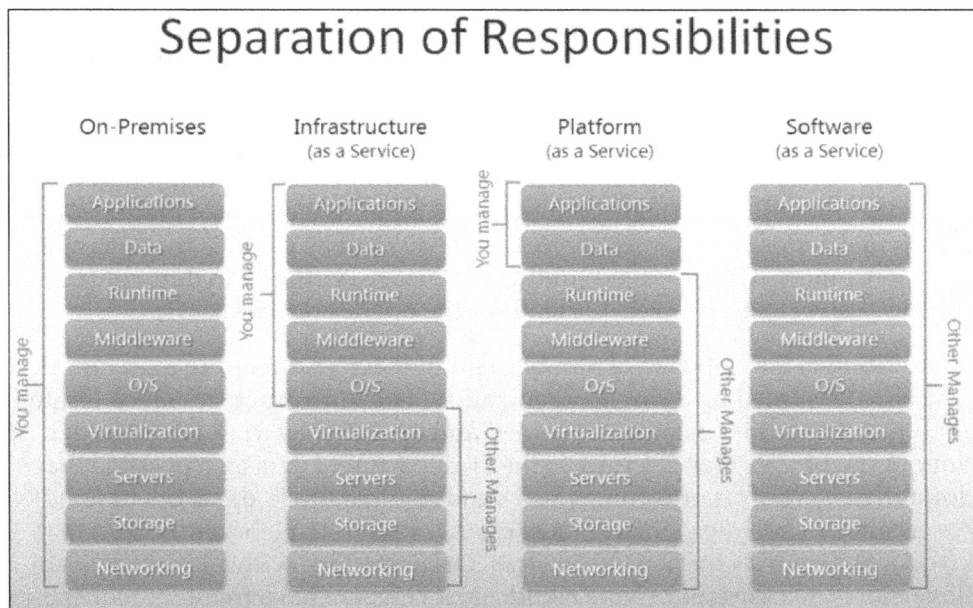

Besides the three service delivery models that are mentioned here, there are many other XaaS offerings:

- **Desktop as a Service**: This focuses solely on delivering cloud-hosted virtual desktops

- **Disaster Recovery as a Service**: This delivers resources that can be temporarily used to host the IT infrastructure and services not available anymore in the primary location

- **Communication as a Service (CaaS)**: This is a rapid expanding service in which Voice over IP services and Unified Collaboration services is offered from the cloud

However, this book will fully focus on the IaaS part of Microsoft Azure. While Microsoft Azure started as a PaaS platform and most of its functionality was targeted at developers, Microsoft Azure IaaS has rapidly evolved towards a mature full infrastructure service offering.

Cloud deployment models

In the previous sections, you learned about characteristics and services. Now, it is time to understand where these characteristics and services live and where the services are made available.

The most commonly used cloud deployment model is public. A **public cloud** means the service is run by an organization that is not a part of the organization to which the consumer belongs. The business objective of a public cloud provider, in most cases, is to make money. Another characteristic of a public cloud is that it is open to multiple consumers. This so-called multitenant usage is offered in data centers that are only accessible to employees working for the operator of the service.

A **private cloud** is the opposite of a public cloud. Services offered in a private cloud are typically consumed by a single organization. The infrastructure can be located either on premise or in a data center owned and operated by a service provider. The provider of the private cloud service is the IT department. It is also possible that the cloud management is outsourced to a vendor while the IT department handles the governance. A private cloud, in most cases, exists in large organizations that have frequent demands for new IT services. Organizations with a lot of software developers are use cases for private cloud, as developers have frequent requests for new virtual machines.

A **community cloud** is an offspring of a private cloud. This kind of cloud is used by a limited number of organizations that offer the same kind of service to their customers. Think about nonprofit organizations, schools, healthcare, or multiple municipalities sharing the same IT infrastructure. Saving on costs while delivering efficient IT services is the main goal of a community cloud.

A **hybrid cloud** is a combination of public cloud services and private clouds. It is not necessary to have a private cloud in order to use hybrid cloud. A hybrid cloud can be a combination of virtualized, on-premises data centers and public cloud services as well. Hybrid cloud can be done on the IaaS or SaaS level. Hybrid cloud can also be seen as a bridge between the public and private clouds, which enables moving workloads between those deployments based on policy, costs, and so on.

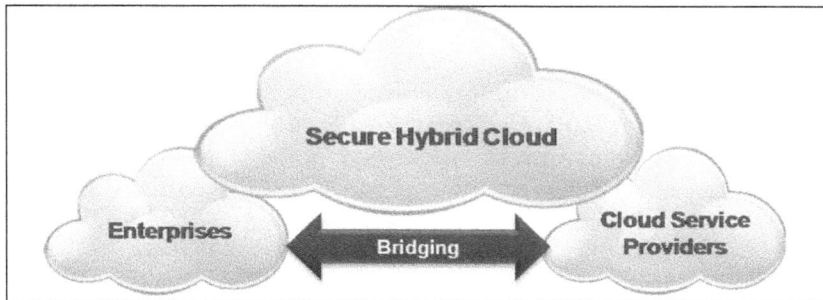

Enabling hybrid cloud became the main focus of many vendors such as VMware and Microsoft from 2012 onwards. They both share the vision that organizations will not move to the public cloud in one big bang. The public cloud, especially when using IaaS, still has a lot of uncertainties and many decision-makers do not know the risks and capabilities of a public cloud.

Hybrid cloud will be a way to get over the security and compliancy concerns that many organizations have on public cloud. Hybrid cloud allows them to enjoy the many benefits of public cloud, while still allowing control over the IT infrastructure and protecting critical services by running those on premise.

Benefits of public cloud

Public cloud has clear benefits that are hard to achieve when using a private cloud. Let's take a detailed look at the benefits of public cloud. These benefits are the reason for all the attention that is being given to cloud computing:

- Scalability and unlimited capacity
- Agility or elasticity
- Insight in costs and no capital expenditure
- Availability
- Business process transformation
- Allows to focus on business, not on management of IT infrastructure or applications

One of the major benefits is the seemingly unlimited number of resources available in a public cloud. We call this cloud characteristic *scalability*. Additional processing power or storage is available on demand when requested; no need to order hardware and licenses, no need to wait for delivery, and no need to install hardware and software. Resources are ready by pressing a couple of buttons.

This offers great opportunities to deal with peaks in demand for resources. Think about a company that starts a new marketing campaign that will run for a couple of weeks. Instead of purchasing additional compute capacity to cover the peak, they just rent the capacity in the cloud: own the base, rent the peak.

Another benefit is agility, or elasticity as it is often called. Using cloud for your IT services means capacity is in sync with demand. Suppose your organization acquires another organization; you need 100 extra desktops and have two weeks to get this organized. Using cloud, the provisioning of those additional desktops is a matter of minutes. The same applies when demand is reduced. Suppose your organization needs to fire 100 employees; if the desktops of those employees are running virtually in the cloud, you can delete the desktops instantly. You are not stuck with assets you paid for but don't need anymore.

Scalability and elasticity is often used interchangeably. However, they are different as explained earlier. Scalability is a feature of the infrastructure that allows the addition of resources to cope with future demand.

Elasticity is the ability of a platform to automatically adapt to changing demand, either by adding workloads or removing workloads.

Availability is another big benefit of cloud. Does your organization have a secondary data center? Is data replicated to another location? Does your data center have enough resiliency when critical components fail? It might have all of these things, but this comes at a high cost. As resiliency is shared by many customers of the cloud service, the provider can offer this in a much more cost-effective way than single-tenant infrastructures.

Another benefit of cloud computing is outsourcing management of the physical infrastructure to the cloud provider. As a cloud consumer using an IaaS service, you only have to worry about managing the operating system and application with its data; there's no need to manage switches, firewalls, routers, servers, load balancers, and so on. To use SaaS, you don't have to worry about managing IT, except maybe managing identity management.

Last but not least, using cloud computing means a shift from investing an amount of money once (CapEx) to operational costs spread over multiple periods (OpEx). It also involves a shift from ownership to subscription. Because costs are now paid on a monthly basis, there is a much better insight into the costs. However, due to the complex cost structure and ease of deployment, there is a high risk that costs will be hard to manage. You have to make sure procedures are in place to monitor the consumption of new services. Most service providers do not offer a possibility to place a limit on the amount of costs per month (spending limit).

Some of the benefits mentioned previously are enablers for business process transformation. Cloud computing allows organizations to make it easier to meet their business goals. For example, because IT services are made available very quickly, products can be brought to market faster or cheaper. Alternatively, as the virtual desktops are running in the cloud, employees can work at any time or any place and are more productive and motivated.

While the benefits mentioned are clear and measureable, other so-called benefits are less clear. Many organizations believe that public cloud is cheaper than doing IT yourself. This is a typical case of *it depends*. For small deployments, cloud might be cheaper. However, for large deployments and especially when large amounts of high performance storage is needed, on-premises IT might be cheaper. It does pay off to do fair cost comparisons.

Cloud computing costs are constructed using the components that are consumed. The components are compute, storage usage, storage transactions, network traffic leaving the data center, support, additional services, and so on.

Keep in mind that when purchasing a storage solution, you pay only once. When consuming cloud storage, you pay each month for the storage and — in many cases — for transactions and data leaving the cloud as well.

Barriers for the adoption of the public cloud

While cloud computing offers many advantages, there are also some barriers for adoption. Some of the top concerns organizations have when using cloud for their IT are:

- Security
- Loss of control
- Compliance
- Network
- High availability
- Inability to audit or examine
- Vendor lock-in

Security is by far the biggest concern especially for organizations outside the United States.. Who has access to my data when it is stored in the cloud? In 2013, we discovered that NSA had access to data in data centers of Microsoft and Google, for example. However, what about other tenants using the same shared infrastructure? What about firewalls and other security appliances? Are they safe? Can they be trusted?

Loss of control is another barrier many organizations see as a hurdle to take on their way to public cloud. All of a sudden, you no longer have physical access to your infrastructure. You cannot touch servers and storage. When something breaks, you have to wait and see whether the service provider is able to fix the issue within the limits as agreed in their Service Level Agreement. You have no means to prioritize actions or get extra people or the information needed to solve the issue faster. Basically, customers have to wait till the provider solves the issue. You may need inbuilt resiliency so that your workloads continue to run somewhere else.

Using public cloud services is only possible using network connections, mainly through the Internet. If the network connection fails, can I still have access to my critical applications? Many organizations are worried about this network dependency.

There have been quite a few outages of public cloud offerings; Amazon AWS had those and Microsoft Azure as well. A leap year bug brought down many Azure services on February 29, 2012. While cloud infrastructures are made highly redundant, when things go wrong, they go badly wrong. Customers are concerned about this. Luckily, some cloud providers are very open about causes of outages. They are willing to learn from mistakes and improve.

Many organizations, such as banks, are only allowed to outsource their IT services when an external auditing firm is allowed to audit the facilities and procedures. This means auditors need physical access to the data center facilities, which is often not allowed.

Microsoft agreed with De Nederlandsche Bank (Dutch central Supervisor for Banks) the right to examine. This means the staff of De Nederlandsche Bank is able to examine procedures of the Microsoft Azure infrastructure. It is also allowed to enter facilities of Microsoft to check if Microsoft indeed complies to policies.

Vendor lock-in is a situation in which a customer will find it very difficult in time, effort, or costs to move to another vendor. Basically, the consumer is involuntary tied to the vendor and has to accept price changes, less than wanted product innovation, or bad customer service. This is sometimes called the "Hotel California" mentality of cloud vendors. "You can check out any time you like, but you can never leave!", the lyrics of the famous song by The Eagles, an American rock band.

Cloud providers are very well aware of this and offer features that give the customer the freedom to move to other offerings.

Challenges of hybrid cloud

Besides the mentioned concerns or fears, there are some additional challenges of using cloud. This section will discuss some aspects of hybrid cloud and public cloud that an organization has to think about before moving to the cloud:

- Control and ownership over data
- Performance
- Feature misalignment
- Application compatibility with cloud platform
- License mobility
- Networking

Data is the main asset of each organization using IT. Without access to data, almost all organizations will sooner or later have serious difficulties in conducting business.

While many cloud vendors make sure data is replicated inside the same data center or even to other data centers, it is still stored on hardware owned by the provider. Also, there is just one logical copy of the data—one copy is not a backup. If the data gets corrupted, the replicas will be corrupted too.

So, every organization needs to make backups. This can be done by storing data on storage provided by the cloud vendor. However, it is still in the same environment run by the same vendor. So, it is better to have an offsite backup. This is a challenge. Not many cloud vendors, especially the larger ones, offer backup to removable media such as tape or external disks. Some software vendors have software that can transfer data between different clouds and an on-premises data center.

If the vendor does not support removable media handling, the only way to have an offsite backup is to transfer backup data over a wide area network to another location—preferably a location managed by another provider or a secondary on-premises location. This might add additional costs for network transfer costs. Microsoft, for example, charges for data leaving the Azure data center. There is no charge for data transfer into the data center.

Guaranteed performance is another challenge. In a multitenant infrastructure without proper measures, there is a risk of meeting the "noisy neighbor." A noisy neighbor is a process run by a single tenant that consumes so much resources that other tenants experience a degraded performance.

Think about a cloud tenant that runs a very IO-intensive database query once a month. As a cloud provider, you do not want other customers to suffer from that query. So, cloud providers need to make sure there is some sort of quality of service on especially storage and on networking.

In most cases, organizations that use hybrid cloud will discover that the features offered by their own on-premises virtual infrastructure are different than the ones offered in the public cloud. Advanced features such as the migration of virtual machines to another host, snapshots, changing virtual disk size, and so on are limited or nonexistent in many public cloud offerings. In the following chapters, we will find out the differences in management experience between on-premises Hyper-V and Microsoft Azure.

So, the integration of private and public cloud and establishing new procedures can be a challenge.

There is a difference in features of on-premises and public cloud, and the underlying virtual infrastructure is very likely to be different.

Basically, there are two architectures used in IaaS platforms: one designed on the principle that the application should deliver resiliency and one that has a lot of resiliency built into the platform.

Software licenses are many times tied to physical servers or CPUs. Vendors still need to do a lot of work to teach customers how licenses can be moved to a different infrastructure. So what if you move your Oracle license to a public cloud? Do you have to make sure that license covers all of the physical CPUs the licensed workload can potentially run on? In the following chapters, we will learn about the strategic partnering between Oracle and Microsoft and what this means for license mobility.

Hybrid cloud potentially allows the movement of workloads between on-premises infrastructures (not private cloud per se) and the public cloud. As explained before, hybrid cloud could be seen as a bridge. However, the network IP addresses used in the public cloud infrastructure will be different than the ones used on premise. Do we need to reconfigure IP addresses in the virtual machines when a virtual machine is moved? In the following chapters, we will learn about technology that enables workload mobility.

Later in this chapter, we will also discuss what happens if your organization needs to exit the cloud provider. However, what if your own organization goes bankrupt and all of the financial data is stored in the cloud? Who is going to pay the cloud provider to make that data available to organizations such as the tax bureau or the curator?

Cattle versus pets

While the infrastructure is important, at the end the application is what matters. Basically, we can divide applications into two categories:

* Those that depend on the resiliency offered by the infrastructure
* Those that have inbuilt resiliency

A famous analogy for this is pets and cattle. Humans have a special relationship with pets. They give their pet a name and have a special bond with the animal. Most people do not have such a bond with cattle. Cattle are for production of meat or milk. If an animal dies, nobody really cares. It is regarded as economic damage but does not affect an individual's emotions.

A "pet type" of application is one where administrators knows the specific name and role of the server by heart. Administrators have a special bond with a "pet type" of application. If the server fails, the application is likely to fail. Examples of such server names are Zeus or Fileserver01.

A "cattle type" of application has multiple instances for the same role. If a server with a middleware role fails, the application will continue to be available because there are multiple servers with same role. Application data is nonpersistent and can easily be provisioned if the server is lost.

Public IaaS architectures are not all the same although they all look similar at first glance; most of them offer a self-service portal, the ability to create/modify/delete virtual machines, and so on. However, there are differences under the hood. Each provider has its own unique sauce added to the IaaS service.

Microsoft Azure was originally designed as a PaaS platform. Business-critical applications that are developed on Azure are resilient by design at the application level. Basically, it means each role (web tier, application tier, database tier, and so on) has at least two nodes. If one node fails, the application will remain available.

Netflix, a US company delivering films and series streamed over the Internet, has a great way to test the availability of their applications. They developed the so-called **Chaos Monkey tool**. Netflix believes the best way to defend against failures is to deliberately create failures, fix them, learn from them, and improve. Chaos Monkey will randomly shut down virtual machines in the Amazon cloud that is used by Netflix to deliver their streaming service. When Chaos Monkey terminates a virtual machine, the Auto Scaling group function of Amazon makes sure an identical virtual machine will be booted up to replace the failed one.

So, Chaos Monkey is a nice way to see whether your application really is cloud-ready (cattle category) or it is a legacy enterprise application (pet).

Later in this book, we will learn about the architecture of Windows Azure and see what kind of applications are most suited to run on Azure.

Using cloud successfully

Many organizations have already started using cloud. Some succeeded in reaching their goals and many failed. This is because designing and building a cloud is seen by many as a technical operation. Cloud is not technical; it is about having the right tools at the right price and moment to be able to do business. IT departments should embrace cloud to make a shift from being a cost center (keeping the lights on) to adding value to the business. They can do that by delivering services, which for instance reduces the time to market for products.

The role of internal IT will change over time from being a supplier of IT services to being a broker. IT will have a more strategic and control function.

Cloud exit plan

We have discussed many of the benefits of cloud computing. However, the balance between benefits and disadvantages might at some time shift to a situation where an organization wants to stop using cloud or switch to another cloud service provider.

There may be many reasons to not continue the cloud service. The reasons can be categorized into voluntary leave or involuntary leave.

Reasons for a voluntary leave can be:

- If the cloud consumer is not satisfied with the quality of the service delivered by the cloud provider — think about performance, response times, available features, and so on
- Not satisfied with the costs of the services
- A merger with another company
- A change in long-term IT strategy

Discontinuing the services of a cloud provider can be involuntarily as well. The main reason for that to happen is when the cloud provider goes broke or decides to discontinue their service.

This happened, for example, in 2013 when Nirvanix ran out of money. Nirvanix had a limited portfolio. It offered only storage as a service. Customers initially got two weeks' notice to transfer their data from the Nirvanix data centers to another location, but the time was later extended to 4 weeks. Some customers had 10 to 20 petabytes of data in use, which was be difficult to migrate within two weeks — especially if there is no plan and when data needs to be moved over limited bandwidth connections.

In April 2011, Iron Mountain, another cloud storage provider announced it would discontinue its cloud-based services. However, customers were given over 12 months to move data to another location.

One of the steps any organization that intends to use cloud-based services should take is to prepare their **cloud exit strategy**. However, less than half of the customers of cloud services actually have an exit strategy. Why is this? Probably it is not cool to have such a plan. The same applies for disaster recovery, backup verification, and so on. Those are all on a top priority to-do list but are the first items to be removed or demoted when time and or budget become issues. A cloud exit strategy should contain information that makes it clear when to exit and how to exit.

Organizations should think about when enough is enough and it is better to exit— think about maximum loss of data, maximum loss of availability, or lost revenue. These need to be monitored to be able to judge whether the service level is breached or not. Do not test only on outages but also on performance. However, in most SLAs of cloud service providers, there is no mention of a guarantee of performance.

Also, try to determine the future of the provider. What is the roadmap? Are new features being added at the same pace as other providers? How frequently does the provider publish press releases announcing these new features? If there is silence for many months, something could be wrong.

So if you decided to move out, there are two options: either back source (bring the workloads back to your on premise infrastructure, the opposite of outsourcing) or find another provider.

One of the advantages of using IaaS over PaaS and SaaS is that you probably do not have to perform any conversion of data. Your data is included in virtual disk files that also contain the application and the operating system. As long as your new cloud provider is able to host that type of virtual disk, file migration is not that difficult. The only challenge is moving the data out and into another location and changing network configuration.

Organizations considering cloud should make sure they are able to import and export data to cloud providers' data centers using external media such as a NAS or a bunch of USB drives. This is the only way to import of evacuate large amounts of data in an efficient and timely matter. Make sure the data on that external media is encrypted when unauthorized staff needs to have access to that media for import or export. Check for RAID compliancy when all the data is on USB drives and one fails.

Export and import operations of data would mean that virtual machines most likely need to be shut down during the export and import operation. It will be very difficult to perform some sort of virtual to virtual conversion between different cloud providers while workloads remain active.

Hybrid cloud to the rescue

Hybrid cloud is seen by many as a way to overcome fear, concerns or barriers preventing the adoption of public cloud computing. A hybrid cloud is one step into the cold water of cloud without getting your feet too wet, and having a way out when things go wrong.

Compare it to starting a relationship with someone without selling your house and moving in with your new partner. Hybrid cloud is like a two-household family; you enjoy each other's company but still have your own habitat that you have control over. It is also a matter of not putting all of your eggs in the same basket. If it is the love of your life you can always start living together.

Using hybrid cloud is the same. It enables you to withdraw virtual machines if services of cloud providers are not meeting expectations or are even terminated like in the case of Nirvanix we mentioned earlier. There is an escape plan.

Another benefit of hybrid cloud is that the organization still employs people with knowledge on infrastructures. Suppose an organization moves its IT fully to a public cloud. It's likely that the number of staff with infrastructure knowledge will be reduced, as the organization does not require that knowledge anymore.

Using a hybrid cloud, IT departments are able to control their IT while at the same time are able to provide an unlimited capacity to their business without having to spend a lot of money on buying new infrastructure.

Hybrid cloud also enables a controlled move towards public cloud. Not many organizations are willing and able to perform a kind of big bang migration scenario in which all of their IT services are moved to the cloud in a short time frame.

It helps when both infrastructures can be managed using the same tools to provide a single pane of glass. In the ideal world there is no difference between features offered by your on premise platform, and the features offered by the platform of the service provider. However, we will soon find out there are some differences.

Hybrid cloud also offers a choice of where to run the virtual machines. Some virtual machines, like those with sensitive data, rather run in the on premise data center that organizations have full control over. Other types of workloads, such as testing and development, can perfectly run in a public cloud.

One of the clearest examples of a hybrid cloud scenario is one where compute capacity is consumed from a public cloud while the data for that compute is located on on-premises storage systems. Microsoft ExpressRoute which offers up to 10 Gbps connections enable these kind of scenarios.

In the next section, we will learn what the vision of Microsoft is for hybrid cloud and what solutions are available to create and operate a hybrid cloud.

Introducing Microsoft Cloud OS

Microsoft strongly believes organizations benefit from using public cloud services mixed with their on premise infrastructure. Connecting on premise with public clouds will give organizations much more efficiency, cost reduction, scalability and agility compared to making use of just an on premise infrastructure. Steve Ballmer, former CEO of Microsoft, called it *the power of AND*.

Microsoft translated their vision on hybrid cloud computing into a marketing campaign in which they mention the Microsoft Cloud OS.

Microsoft Cloud OS is not a product. It is a vision, strategy that is delivered by services and products. The most important ones are:

- Microsoft Windows Server 2012 with Hyper-V
- Microsoft System Center 2012 including Windows Azure Pack
- Microsoft Azure
- SQL Server 2014
- StorSimple

These solutions are either running on premise, in Azure data centers, or in data centers run by service providers. The combination of those solutions is *the power of AND*. The three locations where IT services can be running is a very important part of the vision.

On-premises infrastructures enable control by the IT department. Microsoft Azure enables the cost-effective usage of an unlimited capacity. Service providers offer public cloud services so that customers have a choice of which provider to use, thereby preventing a vendor lock in. Service providers also provide customer intimacy.

So, IaaS services like that of Azure will not be offered by Microsoft exclusively. Any service provider will be able to deliver IaaS with the Azure look and feel and features in their data center. This allows customers to switch from Microsoft Azure to another service provider without changes in the application, data, management, knowledge, and procedures.

Vendor lock-in is pretty much taken away by this. The solution that enables this, that is, Microsoft Azure Pack, will be discussed in the next chapter.

Microsoft hybrid cloud use cases

In this section, you will learn how Microsoft created real value out of their cloud OS vision.

The use cases can be grouped into a couple of categories:

- Test and development
- Backup, archive, and disaster recovery
- Deployment of public-facing applications or split application architecture
- Running desktops
- Cloud bursting

In the following chapters, we will learn a lot more about how to use Microsoft solutions that enable hybrid cloud. For now, I will give you a high-level overview of possible use cases.

Backup and disaster recovery is one of the most common reasons for organizations to use cloud. Instead of owning and maintaining a secondary data center, recovery services can be used on a subscription basis.

Microsoft Azure offers a number of backup and disaster recovery services. Azure Recovery Services enables the storage of backup data on cloud-based storage. It is very easy to direct a Windows Backup agent or a Microsoft DPM agent running in an on-premises Windows Server to cloud-based storage. The advantages of cloud-based storage are an unlimited amount of available storage and cost-effective pricing.

Microsoft StorSimple is a storage appliance that is positioned between the application and Microsoft Azure cloud storage. It has two tiers of fast performance disks inside the appliance that is used on-premises. The third tier is disk storage offered by Microsoft Azure. This tier can be used for archiving purposes. It is still online, but access is slower than the on-premise storage.

Microsoft Azure Site Recovery is a cloud-based orchestration tool for disaster recovery. It enables the orchestrated restart of Hyper-V virtual machines in a secondary data center. This secondary data center can either be a customer managed data center or a Microsoft Azure data center. The execution and configuration of orchestration is done by Azure. Recovery Manager will use a run book to start virtual machines in a predefined order and will perform checks and pauses when manual actions need to be taken. This enables an almost fully automated execution of a recovery.

Besides storing backup data, Azure can also be used as a secondary site for live production data. Active Directory, SQL Server, and DFS file shares can be replicated from on-premise to virtual machines running in Azure data centers. So, all the data available in the primary site is replicated to Azure. If the primary site is unavailable, the services are still available in Microsoft Azure.

Hybrid cloud creates the possibility to create a split application architecture. This enables to run nonpersistent workloads in public cloud, while the critical backend servers are running in a controlled on-premise data center. This gives processing capacity and control over data at the same time.

Another recently added hybrid scenario is the ability to run virtual desktops in Azure. Citrix XenDesktop, a VDI software solution, is now supported on Microsoft Azure. This means it can deliver virtual desktops to end users. Microsoft only allows the usage of Windows Server as a desktop in a multiuser hosted infrastructure. The Microsoft license policy does not allow to use **Virtual Desktop Infrastructure** (**VDI**) using a Windows client operating system, such as Windows 7 and 8, in a hosting provider scenario when hardware is shared between multiple customers.

Another use case is cloud bursting, which means public cloud capacity is used during short and mostly infrequent intervals to cope with demands in peaks. Think about a railway operator who has a timetable that is published online. On a snowy day, when trains are being cancelled, many passengers will be using their mobile devices to query the timetable to check whether their train will be running. This sudden high demand puts a lot of stress on the web server's capacity. It is very cost-effective to have those requests for information temporarily handled by servers running in the cloud. This can quickly be provisioned when demand increases and scaled down when demand drops.

Azure is typically suited for current Microsoft customers using Windows Server, Active Directory, SharePoint, and SQL Server. Microsoft made it easy to connect on-premise instances of these products to instances running in Azure.

Summary

In this chapter, you learned about the development of delivering computing services, which is similar to the way production and distribution of electricity developed from the 1880s until now. We now know the different service and deployment models of cloud computing. Also, Microsoft's vision of hybrid cloud computing and its solutions to enable this vision should be clear now.

In the next chapter, we will focus on and explain the Microsoft solutions that enable organizations to benefit from their on-premise computing resources and those provided in the public cloud by Microsoft Azure.

2
An Introduction to Microsoft Cloud Solutions

In this chapter, you will learn what products of Microsoft make a hybrid cloud and look at the characteristics and functionalities delivered by these solutions. The technical details and how-to's will be described in *Chapter 3, Understanding the Microsoft Azure Architecture*, and the later chapters.

You will learn how the products were developed and also take look at the service levels of Microsoft Azure, the cost structure, supported software, and license mobility.

Last but not least, we will have a fair and unbiased look at what is possible using Microsoft cloud solutions—because it is not only important to understand what a solution delivers, but also what a solution doesn't deliver at the moment.

As described in *Chapter 1, An Introduction to Cloud Computing*, the Microsoft hybrid cloud is made out of a few software components. The ones we will discuss in this chapter are:

- Windows Server
- System Center
- Microsoft Azure
- SQL Server

Cloud first

Microsoft, as a company, is making a switch from being a software company to being a service and devices company. About 5 years ago, each software license Microsoft sold in the enterprise space was used on hardware bought or leased by the customer. With the shift to the cloud, this is changing—along with the features of the Microsoft software.

Microsoft announced it will deliver new features first in cloud and only later in on-premises software. This also means that on-premises software has features to easily connect to Microsoft Azure. For example, an export of SQL Server database can easily be imported into Azure Storage with a few mouse clicks without leaving the SQL Server Management console. Visual Studio has a similar cloud integration.

We have to see how this works out. Currently, software offered in the SaaS model, such as SharePoint Online, Exchange Online, and part of Office 365, are restricted in available features compared to their on-premises versions. For example, SharePoint Online has a lower maximum number of list or library items that a database operation, such as a query, can process at one time. This number is restricted to 5,000 while there is no restriction for SharePoint used on-premises.

> Make sure you know the restrictions of cloud-based applications and infrastructures.

Windows Server 2012

Windows Server 2012 and more specifically the Hyper-V role is the core of the Microsoft hybrid cloud. It will run on-premises in enterprises and in datacenters operated by service providers.

Hyper-V is now a mature hypervisor that offers essential features for the enterprise. Hyper-V is available for free in a product named Microsoft Hyper-V Server 2012. Once installed on a server and booted, a basic command shell interface is presented.

There is no graphical user interface available and no other roles can be installed. However, there are no restrictions from a Hyper-V point of view. All features available in Hyper-V can be used, including clustering, the High Availability feature of Hyper-V. A host running Hyper-V Server can be managed using System Center Virtual Machine Manager. Also this edition does not have the free Windows Server licenses that can be used in the guest operating systems.

For central management of Hyper-V hosts and the virtual machines running on those hosts either Cluster Manager or System Center Virtual Machine Manager can be used. While Cluster Manager offers some basic features, System Center Virtual Machine Manager offers additional features to manage storage, networking, templates, services, role-based management, deployment of physical servers, and a lot more.

System Center Virtual Machine Manager cannot be purchased separately. It comes as part of the System Center Suite. Other components of the System Center Suite are Data Protection Manager, Configuration Manager, Operations Manager, Orchestrator, Endpoint Protection, App Controller, Service Manager, and Windows Azure Pack. An alternative to purchasing the complete System Center suite is purchasing a solution like 5Nine Manager for Hyper-V. This is an easy-to-use and cost-effective management solution for Microsoft Hyper-V. It provides most of the features of Microsoft System Center VMM that SMBs need for everyday Hyper-V management.

Microsoft System Center 2012

Microsoft System Center 2012 is the infrastructure management suite of Microsoft. It contains all the software needed to deploy, operate, and monitor infrastructure components running either on-premises or in cloud platforms.

Obviously, Microsoft provides a good integration between System Center 2012 and Microsoft Azure. We will discuss many examples later in this book.

System Center is a cloud management platform that allows us to create and manage a private cloud. A private cloud allows non-IT staff to provision virtual machines and applications using a self-service portal and a catalog. Strong automation makes sure the requested resources are efficiently made available to the requester with no, or hardly any, involvement of the IT staff.

This book is about the hybrid cloud and not about the private cloud. So, we will not go into the details of the various components of the System Center suite or use case scenarios.

However, let's discuss what the private cloud offering of Microsoft looks like to have a good understanding of the products.

The platform consists of various independent software components that deliver the cloud management functionality when properly connected. These components are as follows:

- Configuration Manager
- Virtual Machine Manager
- Service Manager

- Orchestrator
- Operations Manager
- App Controller
- Data Protection Manager
- Windows Azure Pack

Combined together these solutions form a Cloud Management Platform. These tools can be used to operate a private and hybrid cloud.

In the next sections, we will slightly zoom into the functionalities of the components and especially how they integrate with Microsoft Azure.

System Center Configuration Manager

System Center Configuration Manager (SCCM) is used to deploy operating systems, applications, hot fixes, and other software to clients and servers. It can be used to manage systems such as Windows Server, Mac OS, Linux, and Unix. Also, mobile devices running Windows Phone, Symbian, iOS, and Android can be managed. However, an additional subscription to Windows Intune is preferred for this, since SCCM out of the box only supports older mobile operating systems, such as Windows Mobile 6.1 and Nokia Symbian.

SCCM 2012 SP1 allows us to create a cloud distribution point in Microsoft Azure. A distribution point is a library that contains applications, updates, and more that are ready for deployment to clients managed by SCCM. The advantage of a distribution point in Azure is that it is highly available and reachable from locations all over the globe with just an Internet connection. Data is encrypted before it is transferred to the distribution point.

System Center Virtual Machine Manager

System Center Virtual Machine Manager (SCVMM) has many features. It can be used to deploy physical servers and virtual machines. In this book, we concentrate on the features of System Center that enable a hybrid cloud.

One of the most important features of SCVMM for multi tenant clouds is network virtualization. Basically, this enables the use of IP subnets used by virtual machines, which are totally invisible to the IP-network used by Hyper-V hosts switches and other physical components. Network virtualization is useful for service providers. Two tenants who use the same IP subnets can be hosted in the same infrastructure. It also allows us to move virtual machines between infrastructures that are using different IP-subnets without changes in the IP configuration of the virtual machine.

So, for example, virtual machines can be moved (offline or soon via online Live migration) to a service provider or to Microsoft Azure without adjustment to IP configuration, DNS, and so on.

The best analogy is something we are all used to: when we travel abroad, we can still be contacted on our mobile phone using the same telephone number.

System Center Service Manager

System Center Service Manager (SCSM) allows organizations to manage incidents and problems. It is compliant with Microsoft Operations Framework and ITIL. It provides built-in processes for incident and problem resolution, change control, and asset lifecycle management. Service Manager has a self-service portal that enables end users to report incidents and perform some tasks themselves, for example, resetting passwords.

System Center Orchestrator

System Center Orchestrator (SCO) is an automation tool. Using drag-and-drop, administrators can create runbooks to automate tasks like deploying servers, creating user accounts, and so on. SCO can be connected to many System Center components to automate tasks. For example, it can receive status information from Operations Manager and use that information to instruct SCVMM to deploy additional virtual servers.

System Center Operations Manager

System Center Operations Manager (SCOM), often referred to as Ops Manager, is a monitoring and reporting tool. Using management packs that contain knowledge about applications or operating systems, SCOM reports on the status and condition of several infrastructure components.

System Center App Controller

App Controller is a cloud management portal. It allows administrators and end users to manage private and public clouds. A private cloud is a set of resources abstracted by SCVMM. A public cloud is a set of resources provided by Microsoft Azure or by a service provider. The service provider needs to have the Service Provider Foundation software running. This is a special component of the System Center suite.

In the next chapters, you will learn more about App Controller and how to connect to Microsoft Azure and service providers.

System Center Data Protection Manager

Data Protection Manager completes the datacenter management suite as the backup tool of choice for Microsoft workloads. Through use of the **Volume Shadow Copy Service (VSS)** it provides regular snapshots or full backups of Hyper-V hosts, virtual machines, or SQL/mail databases.

Windows Azure Pack

Microsoft Cloud OS is, as explained earlier, a vision of Microsoft on how to deliver services in a hybrid cloud as seamless as possible. Services can run on-premises, in Microsoft Azure, or in datacenters operated by service providers.

Microsoft offers software that enables service providers to offer Azure-like services in their datacenter. Windows Azure Pack runs on top of Windows Server 2012 Hyper-V and System Center 2012 R2.

It offers four services:

- Virtual machines
- Websites
- Service Bus
- SQL

Azure Pack has an **Application Programming Interface (API)**, so customers can use scripting to perform all kind of management tasks, just as they are used to for Microsoft Azure. For manual management, a self-service portal is available. The user interface of Azure Pack looks similar to the Azure Management Portal.

In contrary to Microsoft Azure, Azure Pack makes it possible to connect to consoles of virtual machines without the need of RDP or network connectivity of the virtual machine. Windows Azure Pack Console Connect works the same way as VMConnect from the Hyper-V Manager console.

Microsoft StorSimple

StorSimple is a stranger in our midst, as this is the only component of the Cloud OS vision that is delivered as hardware. StorSimple highly integrates with cloud-based storage. It can use Microsoft Azure Storage storage services as a cost-effective storage tier.

I have never met a customer who has full control over the growth of data. Each organization is facing growth in the amount of data and the management of that data. End users believe data capacity is unlimited, while the IT management does not have insight if data is really useful or could be deleted.

The shortcut solution to the growing need for storage is simply to add storage. However, the cost of buying and managing storage is expensive. Most data needs a backup as well, which adds to the cost of backup infrastructure.

A common solution to reduce costs on storage is to archive data. About *80 percent of data* is hardly ever accessed, so it can easily be moved to another type of storage.

Microsoft offers a complete solution with the StorSimple appliance. When using StorSimple, virtual machines or physical servers are connected to volumes presented by the StorSimple appliance that is deployed on-premises. The appliance offers two tiers of storage: SSD and SATA. SSD offers the best storage performance, while SATA offers good performance and is cheaper than SSD. The third tier is cloud-based storage. The appliance does auto-tiering such that frequently requested data is located on the fastest tier, while data that is rarely accessed is automatically moved to the cloud storage.

StorSimple is a hardware appliance. Depending on the required capacity, one or more appliances are purchased and connected to the network. If more storage capacity is needed, additional appliances need to be purchased.

It has features such as compression, deduplication, and encryption. As data is kept outside the datacenter, StorSimple can replace traditional tape in certain use cases. Data sent to the cloud is encrypted for security reasons. We know since the PRISM scandal around June 2013 that data could be watched by the NSA without the knowledge of the customer of a cloud provider.

Besides archiving and extension of storage capacity, StorSimple can also be used for disaster recovery purposes. Snapshots can be replicated to Microsoft Azure. When a disaster hits the on-premises datacenter, data can be retrieved from the cloud storage in an alternate datacenter. Instead of having to copy all the data back to the alternate datacenter, initially only the data requested by users is restored.

In a later chapter, you will learn how to use the StorSimple appliance.

Microsoft SQL Server 2014

The Cloud OS vision is not purely focused on delivering an infrastructure platform. Part of the vision is SQL Server 2014. As this book is about infrastructure, I will not go into much detail on SQL Server.

SQL Server 2014 is enabled for use in a hybrid scenario. It means that SQL Server data can be made highly available by using Microsoft Azure as a secondary location to store SQL Server data.

SQL Servers allows us to export a database (data and scheme) and import it into Microsoft Azure in a few simple steps.

Microsoft Azure

So what is Microsoft Azure exactly? To understand Azure we should first have a look at how it all started.

Work started on Microsoft Azure started in 2006 as a project. Microsoft saw how Amazon and Google cloud initiatives got traction and realized it should jump on the cloud train. Amitabh Srivastava of Microsoft was head of the team that had a mission to develop a cloud solution. At that time, Microsoft was planning to offer more cloud services than "just" Hotmail.

The second member of the team was Dave Cutler. Cutler was the developer of VMS and Windows NT. One day, he and a couple of other Microsoft employees were driving in a car heading to a Hotmail datacenter. Cutler saw a really shady strip joint in San Jose called *The Pink Poodle* and thought that it could be a great name for the project.

The other guys in the car said no and thought of a different name. So, the project code name became Red Dog.

While this is the unofficial story, another story tells that the team developing Azure liked a brand of beer called Red Dog.

When Red Dog was announced at the PDC2008 developers conference in October 2008, the new name was Windows Azure. In March 2014 Windows Azure was rebranded to Microsoft Azure to emphasize Azure is a multi-platform cloud. Azure initially was also called by some as *Windows as a Service*. It allowed developers to quickly develop software without the hassle of setting up server hardware, networking, storage, operating systems, and developer tools.

Microsoft Azure was released on February 1, 2010. Initially, Azure was a **Platform as a Service (PaaS)** offering from Microsoft. Developers could access Azure and develop software using a wide range of tools like .NET, PHP, and so on.

It used a hypervisor that was a fork of Hyper-V but written from the ground up, and it used the VHD file format like the Hyper-V part of Windows Server.

Developers were limited in their choice of tooling as only Microsoft-supported tools were offered. It was not possible to control at the operating system-level. There were a few roles active as virtual machines; the worker role that was a virtual machine acting as an application server and the web role. This was a virtual machine running a web server.

The limited selection of developer tools was raised when Azure Virtual Machines were introduced. A new offer went live in April 2013 and gave the opportunity to provision virtual machines running Windows Server-based or Linux-based operating systems. Besides control over the operating system, Azure Virtual Machines also enable the management of networking. Customers can now control network connections between virtual machines by using a VLAN type of separation. They are also able to control access to network ports in the guest operating system.

In January 2015, Microsoft Azure runs in 17 regions (one or more data centers) located in four continents. Each continent (except South America) has at least two regions for data redundancy.

> New functionality is added almost every three weeks! While I did the most to keep this book as up to date as possible, it is very likely Microsoft has added new features to Azure that are not mentioned in this book. See the errata page on the Packt Publishing website (www.packtpub.com) ( ) for up-to-date information.

Microsoft Azure Services

As you learned before, Azure started as a platform for developers. Most functionality is still targeted at developers and to make applications running in the cloud accessible for consumers. In this section, we will shortly discuss those services to give you a better understanding of what Azure has to offer.

Basically, there are three main services offered by Azure:

- Websites
- Cloud services
- Virtual machines

Azure can be seen as a box full of Lego bricks. An Azure customer can choose which bricks to use for the application they require. Azure offers several of those bricks that are called *services* by Microsoft. Each service has its own pricing and Service Level Agreement and can be purchased separately. These can be categorized into four classes:

- **Compute services**: websites, virtual machines, mobile, and cloud services
- **Data services**: Backup, Cache, Site Recovery, and HDInsight
- **App service**: Media services, messaging, and Active Directory
- **Network services**: Virtual Network and Traffic Manager

As this book is solely focused on the **Infrastructure as a Service (IaaS)** features of Azure, we will not go into the details of each service in this book.

Using these Azure services, the following use cases can be built:

- Web Sites
- Mobile apps
- Dev/test
- Big data
- Media
- Storage, backup, and recovery
- Identity and access management

To get to know the Azure use cases in detail, we will discuss each of them in depth.

Web Sites was one of the first features available when Azure became available to public in 2010. Web Sites allows customers to deploy websites on Azure. Provisioning is made very easy using preconfigured virtual machine images. Many tools to create web-based applications are supported. To cover peaks in demand, bursting can be configured.

Mobile Apps services allow developers to support apps running on mobile devices. The backend for these apps are different from websites. Mobile Apps allows support for Software Development Kits of mobile platforms such as Windows Mobile, iOS, and Android. It allows us to send push notifications to mobile devices and is able to authenticate platforms such as Facebook, Twitter, and Microsoft.

Big data is a service that offers Hadoop software to perform data analytics. Hadoop is one of the best known software for analyzing all sorts of data. The service is called HDInsight by Microsoft.

On-demand and live streaming of media content such as video is offered by Media Services. Customers can upload, convert, and encode all kinds of media.

Storage, backup, and recovery allows us to store data into Microsoft Azure. This can be live data, backup data, or archival data. Recovery allows us to perform an orchestrated recovery of datacenters running System Center by Microsoft Azure. You will learn more about this in one of the next chapters.

Identity and access management services enable users to authenticate to Microsoft Azure Directory Services. Two-factor authentication is supported. On-premises Active Directory can be extended to Azure. Single sign-on is supported when Federation Services is used. You will learn more about authentication in the next chapters. Access management allows users to have single sign-on access to SaaS applications once they are authenticated to Windows Azure Active Directory.

Dev/test is all about the ability to quickly deploy virtual machines with preconfigured software. Microsoft made many software tools available that are preinstalled in a virtual machine image. Getting access to these applications is as simple as selecting the image, selecting the size of the virtual machine, selecting the location, and done!

Some examples of the software available in virtual machine images are Oracle WebLogic and Ruby on Rails.

When these images are not sufficient, there is also a library full of images. These are not stored in the Microsoft Azure datacenters but need to be downloaded. When even this does not meet the requirements of the needy customer, you can always upload your sysprepped company image or a prepared .vhd virtual disk to implement in the Microsoft Azure Cloud.

Stateless versus stateful virtual machines

As described earlier, Azure offers two models of cloud computing: PaaS and IaaS.

Services offered in PaaS run in a virtual machine, but the consumer is not aware of this. They don't have to create a virtual machine, networking, or storage and are also not able to manage the operating system. Patching and updates on the operating system are done by Microsoft. Microsoft does this by deploying a new operating system with the latest patches.

Virtual machines in PaaS are stateless, which means if the host crashes, a new virtual machine will be created. All data on the crashed virtual machine, however, is lost. Data in this model needs to be stored in Microsoft Azure Storage, which is persistent storage.

This model does not work in IaaS. So, here the virtual machine is stateful.

Microsoft Azure Infrastructure Services

Microsoft Azure is a service name. It provides virtual machines and virtual networking. But it goes a bit further in available services than the average IaaS offering. Azure Infrastructure Services also offer a SQL server running inside virtual machines which allows you to use Microsoft Azure as a DR site. It is also possible to connect an on-premises Active Directory with Microsoft **Windows Azure Active Directory (WAAD)** to provide single sign-on for applications running on Azure.

Microsoft Azure Virtual Machines

The Azure Virtual Machines service allows us to create, delete, and modify virtual machines running a selected number of operating systems. Currently (January 2015) supported operating systems are Windows Server 2008, Windows Server 2012, Windows Server 2012 R2, and 6 different Linux distributions.

Virtual machines come in fixed sizes. Generally, these are called "t-shirt-sized virtual machines." Currently (January 2015), there are 23 choices of configurations, and each configuration is a fixed number of virtual cores and virtual memory. Virtual machine configurations are grouped in A, D and G series.

It is not possible to configure specific preferences for the number of virtual processors, amount of internal memory, or the disk size of the operating system disk. Customers are able to add additional virtual disks, but the maximum number of disks that can be added to the virtual machine depends on the size of the virtual machine.

Microsoft Azure Storage

Microsoft offers cloud-based storage. Storage capacity can be used by customers without the need to consume processing, as in the case of virtual machines. Azure storage can be used for backup purposes for storage of virtual machine data, SQL Server, SharePoint data, and so on.

Data can be accessed by customers using a REST API. That is a standard protocol of accessing various sources. Using the REST API, it is very simple for applications to connect to Microsoft Azure. Data located on Azure storage is stored three times in a single datacenter; this way, the data is protected from the failure of a single disk. Thanks to geo-replication the data is replicated to yet another location. If enabled (which is the case by default), geo-replication will replicate the data to another datacenter in the same region.

In the next chapter on Microsoft Azure architecture, you will learn about storage in detail. You will learn about storage accounts, IOPS, best practices, and so on.

Azure Virtual Network

Azure Virtual Networks allow customers to extend their on-premises infrastructure to Microsoft Azure. Azure Virtual Networks offer functionality like **site-to-site (S2S)** VPN, point-to-site VPN, and internal cloud networking.

Azure customers can set up a secure connection over the Internet using a S2S VPN between Microsoft Azure and an on-premises location. At the moment, only one S2S connection can be set up per subscription.

A secure connection between desktops/laptops and Microsoft Azure can be set ( ) up as well without installing a VPN client to the corporate network. This point-to-site connection will be described later.

Virtual machines running in Microsoft Azure will require a network connection to communicate with each other, and they will need IP configuration as well.

Microsoft Azure has dynamic IP addresses for virtual machines. The addresses are fixed to the virtual machine as long as the cloud service to which the virtual machine belongs to is active.

In September 2013, Microsoft announced that Microsoft Azure will be connected to the AT&T network. As many datacenters of US organizations are already connected to the AT&T MPLS VPN network, this means a very easy connection to Azure. Besides easy on-boarding to Azure, it will also provide additional security benefits, reduced latencies, and faster data transfers.

Microsoft Azure Directory Services

Almost all enterprise applications require some sort of authentication. This enables control over who has access and permission to the application.

Microsoft Active Directory is used by many organizations worldwide for identity management and access control. A multitenant version of Active Directory called Windows **Azure Active Directory (WAAD)** is available in Microsoft Azure. It is a very important component of many online Microsoft services. Examples of these services are Office 365, Dynamics CRM Online, Windows Intune, and other (third-party) cloud services.

On-premises Active Directory hosted on Windows Server can be synchronized with WAAD. The process of setting up WAAD and directory synchronization with on-premises Active Directory will be described later in this book.

To enable single sign-on for on-premises users to services running in Microsoft **Azure Active Directory Federation Services (ADFS)** needs to be installed on-premises. ADFS is a kind of proxy between the AD and the Microsoft Azure AD. It does not relay the username/password, but it uses a ticket to authenticate to Azure services.

For an even higher level of security, Microsoft has developed multifactor authentication. Users don't just use their credentials to log on to a server or service, but they must additionally authenticate with another device (another factor), with an app or by responding to an automated text message, before access is granted.

Azure Preview

New features in Microsoft Azure do not come available as a beta. Microsoft adds new features in an extremely rapid pace of about every three weeks. Most new features are first being made available as a Preview. Sometimes, the Preview is open to the public and sometimes usage of the Preview is limited. An example of a limited Preview was Azure Site Recovery.

Like in a beta of any Microsoft software, you should not use Preview features in any production environment. The Preview is meant to do research on the new feature before it eventually becomes generally available. It is also much appreciated when Preview users provide their feedback to Microsoft.

Azure Previews are likely to become generally available at some time. However, there is no guarantee.

An overview of Azure Preview features can be found at `http://www. windowsazure.com/en-us/services/preview/`.

Best effort versus reliable clouds

Not every IaaS cloud service is the same. There are some fundamental differences between IaaS clouds. The main difference is in the architecture of the platform. Gartner has named the two most common architectures a *best effort cloud* and a *reliable cloud*. Other names for these different types of clouds are *designed for failure* versus *enterprise* clouds or *stateless cloud service model* versus *stateful cloud service model*.

A designed for failure cloud has been designed for running applications that have resiliency built into the application. This means that when a particular part of the application fails, the application continues to be available. This comes down to an application made up of many different virtual machines. Think about an application with a web tier, an application server tier, and a database tier. Each tier has at least two nodes so that if one node fails, the application will continue to be available.

A best effort cloud uses commodity hardware with no redundancy built into the hardware. For example, there is only one power supply, and a single fan for cooling. There is a single top-of-rack switch, no live migration of virtual machines, and so on. In some cases, the cloud provider does not have a Service Level Agreement available for single instance virtual machines.

As virtual machines are nonpersistent, there is no need for backup virtual machines. Backup at the storage layer is good enough.

Microsoft Azure is an example of a best effort cloud. In the next section, you will learn why.

A reliable cloud has been designed to host legacy, non-cloud ready applications that have single points of failures built into the application. In this cloud, the infrastructure is designed such that it provides resiliency for the application. An enterprise class with redundant components is the server hardware used. The cloud platform provides high availability and fault tolerance.

Virtual machines are persistent and a frequent backup is required. VMware vCloud Air and other VMware vClouds are examples of reliable cloud platforms.

Microsoft Azure is a best effort cloud

Microsoft Azure is designed for cattle type applications. We discussed cattle versus pets in *Chapter 1, An Introduction to Cloud Computing*.

Azure does not have facilities to move virtual machines without downtime to other nodes in case of planned maintenance. Virtual machines will restart when Microsoft installs updates on the nodes. For this reason, Microsoft does not have a Service Level Agreement for single-instance virtual machines.

For customers to get guarantees on availability via an SLA, there needs to be at least two instances serving the same application role that are required to be part of the same availability set. In the next chapter, we will discuss availability sets.

Microsoft also does not support the Windows Server Failover Clustering role in virtual machines running on Azure. The only exception is SQL Server AlwaysOn Availability Groups, which are fully supported by Microsoft. So Windows clustering cannot be used to have redundant instances. This restriction means that many traditional applications will not be the most obvious choice to move to Microsoft Azure. If the application runs on a single virtual machine only, Microsoft will not offer an SLA on the virtual machine. Customers will need to rearchitect those traditional applications to be able to run on best effort clouds.

The result is that many traditional applications currently in use will have to be rewritten if they are to be deployed on Microsoft Azure and require high availability.

Microsoft is working on a solution for downtime because of planned maintenance on Azure hosts. The technology will be some sort of hot patching. This will allow installation of hotfixes on Azure hosts without the need to reboot the host. At the moment no information is publicly available on this new technology Microsoft is developing.

An alternative to rearchitecting the application or acquiring a new application is to use a reliable cloud platform like VMware vCloud Air.

Dedicated versus private virtual clouds

Cloud service providers sometimes offer their customers two options in their IaaS offering:

* A dedicated, private cloud
* A shared cloud

Private cloud hosting or *dedicated cloud* means the virtualization host machines exclusively run virtual machines of a single tenant, and there is physical isolation at the compute level. Storage, networking, and other components are mostly logical, isolated using virtual LAN and virtual storage features. Without logical isolation, this will be a very expensive kind of cloud.

The advantage of this kind of cloud is on security and performance. Some organizations do not want shared processing by multiple tenants. They believe there is a risk other tenants might be able to look into virtual machines of other tenants. Another aspect is performance.

The third possible reason for using a dedicated cloud is compliance requirements regarding licensing. Some vendors believe their customers need to license the number of CPU sockets that a virtual machine can possibly run on. When using a dedicated cloud, the potential number of CPUs is restricted and is easy to count in a license assessment.

In shared cloud processing, resources are shared between multiple tenants. This makes this offer cheaper than a dedicated cloud. Virtual machines of multiple tenants are processes on the same host. Tenants do not have any control over where their virtual machines are running.

Microsoft Azure does not offer a private/dedicated cloud. Compute, network, and storage resources are logically isolated. So, virtual machines of multiple tenants will share the same Azure host.

Use case scenarios for Microsoft Azure

In the previous section, you learned that Microsoft Azure is not well suited to run legacy, traditional stateful applications which rely on single nodes. You can easily recognize that type of application. If you are afraid to stop a virtual machine that serves an application, that application is a legacy, not a cloud aware application.

So what are the use case scenarios for using Microsoft Azure in general and in a hybrid cloud scenario in particular? We will answer this question in the following sections.

Test and development

Azure offers a lot of facilities for software developers. Images complete with operating systems and applications such as SQL Server, SharePoint, or Oracle databases can be deployed with a few mouse clicks. Several developer tools are available. The best thing for dev/test scenarios is that when Microsoft Azure VMs are shut down, Microsoft stops billing you for them. So, when developers need a virtual machine for programming and another virtual machine for testing the code, they can stop working when they leave the office and their expenses (for compute resources) stop when they turn off the lights in their office.

Temporary processing power

Microsoft Azure provides lots of processing power that can be provisioned very quickly. There are many use cases in the medical world where applications are running in Azure that perform analytics on DNA or medicines. Instead of days of calculations in an on-premises infrastructure, calculations in Azure can be done in hours. This happens without the capital investment needed for on-premises compute resources.

Cloud bursting

Some information of services available via Internet have temporary peaks in demand. Think about web shops that get a lot of additional page views in the weeks before Christmas, or websites of events like the Olympic Games. Another example is the website of the Swedish organization that awards the Nobel Prize.

Demand peaks only during a couple of week per year. It does not make sense to invest into infrastructure just to handle these peaks. Microsoft Azure is a perfect cloud platform for use during peak demand on web services.

Windows Server and Data Protection Manager cloud backup

There are many use cases for using Microsoft Azure as an offsite location for storage of backup data. Azure could potentially replace backup tapes. Storage on disk is much more efficient and easier to handle. There is one caveat and that is the restore time. If you need to restore lots of data back from Azure, it can take a lot of time.

Backup data created by Windows Server backup and Microsoft Data Protection Manager can be stored in Microsoft Azure using a standalone backup agent.

SQL Server cloud backup

Microsoft makes it very easy for customers to store backup data of on-premises SQL Server in Microsoft Azure. SQL Server 2012 and 2014 offer a built-in ability to store SQL Server backup in Microsoft Azure. The backup data is encrypted.

For versions like SQL Server 2008 and earlier, Microsoft offers a standalone tool that is able to automatically store, compress, and encrypt SQL Server backup files in Microsoft Azure. Configuration of backup to Azure from the SQL Server user interface is very straight forward

StorSimple seamless backup

StorSimple is a hardware appliance which serves as a local storage device. It offers several storage tiers. One of the tiers is Azure storage. The StorSimple device will automatically move infrequently used blocks of data to Microsoft Azure, thus reducing on-premises storage costs.

Besides backup, the StorSimple appliance is also useful for disaster recovery. Full backups can be stored in Azure. When on-premises storage is unavailable, the StorSimple device can be used to restore access to data in minutes without having to perform a full restore. The device will copy only the hot data to the on-premises StorSimple device.

A use case for StoreSimple in the medical field could be built around X-ray scans. These scans need to be available to doctors for long periods after a patient leaves the hospital, but when an unfortunate person returns with another broken limb after years of good health, the specialist should be able to consult the earlier data. This data doesn't need to be on-site, but should be available to the doctor as if it were on site.

SQL Server cloud replica

SQL Server 2014 offers the ability to use a SQL Server 2014 running as a virtual machine in Azure as a replica. This offers a cost-effective disaster recovery solution for SQL databases.

DFS cloud replica

Windows Distributed File Shares can be replicated to a DFS server running in Azure. This enables easy offsite storage.

Disaster recovery

Azure Site Recovery allows for an orchestrated failover in case of a disaster. It also enables Azure as a target for replication. If a customers' primary on-premises datacenter is protected by Hyper-V Replica and managed by System Center, Azure Site Recovery can perform a fully automated failover to the customers' secondary datacenter. No customer data is stored in Microsoft Azure, just the metadata of the infrastructure, such as virtual machine names and network names.

In the next chapters, we will go into the details of the scenarios described earlier. You will learn about the benefits, the caveats, and how to install and manage.

On-premises and cloud feature misalignment

It is likely that Microsoft customers using Hyper-V and System Center on-premises will consider Microsoft Azure as their preferred cloud platform for hybrid cloud. Microsoft does a lot of promotion of its Cloud OS vision and makes sure System Center integrates nicely with Azure.

While a seamless experience for management of both on- and off-premises might be very obvious, there are some caveats. The caveats are in the missing features in Azure on virtual machine management compared to what Hyper-V has to offer.

Despite Microsoft Azure running Hyper-V on the nodes, there are quite some differences in management features between on-premises and Microsoft Azure. This is partly caused by the mixture of Windows Server 2008 R2 Hyper-V and Windows Server 2012 Hyper-V deployed in Azure datacenters. The exact percentage of 2008 versus 2012 Hyper-V is not made public by Microsoft.

So let's have a look of what Azure is missing at the moment (January 2015) for the management of virtual machines:

- There is no VMConnect capability for console access to the virtual machine as there is with Hyper-V. The virtual machine in Azure can be managed remotely using **Remote Desktop Protocol (RDP)**, PowerShell, or Server Manager. However, these all need a working network connection. If the network connection is not available, there is no way anymore to manage the virtual machine. Microsoft is working on a way to reset the network if an administrator made a mistake so RDP access is not possible anymore..

- No live migration for planned maintenance. Azure customers are not able to use the Hyper-V Live Migration feature to move a virtual machine to another host. Simply because Azure does not offer Live Migration. This is because of the stateless architecture of the platform. If an application depends on a single virtual machine, the application will be offline when Microsoft performs maintenance on nodes. Another reason for Microsoft not to offer Live Migration on Azure is the amount of network bandwidth required for Live Migration. Image all those virtual machines moving to other servers. Microsoft need that east-west network bandwith for regular network traffic generated by customers. Microsoft is working on a solution. Little is known at the moment (January 2015) about this solution. It is based on a new technology which enables a fast switch from an old host operating system to a new, patched operating system. The virtual machines on that host will not have downtime during the switch or very limited downtime.

- There are no checkpoints/snapshots. Currently, it is not possible to make a point in time backup of a running virtual machine using checkpoints. A checkpoint, also can be very handy in situations where a rollback to a known good state is required. Microsoft is considering adding a snapshot feature in the future.

- There is no VDHX support. Virtual disks in Windows Server 2012 Hyper-V can be as large as 64 TB when the VHDX format is used. However Azure does not support VHDX. It is currently limited to VHD format only.

- There is no resize of VHD files. Azure does not allow an online change in the format of a VHD file.

Microsoft Azure security

No book on public cloud computing is complete without a chapter on security and compliancy. Security means doing the best possible to prevent unauthorized access to data and components publishing that data.

Microsoft Azure datacenters are not accessible for unauthorized persons. The only persons allowed to enter the datacenter are security guards and Microsoft staff responsible for operating the infrastructure. Customers are not allowed to enter under any circumstances.

Azure datacenters have a ISO 27001 certification. Each year, a third-party auditing company checks if Microsoft complies with its security policy.

To allow Dutch financial organizations to use Azure, the Dutch bank regulator De Nederlandsche Bank (Dutch Central Bank) has a right to examine Microsoft Azure.

Azure runs in many datacenters worldwide. Two datacenters are located in Europe: one in Amsterdam and one in Dublin. Besides being close to European customers and thus limit latency, it is also required for certain European organizations that data stays within EU boundaries. Azure complies with the EU-US Safe Harbour Framework.

Other certifications are:

- SSAE 16/ISAE 3402 SOC 1, 2, and 3 (this replaces SAS70)
- HIPPA/HITECH
- PCI Data Security Standard Certification (this is a certification required when credit card payments are processed)

The infrastructure under management of Microsoft is protected against unauthorized access. Network access is routed via firewalls, and the physical network is separated using VLANs. Network traffic from the Internet is encrypted using HTTPS and using VPN.

Microsoft does not encrypt replication traffic going to another datacenter yet. Also, data stored on Azure storage is not encrypted by Microsoft. Encryption needs to be done by tooling running on-premises.

Luckily, many of Microsoft's software solutions encrypt data on-premises before it is stored in Azure. System Center Configuration Manager, Data Protection Manager, and StorSimple all encrypt data.

Two-step authentication to the management portal is possible. To access data on the storage system, a complex key (Shared Access Signature) that is used like a password is required.

Microsoft support on Azure

When organizations use Azure IaaS they are themselves responsible for management of the operating system and all the software running on top of that. Microsoft is responsible for management of the virtualization layer and anything below that layer (IT infrastructure). So, when things look broken or organizations have an issue with the components Microsoft is responsible for, you need to contact Microsoft support.

You do need a support contract to be able to get support. Contracts are available in various forms. Microsoft Support can be contacted over the phone or by submitting a support request.

T-shirt virtual machines versus tailor-made virtual machines

Virtual machine sizes are offered by many cloud IaaS providers as t-shirt sizes. That means the configuration of virtual machines memory, number of virtual processors, and hard disk size is limited.

Most likely they do that for their own benefit. Having a limited number of sizes makes it possible to maximize the utilization of the hosts and reduces what is called cutting waste. A fully utilized host makes the most revenue and enables to reduce costs and be competitive.

Virtual machine size offerings are often named like extra small, small, medium, large, and extra-large. Microsoft initially started with naming their virtual machine sizes like this, but later realized this naming has its limits. What about a super-super-large virtual machine name. So, Microsoft switched to names like A5, A6, A7, and so on.

The disadvantage of t-shirt sized virtual machines is that you are probably going to pay for resources you are not going to consume. For example, you need 32 GB of internal memory and two cores, but the provider only offers 32 GB and four cores.

Other IaaS providers like VMware vCloud Air offer a custom sized virtual machine. Customers can configure any combination of number of cores, internal memory, and disk size.

Microsoft Azure cost model

Cloud computing has different cost models:

- Pay-as-you-go
- A commitment consumption-based plan
- Free, on demand, reserved capacity, spot capacity dedicated

Amazon EC2 calls virtual machine capacity that is reserved but not yet used *Reserved Instances*. Customers who bought a reservation but did not use all of it can sell it to other customers in the Amazon EC2 Reserved Instance Marketplace.

When customers choose the pay-as-you-go model, they pay only what they consume. A virtual machine that is switched off is not billed for processing. However, the virtual machine still has storage allocated, so billing for storage will continue while the virtual machine is switched off.

Pay-as-you-go is unpredictable for cloud service providers. They cannot predict how much revenue they will make exactly. They also do not have a good estimate on the number of resources they have to allocate.

So an alternative is a *plan*. In this model, the customer pays in advance and commits to consuming a certain amount of resources. For this commitment, the customer gets a discount. The discount is increased when the commitment is higher.

Microsoft Azure has a spending limit. This means a customer can set a limit on the amount of costs per month. If a particular service is consuming more than expected, the service will be paused when the spending limit is reached.

Obviously, some caution needs to be taken. You do not want your web shop to be shut down because the spending limit was reached and the cloud platform has paused or stopped servers hosting the website. Microsoft charges by the minute and not by the hour, like many other providers.

Also, the average usage over a certain time frame is calculated. Suppose a customer has 100 GB of data at the first of the month and 200 GB at the end of the month, Microsoft will bill 150 GB for the whole month.

Microsoft Azure service-level agreement

The cloud consumer wants to have a guarantee that their services will be available for a certain amount of time. If not, there should be some sort of compensation. Agreements on the availability are documented in Service Level Agreements (also called SLAs).

SLAs are not sexy. I have seen many providers with an unclear SLA and customers not worrying about it. If you are a customer of a cloud service provider, you should be concerned about a SLA: know what it says, what the maximum downtime is, and how the service provider compensates for this.

Each SLA of a cloud provider is different. For one provider, the SLA is effective for the complete virtual machine, including dependent services such as storage and networking, while for another provider, the SLA only covers the virtual machine and is not applicable to virtual machine storage. Some are measured in years and some in months of availability.

As Microsoft Azure offers various services, each service has its own SLA. The following SLAs are available for:

- Virtual machines
- Cloud networking

- Cloud services
- On storage
- Multifactor authentication
- Websites
- SQL database
- SQL Reporting
- Caching
- CDN
- Service Bus

Microsoft uses a whole year in their SLA availability. 99.95 percent means a maximum of 263 minutes of downtime per year. An availability of 99.9 percent means 526 minutes of downtime per year.

Most of these services offer a 99.90 percent availability. For cloud services and Virtual Machines Microsoft even offers an availability of 99.95 percent. The caveat here is that to get this availability, virtual machines need to have to have at least two instances deployed in the same availability set. We will discuss this in detail in the next chapter.

To calculate the maximum downtime per year customers need to add the various Azure components of which their service is depending on.

For example, consider a customer who is using two virtual machines. They depend on the virtual machines (99.95 percent), storage (99.9 percent), cloud networking (99.9 percent), and cloud services (99.95 percent) Azure services.

So, the maximum downtime of the customer service without Microsoft having to credit is 1576 minutes per year (*263 + 525 + 525 + 263 = 1576*), which equals over 26 hours per year.

Microsoft software support

As Microsoft Azure is a Microsoft product, it doesn't automatically mean that all Microsoft software is fully supported to run on the Microsoft Azure platform.

However, most Microsoft software is supported. Supported means that customers can call Microsoft support and will get full support if their software is running on Microsoft Azure.

Windows Server 2008 and later is supported. There are a few roles that are unsupported:

- Dynamic Host Configuration Protocol Server
- Hyper-V
- Remote Access (Direct Access)
- Rights Management Services
- Windows Deployment Services

Besides the aforementioned roles, Microsoft also does not support the following features:

- Bitlocker drive encryption (on the operating system hard disk, but it can be used on data disks)
- Windows Server Failover Clustering (except for SQL Server AlwaysOn Availability Groups)
- High Availability and Disaster Recovery for SQL Server in Microsoft Azure Virtual Machines
- Internet Storage Name Server
- Multipath I/O
- Network Load Balancing
- Peer Name Resolution Protocol
- SNMP Services
- Storage Manager for SANs
- Windows Internet Name Service
- Wireless LAN Service

At the moment (January 2015), Microsoft supports the following software on Azure:

- SharePoint (2013 and 2013)
- SQL Server (2008 and later)
- BizTalk (2013) and Dynamic NAV
- System Center 2012 SP1 App Controller
- Operations Manager
- Orchestrator
- App-V and Service Manager

- Dynamics GP
- Team Foundation Server

Exchange Server, Dynamics CRM, and Dynamics AX are currently in validation for support by Microsoft to be run on Microsoft Azure.

Other vendor software support

When server virtualization was new, many software vendors were reluctant about supporting their software when it was running in a virtual machine. Some vendors were only willing to give support if the customer was able to prove the issue was not related to virtualization. In some cases, they even had to perform a virtual to physical conversion of their workload as evidence. Oracle was one of those companies that clearly stated that in rare cases the customer had to perform such a conversion.

Software vendors nowadays are less reserved in supporting their software when it runs on cloud platforms and Microsoft Azure in particular. Microsoft has put in a lot of effort to make sure vendors support Azure. Many large software vendors support Azure, for example, SAP, Citrix, and Oracle. Oracle announced that it will fully support customers running their software on Microsoft Azure and Hyper-V.

Microsoft software license mobility

While software is in many cases supported by the vendor to be run on Microsoft Azure, there are some complications with licensing.

Basically, there are two scenarios. Customers can create a new virtual machine in Azure and one of the many available images. An image is a virtual machines that has operating system and application software preinstalled. The customer pays a fee for using the operating system and a fee for using the application; no hassles with license management here.

The second scenario is where the customer is either moving a current server or application from on-premises to the cloud including a license, or wants to create a new server in Azure using his own application license.

This second scenario called *bring your own license* is often very complicated. It is like your pension. Very important, but not sexy and very complicated. Many people trust that their pension is okay, but some will find out it is not when an audit is performed. When you find this out, it usually takes lots of time and effort, and thus money, to correct the situation.

Charging for the use of software is often still based on the usage of the numbers of sockets in a physical server. License agreements often do not allow software to be used in a multitenant environment. Both restrictions are a big issue in cloud infrastructures. A virtual machine can potentially be running on many physical servers during its lifecycle. If a customer is charged for each and every socket the software has run on, the charge will be enormous.

Finally, when a license forbids the usage in a multitenant environment, the software cannot be used in many cloud platforms. Compute resources in Microsoft Azure are always shared by multiple tenants/customers. Other cloud platforms offer a choice between dedicated cloud or shared cloud.

When a custom-made virtual machine image containing Windows Server is uploaded to Microsoft Azure, Microsoft provides the license key for that instance. When a Windows Server virtual machine originally created in Microsoft Azure is moved to on-premises, the customer needs to assign their own license to that instance when running the virtual machine on-premises.

I could dedicate a whole book on software licensing but that is out of the scope of this book. Here are a few important remarks about Microsoft software license mobility:

- License mobility is only eligible for Microsoft SQL Server, SharePoint, Exchange, System Center, and Lync Server.

- All other Microsoft software running in a multitenant cloud environment needs to be licensed using the **Service Provider License Use (SPLA)** licensing. This means the tenant is charged in a pay per use model for usage of the Microsoft software. The provider will collect the charge and will pay Microsoft for the usage of the license.

- Customers cannot transfer Windows Server licenses to the cloud. Also, Microsoft desktop operating system licenses cannot be transferred to cloud platforms.

- Software assurance is required for License mobility. Customers with the following Volume Licensing agreements have License mobility: Enterprise Agreements, Enterprise Subscription Agreements, and Microsoft Open Value Agreements.

- License mobility through Software Assurance allows us to use the customer owned license to run application software on shared hardware owned by a provider. However, despite sharing hardware, such instances must be dedicated to a single customer, and cannot be shared with other customers.

- Customers are not allowed to move licenses to any cloud or service provider. The provider should be an Authorized Mobility Partner of Microsoft.

- Customers must request Microsoft within 10 days of deploying their license on a cloud platform for confirmation the license is eligible for License Mobility.

- Microsoft licenses must be assigned to a cloud platform for at least 90 days.

Bring your own application license

Very few vendors have yet made firm statements that customer purchased software licenses can be used in cloud environments as well. Oracle allows you to bring your own license or license mobility for their products on both Azure and Amazon. Depending on the Oracle software, four virtual cores are counted as one socket, which is the equivalent to one processor license.

Trying Microsoft Azure

Now that you know a lot about the functionality of Microsoft Azure, you might be interested in trying Azure yourself. Microsoft made it very easy to try Microsoft Azure. Customers get a free trial for 30 days and a credit of $200/€150.

Within a few minutes from now, you will be able to log in to a Windows of a Linux server running in Azure.

The requirements to subscribe for a free Azure subscription are as follows:

- A credit card, which is used to authenticate you. It will not be charged.

- A Microsoft (LiveID) account.

- A mobile phone to receive an authorization code via SMS.

You will not be charged on the credit card. If the credit given by Microsoft has reached the value of zero, the trial stops.

To try out Azure go to `http://www.windowsazure.com` and click on **Free Trial**.

Microsoft customers who have an MSDN subscription with Visual Studio receive free Microsoft Azure usage credits per month and discounts on services like Virtual Machines. The free usage credits range from $50 to $150 per month.

This offer is only valid for test and development usage. If Microsoft finds out that the free Azure credits are used for production or are running over 120 hours, Microsoft has the right to terminate virtual machines or other Azure services.

If you are a student without a credit card, Microsoft offers a free 180-day Azure Academic Pass. You can apply for an Educator Grant of Microsoft Azure Academic Passes at `http://www.windowsazurepass.com/azureu`.

Note that Microsoft does not provide technical support for customers using the MSDN credits. Those customers are entitled for support on billing only. The response time is 8 hours.

Summary

In this chapter, you learned about the Microsoft Cloud OS vision of Microsoft and how this is translated into real-world solutions. We discussed the various components of System Center. You also learned that there are two types of clouds and that Microsoft Azure is a "best effort" cloud. We also discussed license mobility and the restrictions, which are very important.

The next chapter will be the first in this book where we will take a closer look at the technical side of things, and you will learn about the architecture of Microsoft Azure.

3
Understanding the Microsoft Azure Architecture

In this chapter, we will go through the various components of the architecture of Azure. This will provide a high-level understanding of the architecture. You will also learn about the features offered by Azure for computation, storage, and networking.

A look under the hood of Microsoft Azure

A good understanding of the architecture of the Microsoft Azure platform is important to understand what is going on "under the hood". This will help us in the design of our virtual infrastructure running on Azure hosts, stored on Azure Storage, and connected by Azure Virtual Networks. It will also help us to understand what kind of availability we need to create for applications running in Azure.

Data centers and regions

Microsoft Azure is available in many data centers located in many continents. Each datacenter also houses other Microsoft online services besides Microsoft Azure services, such as Office 365, Bing, Xbox Live, and so on. Actually, many Microsoft cloud services are hosted on Azure. The average Microsoft datacenter is about 7 to 10 times the size of a football field. Each datacenter is home to thousands of servers and many petabytes of storage. The maximum capacity of an Azure datacenter is around 100,000 servers.

Data centers are grouped into major geographical regions. In most cases, a single region is a continent. Azure is currently available in regions located in North America, Europe, Asia, and Brazil.

Each region has at least one datacenter. Each region is paired to another region with a minimum distance of around 500 miles. This is done so that hurricanes, floods, and other natural disasters will not destroy two regions at the same time.

Current operational regions are:

- Europe West (Amsterdam) paired to Europe North (Dublin)
- US West (California, exact location not disclosed) paired to US East (Virginia)
- Asia Pacific Southeast (Singapore) paired to Asia East (Hong Kong)
- US North Central (Chicago, IL) paired to US South Central (San Antonio, TX)
- Brazil South (Sao Paulo State) paired to US South Central (San Antonio, TX)
- Japan East (Saitama Prefecture near Tokyo) paired to Japan West (Osaka Prefecture in Kansai)
- Australia East (Sydney) paired to Australia Southeast (Melbourne)
- US Central (Iowa) paired to US East 2 (Virginia)

In China, two regions are running Microsoft Azure services. The northeast region is located in Beijing while the east region is located in Shanghai. The data centers in these regions are not operated by Microsoft itself. Microsoft licensed the technology, know-how, and rights to operate and provide Office 365 and Microsoft Azure services in China to 21Vianet. This is the biggest Internet datacenter services provider in China.

Microsoft Azure customers outside China are not able to use the China regions' data centers for consumption of services. These two Chinese regions are isolated from the Microsoft operated regions mostly for political reasons. The Chinese government wants to have control over network traffic leaving and entering China.

The following map shows all Azure data centers worldwide as of summer 2014:

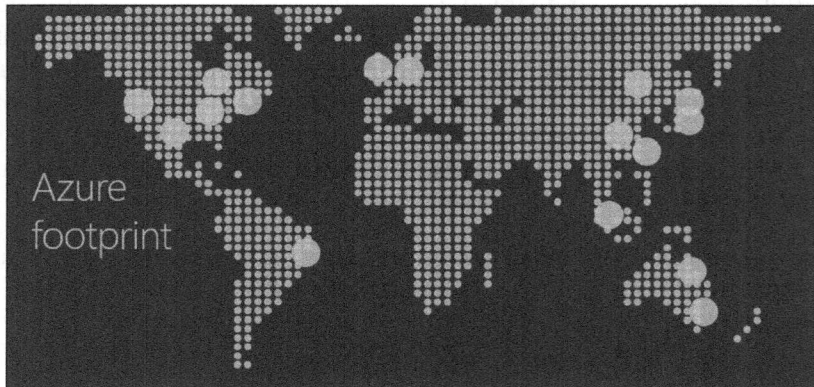

Each region is paired to another region. The pairing of regions is for redundancy reasons. By default, when data is stored in a Microsoft Azure region, it is replicated to the paired region. Data is asynchronously replicated. This means data is stored by the application. The storage layer confirms that the data has been written. Then, the Microsoft storage software will make sure the data is replicated to the paired region with a delay of about 15 minutes.

Customers can enable or disable this **geo-replication** feature.

Microsoft will not transfer customer data outside the major geographic region. So, data placed by customers in the European region will stay in Europe and will not be transferred to, for example, North America.

Besides large data centers, Microsoft also has 24 **Content Delivery Networks** (**CDN**) worldwide. These CDNs are small locations that cache certain content. The main purpose of a CDN is to reduce latency and enhance the user experience.

Developing Microsoft Azure is one of Microsoft's biggest priorities. In 2014, the company spent three billion US dollars on investments in infrastructure for data centers.

Microsoft also adds new services and enhances current services at a rapid pace. In a periodic interval of about three weeks, new enhancements are made available.

Zones

Regions are grouped into zones. Zones were created to charge outbound data transfers. Data that goes outside an Azure datacenter is charged by Microsoft.

The costs for outbound data transfers depend on the location of the datacenter. In the United States and Europe, costs for bandwidth are lower than in Asia and Brazil. Currently, Azure has three zones:

- **Zone 1**: US West, US East, US North Central, US East 2, US Central, US South Central, Europe West, and Europe North
- **Zone 2**: Asia Pacific East, Asia Pacific Southeast, Japan East, and Japan West, Australia East, Australia Southeast
- **Zone 3**: Brazil South

Servers used in Azure

Now that we know about the data centers and locations, let's have a look inside the data centers.

Microsoft operates a lot of data centers worldwide to provide various services, such as Office 365 and Microsoft Azure. Some of the data centers use containers similar to sea-containers, which are standalone units containing processing, storage, and networking.

However, in most Azure data centers, servers are not located in containers because of cost constraints. Azure servers are placed in racks. Microsoft Azure is designed such that the application running on top of Microsoft Azure provides resiliency. This type of cloud is named a **best effort cloud**.

This architecture makes sure the platform is relatively simple and cost-efficient. Physical servers that host the Azure virtual machines are industry-standard hardware with hardly any built-in redundancy. So, the servers of brands like Rackable Systems do not have redundant power supplies and redundant fans, for example. This keeps the costs low. Originally, Microsoft used AMD processors. Later, Intel processors were added.

The vision of Microsoft is to invest in facility redundancy instead of server redundancy. Millions of dollars spent on server hardware or network redundancy will prove to be worthless when a complete datacenter is lost because of fire or no outside world connection. Server and network redundancy adds complexity.

The network inside an Azure datacenter is a flat network. It means that each component in the network has multiple connections to other components.

Each datacenter contains many racks full of servers. Most servers are blades. Each rack is installed with a single top-of-rack switch. Each rack contains about 90 servers. These racks are grouped into clusters, or **stamps**, as Microsoft likes to call them.

Each stamp has about 1000 servers/nodes. The reason behind using stamps is partitioning. Partitioning is done to keep availability at a high level. By partitioning, the impact of a failure is reduced to a part of the datacenter.

Each datacenter also has multiple racks for storage with two top-of-rack switches in each. Each storage rack contains 36 storage cabinets. Microsoft uses storage stamps for grouping different racks. A storage stamp typically contains 10 to 20 racks. Each rack is a fault domain. As data is by default stored in three different copies, each copy is stored in a different storage stamp.

Top-of-rack switches are connected to multiple switches which form the cluster spine. The datacenter spine switches are located above the cluster spine level of switches.

Hypervisor used in Azure

Now that you have learned how an Azure datacenter is built using server hardware, network, and storage, it is time to learn about the software. The "secret sauce" of Microsoft Azure is the software used by Microsoft to manage a massive cloud service such as Azure. This software enables Microsoft to offer a dynamic, self-service cloud with a minimum number of administrators.

Each Azure host runs a hypervisor. From the launch of Azure to the first half of 2012, a hypervisor very similar to Windows Server 2008 R2 Hyper-V was used. In 2013, Microsoft started upgrading hosts to Windows Server 2012 Hyper-V. It is unclear what percentage of servers are now running Windows Server 2012 Hyper-V. In summer 2014, Microsoft started to rollout Windows Server 2012 R2 Hyper-V.

When new server hardware has been installed and is ready for use, it boots from the network using PXE. PXE is a network protocol that allows a server or desktop to load an operating system over the network. It then loads Windows PE as a maintenance operating system. This cleans the local hard disk of the host and loads the host operating system from a VHD image over the network. Then, the maintenance operating system loads Hyper-V.

One of the reasons behind using network boot instead of local install is the ability to return to a good state. The VHD image is very well tested. If anything gets corrupted on the host, the clean VHD image can be used to restore the state of the server.

When security patches become available for the host, they are built into a new version of the VHD image. This image is then deployed to the hosts in a highly controlled manner.

Each host, or **node** as we will call them from now on, runs a special piece of software called the Host Agent or **Fabric Agent** (**FA**). The FA communicates with each virtual machine running on the node. Therefore, each virtual machine has a guest agent installed.

The nodes that are running Hyper-V are not members of a Windows Failover Cluster. Azure uses its own clustering technique.

Each node runs a maximum of 12 virtual machines when the server only hosts the "extra small" virtual machines.

The following image shows the various software components of Microsoft Azure:

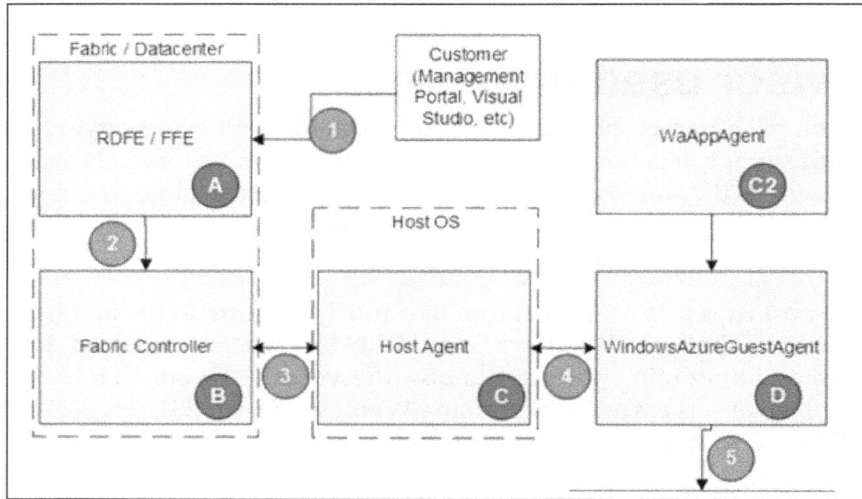

The Fabric Controller

The **Fabric Controller** (**FC**) is a step higher in the software stack. This is the brain of Microsoft Azure. The FC is what the kernel is for an operating system. It is responsible for blade provisioning, blade management, service deployment, monitoring and healing of services, and life cycle management.

The FC not only manages servers, it also manages storage, load balancers, switches, and routers. FCs run as software appliances and are based on a modified Windows Server 2008 instance.

The FC monitors nodes via the FA running in each node. The FC also monitors the guest operating system. If there is no heartbeat received by the FC, it will either restart the guest or the complete node in case the heartbeat of the node is lost.

If the FC detects a hardware failure of the node, it will reallocate the guest to other nodes and mark the node as "out for repair".

It is situated between the datacenter fabric (servers, network, and storage) and the services running on the fabric. The FC runs in five to eight instances that are distributed over at least five fault domains. One FC has the primary role, while the others are replicas. The state of the nodes is replicated over all FCs so each has 100 percent up-to-date status information. If all FCs go down, all Azure services will continue to be available; however, provisioning and fault tolerance will not be operational anymore.

For security reasons, the communication between FCs and the storage and compute nodes is over an isolated VLAN. This VLAN is not used for network traffic originating from Azure customers.

Red Dog Front End

Now that we know the role of the FC, we can take another step upwards.

While the FC controls nodes inside a datacenter, a process running above it controls placement in data centers and clusters. This process is called the **Red Dog Front End** (**RDFE**). The name comes from the initial project name of Azure, Red Dog.

The RDFE is responsible for publishing the publicly exposed Service Management API, which is the frontend to the Management Portal and tools such as Visual Studio, **Azure Cross-Platform Command-line Interface** (**X-Plat CLI**), and PowerShell, which communicate with the RDFE for queries and to submit tasks. An example of such a task is *create virtual machine* or *create storage account*. The RDFE instructs the FC in one of the clusters to perform a certain action.

The Azure management portal instructs the RDFE using APIs. The API-release that the RDFE is publishing is a single point of failure in Azure. There is only a single software version of the RDFE operational at the same time. This release is active in all regions. If Microsoft makes a mistake in updating the RDFE software, all regions are affected.

The reason behind having a single software version is that Microsoft wants to provide the same release of APIs to all customers. If there was a kind of rolling upgrade, there would be two different APIs operational at any given time: the previous release and the updated release.

The API is updated frequently. So, when using the API, a version request needs to be inserted in the code. For an overview of updates of the Service Management API, visit http://msdn.microsoft.com/en-us/library/azure/gg592580.aspx.

Now that we have enough information on what is located under the hood of Microsoft Azure and what it looks like, the next few sections will explain how we can manage the availability of virtual machines.

Fault domains

As you learned earlier, Microsoft Azure is designed such that the application provides resiliency. When hardware fails, the application should be clever enough to make sure it remains available.

While server hardware and top-of-rack switches are not redundant, Microsoft Azure has some resiliency built into the platform to protect it against hardware and software failures.

Azure provides so-called **fault domains**. Fault domains protect services for unplanned downtime.

A fault domain is a unit of failure that has single point of failures in it, such as server or storage nodes or networking and power unit rack switches. A fault domain consists of one or more racks. If, for example, a switched rack power distribution unit fails, all components in that rack will be without power. Also, a failure of a top-of-rack switch will lead to network isolation of all virtual machines running on nodes in that rack. The same rule applies to storage. As data is stored at three different places in a datacenter, this is done in three different fault domains.

You, as a customer, do not have control over the number of fault domains your virtual machines are placed in. Three virtual machines, all part of the same availability set, can be placed by the FC in two different fault domains.

The Azure Management Portal shows in which fault domain a virtual machine is running. To check this, you can select **Cloud Services**, click on the name of the cloud service serving the virtual machines, and click on **INSTANCES**.

To be able to make an application resilient on Azure, at least two instances of each role need to be running. Azure customers are able to control placement of virtual machines in different fault domains by using availability sets.

The following screenshot shows the columns named **UPDATE DOMAIN** and **FAULT DOMAIN**:

NAME	STATUS	SIZE	UPDATE DOMAIN	FAULT DOMAIN
sp3	Running	Medium	0	0
dc1	Running	Small	1	1
dc2	Running	Small	0	0
ex1	Running	Medium	0	0
sp1	Running	Large	0	0
sql1	Running	Extra Large	0	0

DASHBOARD   MONITOR   SCALE PREVIEW   INSTANCES   LINKED RESOURCES   CERTIFICATES

Availability set

Azure **availability sets** are used for two reasons:

* Availability of virtual machines
* Scaling of applications

When two or more virtual machines are members of the same availability set, the Azure FC will make sure those virtual machines are processed by different fault domains. An availability set does not span multiple cloud services. Cloud services are explained in more detail later in this chapter. A cloud service can be seen as a container that contains multiple virtual machines hosting the same application.

So, for example, when you use 10 virtual machines that are all part of the same availability set, five of those virtual machines will be part of fault domain number 1 and five virtual machines will be part of fault domain number 2. This means that if a hardware failure causes a rack to go down, in a worst case scenario, 50 percent of the capacity of your application is temporary lost. At the time of writing this book, there are no more than two fault domains.

> Ensure that you create an availability set first, then create new virtual machines, and only then add those to the availability set during creation. If you create virtual machines first and later add those to the availability set, the virtual machine will immediately reboot after being added to the availability set.

The following image shows two fault domains and an availability set consisting of two virtual machines serving the same application:

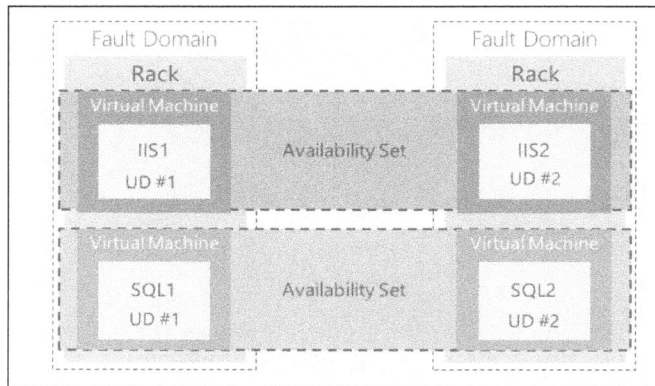

Rebooting is required to place a virtual machine (now part of an availability set) in another fault domain. Azure does not provide a live migration feature that could prevent a shutdown of virtual machines.

A second reason to use availability sets is scaling up or down of applications. Suppose the load on an application increases, for example, an e-commerce website has an increasing number of visitors in the weeks before Christmas.

This peak can automatically be covered by Azure by starting additional virtual machines or web servers. Azure will monitor the average CPU usage of virtual machines that are part of the same availability set. If the CPU usage reaches a value set by the administrator, additional virtual machines will be started. The reverse happens when the CPU usage drops below a threshold.

The advantage of this autoscale feature is that Microsoft does not charge processing costs for virtual machines that are not running. Keep in mind that storage charges still apply!

It is very important to only place virtual machines with the same role in an availability set. Therefore, place only web servers in the `webservers` availability set and place only database servers in the availability set named `database servers`. Do not mix these, since your service within the availability set, let's say a web frontend, is available through a single public IP address.

> An availability set is part of a cloud service. So if you place two virtual machines in different cloud services, those virtual machines cannot be part of the same availability set.

Update domain

An update domain has a function similar to that of the fault domain. However, an update domain protects virtual machines for **planned** downtime.

The reason behind having update domains is that Microsoft frequently needs to update the software running on nodes. This is done once every one to three months, just as many on-premises Windows Server installations. The updates are done sequentially using groups of storage or compute nodes, one at a time. Upgrades and updates are first applied to the first group, then to the second group, and so on.

Update domains consist of multiple racks.

When an Azure node is being updated, virtual machines running on that node are not available. The node will reboot, causing the virtual customers to reboot as well. There are no plans made available by Microsoft to indicate when this happens for virtual machines that are part of an availability set.

Microsoft does plan the maintenance on hosts running single instance virtual machines. However, single instance virtual machines are those that are not part of an availability set. Microsoft communicates a date and time window to the customer. The time window is about 8 hours. Maintenance is done region-wise. Also, updates in subregions that are paired will not be done at the same time. For example, updates in the Amsterdam datacenter will be done on a Monday and for the Dublin datacenter on a Friday.

For updates on virtual machines that are part of an availability set, it is very hard for Microsoft to predict in which time window a certain server will be shut down for maintenance. Even the exact day is hard to predict. The progress of updating all the data centers strongly influences the speed of progress.

The downtime of virtual machines that run on a server that was updated can be up to 15 to 20 minutes. As explained in *Chapter 2, An Introduction to Microsoft Cloud Solutions*, Microsoft is working in a hot patching technique which allows virtual machines to remain operational when Azure nodes are patched.

This segmentation of updating nodes is done for two reasons. First reason is that when Microsoft applies upgrades to nodes, in many cases the nodes will require a reboot. To prevent all Azure nodes to go into reboot, the upgrades are done in groups. Microsoft starts upgrading nodes on the first group, does a reboot, and monitors if all nodes come up and behave normally. If this is the case, upgrades are applied to the next group and this process continues until all nodes are upgraded.

The second reason behind using update domains is to prevent a faulty update from bringing down major parts of the Azure infrastructure.

Azure customers cannot determine which virtual machines are part of which update domains. They can, however, instruct the FC how much percentage of their servers can be taken down when Microsoft updates nodes. This is done by configuring the Microsoft Azure Service Definition Schema file. However, this file is used when using Azure in a PaaS model.

When using virtual machines, each virtual machine placed in an availability set will not only be placed in a unique fault domain, it will also be placed in a unique update domain.

In Azure IaaS, the number of update domains used cannot be controlled by the customer. Azure will use five update domains for virtual machines that are part of the same availability set. This means that for an update, a minimum of 20 percent of the capacity will not be available during the update process.

A single upgrade domain can span multiple fault domains, and multiple upgrade domains can live in a single fault domain. This means there is no guarantee that all instances from a single upgrade domain will be placed in different fault domains.

Affinity group

Another method by which customers can control placement of processing and storage is by using affinity groups. An affinity group can be used by customers to have control over:

- Latency
- Costs

An affinity group can be used to place virtual machines and storage close to each other in the same datacenter. Since an Azure datacenter is a very large facility, latency between two virtual machines running at each end of the datacenter can be high. The affinity group will make sure both storage and processing will be placed close to each other.

First create an affinity group and then place network, storage accounts, and virtual machines in this affinity group. Once a virtual machine has been created, it cannot be added to another affinity group.

The name of an affinity group has to be unique within an Azure subscription. Each virtual network needs to be member of an affinity group.

Affinity groups can only be used to place storage and virtual machines close to each other. This is because of the way Azure services are housed. Services are housed in containers. This is not the sea container type that Microsoft uses for other data centers. An Azure container is just a collection of racks and clusters. Each of those containers have specific services, for example, compute and storage, SQL Azure, service bus, access control service, and so on. As we can see, only compute clusters and storage clusters are part of the same container.

The second function of affinity groups is control of costs. Microsoft charges for network traffic leaving the datacenter. Suppose the web tier of an application is running in the Amsterdam datacenter while the databases are running in the Dublin datacenter — this has an effect on the costs.

Microsoft Azure Storage

In this section, we will have a look at storage of Microsoft Azure. The storage service is named **Microsoft Azure Storage**.

Azure Storage is built using **just a bunch of disks (JBOD)** arrays with disk controllers running in software. You could see this as software-defined storage. Azure storage can be accessed directly using a URL. So, even when no virtual machines are used by a customer, storage can still be accessed. This kind of publishing data can be compared to, for example, CIFS shares on certain enterprise storage arrays. The storage arrays can directly present file shares to Windows servers or Windows desktops; there is no need to have a Windows server in-between the client and storage layer.

Azure Storage is very scalable. There is no limit to the amount of storage that can be used. There is a limit on performance in the storage account however.

When we look at the lowest level of storage, there are two ways to deliver raw storage capacity:

- By using local storage
- By using shared, distributed storage

Local storage

Local storage is provided by the physical servers. A set of around five hard disks located in each server contains a volume and is made available to the virtual machines running on the host.

Azure uses local storage to store nonpersistent data. That means the data is lost when the host crashes or needs to be reimaged using a fresh Windows server image.

Local storage is used for the PaaS server of Azure to store operating system virtual disks. The PaaS and IaaS services use local storage as well to store the virtual disk that holds the Windows pagefile. This is the D: volume that each virtual machine in Azure has.

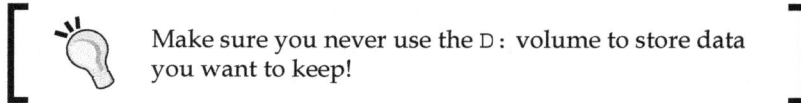

> Make sure you never use the D: volume to store data you want to keep!

Also, the host cache uses the local storage on the host.

Shared storage

A major component of every datacenter is the storage system. Microsoft Azure does not use the type of storage arrays we are familiar with, for example, EMC, NetApp, or HP LeftHand. This type of storage does not scale and is not able to handle the types of files used in a cloud. It is also very expensive.

Microsoft developed its own distributed storage. This is called Microsoft Azure Storage. It is a durable filesystem. Data is stored in a datacenter at three different locations. Geo-replication is enabled by default for a storage account, which means the data is replicated to the paired region and stored there as well on three different locations. So, by default, data is stored using six copies.

Azure Storage is a very complex and sophisticated way of storing data in a resilient way. This chapter will give a high-level overview of Microsoft Azure Storage.

Microsoft Azure Storage uses cabinets full of hard disks in a JBOD configuration. Racks are filled with those storage cabinets. A group of multiple racks is called a storage stamp.

Storage cabinets or nodes are similar to compute nodes controlled by the FC. There is a separate FC per storage stamp in order to prevent certain classes of errors from affecting more than one stamp.

All handling of storage is done by software-based controllers.

Azure's storage architecture separates the logical and physical partitioning of data into separate layers of the system.

The following image shows the layers used in the Azure Storage architecture:

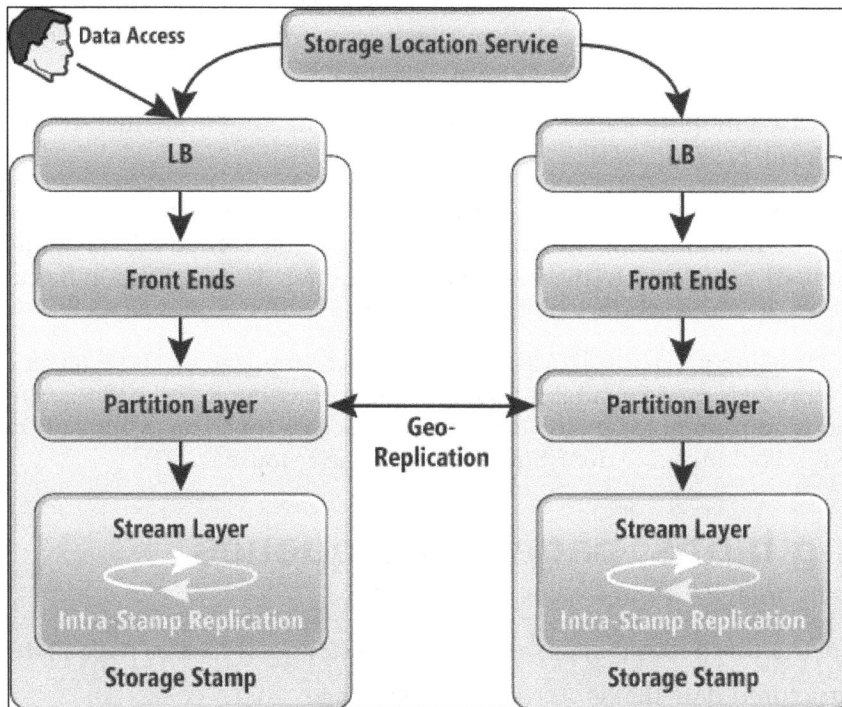

There are three layers in the preceding image:

- **Front End (FE) layer**: This serves as a type of router for data. The FE knows which partition server is responsible for a certain amount of data. The FE redirects transactions to the partition server responsible for controlling (serving) access to each partition in the system.

- **Partition layer**: The partition layer has partition servers. A partition server can be best seen as a controller for LUNs in enterprise storage. In Azure, we talk about partitions instead of LUNs. The partition server is aware of what type of data is processed. It understands blob, table, and queue storage types.

- **Stream layer**: This is also called the **distributed and replicated file system (DFS)** layer. This layer stores the data on disk and is responsible for the distribution of data over storage servers for resiliency. There are many DFS servers active in Azure. The DFS layer stores the data in "extents". This is a unit of storage on disk and a unit of replication, where each extent is replicated multiple times. The typical extent sizes range from approximately 100 MB to 1 GB in size. The stream layer is also responsible for geo-replication.

The servers used in these three layers are placed in the fault domains. At the filesystem-level, NTFS is used.

Data is stored in a single datacenter at three locations for resiliency. Each location is in another fault and update domain. If geo-replication is enabled, the data is asynchronously replicated to the secondary datacenter. The replication has a delay of 15 minutes. In the secondary datacenter, there are three copies as well.

Azure DFS is using journaling for the writes that are replicated. The data stored by Azure storage is made available over the network using REST API instructions. There is no requirement for a virtual machine to access this data. Microsoft uses hardware load balancers to distribute load over the resources.

Storing blobs, pages, and queues

Azure offers storage for three types of data:

- Unstructured files that are stored as blob storage (block or page blobs)
- Structured data that is stored as table storage
- Messages stored in queue storage

Data and messages are data types in use for the Platform as a Service model in Azure. These are very useful for applications being developed on Azure. Virtual machine data as well as backup data is stored as blob storage.

Blob storage can be best seen as a filesystem in the cloud. Blobs allow you to access individual files over the Internet. A blob is just like a text file, VHD file, or any other unstructured file on a regular filesystem. Also, each file stored in a blob has a URL associated with it. In this way, each file can be modified using HTTPS. Data can be read or modified using the REST API. There is versioning, so older versions of files can be retrieved. This can be extremely useful when you need to restore an older version of virtual disk files, for example.

Blobs are suitable for random read/write payloads and can be a maximum of 1 TB in size. A common use case of a page blob is a VHD mounted as a drive in a Microsoft Azure role.

Block blobs are useful for streaming.

Data cannot be encrypted automatically by instances in Azure storage. If customers want to encrypt data, it should be done by the appliance or application. For example, StorSimple, the Microsoft hybrid storage solution, will encrypt all outgoing data that is sent to the supported cloud platforms.

Each blob is linked to a disk object. The "disk object" kind of storage connects the blob storage to a service in Azure. The disk object is the glue that connects the virtual machine to the VHD. If the disk object is deleted, the connection is broken. However, the VHD file remains on the storage and can be reused.

Blobs are organized in containers. Containers can be seen as folders, as we know from Windows NTFS. Virtual machine disk files (VHD) are automatically created in a container named vhds.

Each container has an **access control list (ACL)**. The default access for a container is private, which means only the owner of the storage account can access the data.

The Public blob access option allows public read access to the blob. However, the container properties cannot be read by this role.

A blob file can have multiple snapshots. A snapshot can be seen as a point-in-time copy of the file. It allows us to restore a previous version of the blob file. It works the in the same way as snapshots of virtual machines.

A blob cannot be removed as long as the blob has snapshots. In the Azure Management Portal, you are not able to manage snapshots. Snapshot management can be performed using scripts, or third-party tools can be used. Storage tools will be discussed later in this chapter.

Storage account

Storage and compute in Microsoft Azure are different services. This means a customer can use only storage without having to create virtual machines or another Azure service first. For example, a customer who uses StorSimple to back up data to the cloud only consumes disk storage.

To access the data located in Azure, customers need to have a storage account. A storage account is like an account for Active Directory—a key to authenticate.

A storage account needs to have a unique Azure name. If another Azure customer already took your favorite storage account name, you are out of luck and you will need to find another name.

The reason for the requirement of a unique storage account name is that the storage account has a URL such as `<yourstorageaccount>.<type of storage>.core.windows.net`.

Storage in Microsoft Azure can be accessed over the Internet using the REST API or PowerShell scripts. To reach the data, the URL is used.

When the very first virtual machine is created in an Azure subscription, a storage account is created automatically. However, Microsoft Azure randomly creates a storage account name. A storage account has an account name and two 512-bit string access keys (primary and secondary). The secondary access key is a backup for when the first one is lost or otherwise not useable.

The access keys have a function just like a password for a regular user account stored in Active Directory.

For ease of management, I advise you to create a storage account first and give the account an easy to distinguish name.

For an Azure subscription, the maximum number of storage accounts has a maximum of 100 storage accounts per Azure subscription. Customers are not charged for the total number of storage accounts they have. Each storage account is currently limited to a maximum amount of data per storage account, which is 500 TB.

When a virtual machine is provisioned for the first time, a storage account is automatically created using the wizard.

Storage accounts have limits. It is important to understand those limits. By using multiple storage accounts, storage performance can be improved.

Max. IOPS per storage account	20,000 per SLA
Maximum IOPS for persistent disk	500
Maximum capacity per storage account	500 TB
Transactions	20,000 entities/messages/blobs per second
Bandwidth for geo-redundant storage account	Ingress – up to 5 Gigabits per second Egress – up to 10 Gigabits per second
Bandwidth for a Locally Redundant storage account	Ingress – up to 10 Gigabits per second Egress – up to 15 Gigabits per second

Do not place more than 40 highly used VHDs in an account
to avoid the 20,000 IOPS limit.

When we look at the virtual disk level, each virtual disk of a virtual machine is able
to deliver 500 IOPS and 60 MB/second for no caching disks for I/O of 64 KB or less.

At the time of writing this book, the 500 IOPS is not capped. However, it will be
capped to give a consistent performance.

Microsoft is working on enabling Quality of Service for disk I/O. This will mean that
customers can select the maximum number of IOPS and will be charged accordingly.

Disks

In the previous sections, you learned about local storage and Microsoft Azure
Storage, which is a distributed storage system. You learned that Microsoft offers
three types of storage: blob, page, and queue storage.

Azure virtual machines use virtual hard disks to store data. These disks are stored
as VHD files. VHD is storage as a page blob.

Basically, this is the same as how Hyper-V uses VHD files. Each disk volume of a
Hyper-V virtual machine uses a VHD file.

From the Azure Management console, you are not able to see VHD files. You will
need an Azure storage browser to see the VHD files located in the storage account.

However, a VHD is not directly connected to an Azure virtual machine. Azure
virtual machines use an object named `Disks`.

Microsoft Azure has three types of disks:

- Operating system disks
- Temporary disks
- Data disks

There is a one-to-one relationship between the VHD and the disk. A disk can be
attached to a virtual machine or can be disconnected from a virtual machine.

The default naming convention of a virtual hard disk containing an operating system that is deployed using the image gallery is as follows:

```
<cloud service name>-<virtual machine instance name>-<year>-<month>-
<day>.vhd
```

For example, a virtual machine instance with the name `Fileserver01` that is part of the cloud service named `production001` that is created on November 1, 2013, will have a VHD named `Production001-fileserver01-2013-11-01.vhd`.

You cannot adjust this default naming convention.

Windows Server operating system disks are always 127 GB in size, and similar to all Azure disks, they cannot be resized using the Azure Management Portal.

> It is *very* important to define a naming convention for additional disks added to the virtual machines. Without a proper naming convention, it will be difficult to associate which VHD and which disk belongs to which virtual machine.

The temporary disk is always automatically assigned the letter D: when a virtual machine is deployed from the Azure Management Portal. The D: volume is a nonpersistent disk. The data stored on this disk is lost in the following situations:

- When the virtual machine is assigned to a different host. This can happen when the host has been shut down and is restarted for maintenance reasons. The FC will run the virtual machine on a new host.
- When the size of the virtual machine is adjusted by the administrator.
- When the hosts crashes.
- When the host is shut down for maintenance and a new image is installed.

Data disks are used to store anything. The maximum size of a data disk is 1 TB. In Windows Server Manager, however, you can combine several 1 TB disks to create a larger volume.

Each virtual machine can have a number of data disks. The maximum number depends on the size of the virtual machine.

The following table shows the available virtual machine sizes and the maximum number of data disks that can be attached to that virtual machine:

Virtual Machine Size	Maximum Data Disks
Extra Small	1
Small	2
Medium	4
Large	8
Extra Large	16
A6	8
A7	16

A data disk can be an empty disk. You simply use the Azure Management Portal to add an empty disk.

You can also add a disk that you uploaded yourself, for example, a disk that contains your corporate image, custom software, or data you need to share. There are several ways to upload data disks. You can use PowerShell or third-party tools. In the next chapter, we will explain how to do this in detail.

You create a disk from a VHD; think about using the uploaded VHD as a template.

Disk caching

Disk caching improves performance. When caching is set to `active` on a disk, the local disk of the Azure server stores reads and writes coming from Microsoft Azure Storage. So, by using local server attached storage as a buffer, data does not have to go to / come from the Microsoft Azure Storage systems that can be located somewhere else in the datacenter.

Disks can have one of the following three caching modes:

- **ReadWrite**: This is the default mode for the operating system disk. This can be set to data disks as well.
- **ReadOnly**: Set to operating system and data disks.
- **None**: This is the default setting for data disks.

Containers

Containers are like folders in any filesystem, such as FAT or NTFS. Containers are used to organize files. The second purpose of containers is to set access control to certain files.

Images

Images are used to deploy new virtual machines. Basically, images have the same functionality as templates used in Hyper-V or other x86-based hypervisors.

There are three types of images that can be used:

- Microsoft images
- Community images
- Your own images

Microsoft has a lot of "off the shelf" images available in the Azure Management Portal. These are either just Windows Server or Linux installations, or a complete operating system with SharePoint, SQL server, or Oracle databases.

At the time of writing this book, there are 126 different images available. Images allow you to quickly deploy server instances. In the Azure Management Portal, these images are listed as *platform images*.

You can simply select an image from the image gallery named *Windows Server 2012 R2* or *SQL Server 2012 SP1 Web on Windows Server 2008 R2*.

A second image source is VM Depot. It is a community-driven catalog of preconfigured operating systems, applications, and development stacks that can easily be deployed on Microsoft Azure. These images are based on the Linux distributions Centos, openSUSE, SUSE Linux Enterprise Server, and Ubuntu.

You can either select an image from the Azure Management Portal or go to `https://vmdepot.msopentech.com/List/Index`, where you will find a lot of images.

Be aware that these images are supplied by the community. VM Depot is managed by Microsoft Open Technologies Inc., a subsidiary of Microsoft. They do not screen the images for security. You are responsible for making sure the image does not harm the security of your environment.

A third way of using images is to create images yourself. You can customize a virtual machine image, run `sysprep`, and then create an image of it. Images are based on an existing VHD (which is short for virtual hard disk) files.

Copy of blob storage

Azure storage has an interesting feature that allows us to save copies of files. Instead of a real copy where two separate files are created, Azure keeps a history of a file when a copy is done. It is the same as using snapshots to create a point in time of a virtual machine. Snapshots can be promoted in such way that the snapshot becomes active.

Blob lease

When a blob is created, an infinite lease is set on that blob. The goal of the lease is to prevent storage from being deleted while somebody is using the storage.

Protection of data

Data is protected by default in Microsoft Azure Storage. Each block of data written to a VHD file is triple-replicated to three different storage stamps located in the same datacenter. A storage stamp has the same functionality as a fault domain. If a single point of failure fails, the data is always available in two other locations.

When a storage account is created, you have an option to enable geo-replication. Geo-replication replicates the data to another region. This protects the data from a failure of a complete datacenter.

Data that is protected by geo-replication is stored at three different locations in the other regions. Geo-replication is enabled by default. However, the costs for storage are higher than when geo-replication is disabled.

Replication is performed asynchronously. The delay is about 15 minutes. This means that if the primary storage location is not available and Microsoft decides to failover, customers will lose about 15 minutes of data.

The data is stored at several locations for the purpose of disaster recovery. It is not a backup. If you delete the data, it is deleted from all the locations.

Customers are not able to actually failover to the replicated data if they want to. Only Microsoft staff is able to failover to another datacenter if the data is unavailable in the primary location.

Securing data

Data stored in Azure Storage is not encrypted by default by Microsoft. You have to take your own actions to prevent others from peeping into your data.

Data stored by SQL Server, **System Center Data Protection Manager (DPM)**, and server backup can be encrypted if needed.

Also, BitLocker can be used to protect data of virtual hard disks. However, Microsoft only supports using BitLocker Drive Encryption on data drives and not on operating system disks in Microsoft Azure.

Storage protocol

Microsoft uses a protocol to access Microsoft Azure Storage from nodes that Microsoft developed itself. Protocols like NFS or iSCSI are not used. The protocol used by Microsoft is based on the REST API. The network traffic uses SSL certificates for encryption. These certificates are stored in the Secret Store. This is a vault internally used by Microsoft to store certificates. Both Microsoft Azure and its customers use certificates to access services running on Azure. These certificates are handled by the Secret Store such that the Microsoft staff do not have direct access to certificates for security and compliancy reasons. One of the tasks of the Secret Store is to monitor the expiration date of certificates and alert the Microsoft Azure Storage service team in advance when certificates are about to expire.

Costs of storage

Microsoft Azure Storage is a thinly provisioned filesystem. It only writes actual data.

Microsoft only charges for the actual consumption of data. So, for example, when you have a 1 TB disk assigned to your virtual machine but you are actually using 500 GB, you are charged for 500 GB.

As you might have noticed, each Windows Server operating system disk is 127 GB large when deployed form the image gallery. However, you only pay for the actual data you write to disk.

There is a small caveat in certain operating systems.

Suppose you have a 40 GB volume with 20 GB of actual data. Now, you write an additional 10 GB of data and then delete 5 GB of data.

Since September 2013, Microsoft Azure has supported TRIM. It enables the operating system to tell the storage system that the operating system deleted data. The storage system then knows it does not have to allocate data for that operating system:

- This is supported by Windows Server 2012 and 2012 R2 for both operating system and data disk
- For Windows server 2008 R2, TRIM only works on the operating system disk
- Linux currently does not have TRIM support
- TRIM is only supported on ATA disks

Azure storage tooling

The Azure Management Portal provides some basic management on storage. Basically, disks can be created or deleted.

Cerebrata Azure Explorer is a free Windows tool that allows many actions on Azure Storage. It is very simple to upload files, delete files, download files, and rename files. Visit http://www.cerebrata.com/labs/azure-explorer for more information.

CloudXplorer by Clumsyleaf is another nice tool. There is a paid and a freeware edition available at http://clumsyleaf.com/products/cloudxplorer.

There are many other paid software solutions available.

Networking

Besides understanding how Azure Storage works, understanding the networking aspect is just as important.

We will discuss two parts of networking in Azure: the part under the hood that is not visible to Azure customers, as well as the part that customers have control over.

Azure networking under the hood

Initially, when Azure was released in 2008, the network was a North-South design. Traffic originating from a server went North via several layers of switches and then South to the destination server. This design did not scale very well.

So, soon after the first release, Microsoft completely redesigned the network. All servers have at least 10 Gbps connection to multiple switches. In 2014, Microsoft even introduced new virtual machine sizes offering 40 Gbps InfiniBand network connections. Now, the network offers multiple connections from a single node to switches.

The following image shows the current Azure network diagram. On top of the Azure hosts, three layers of switches are seen.

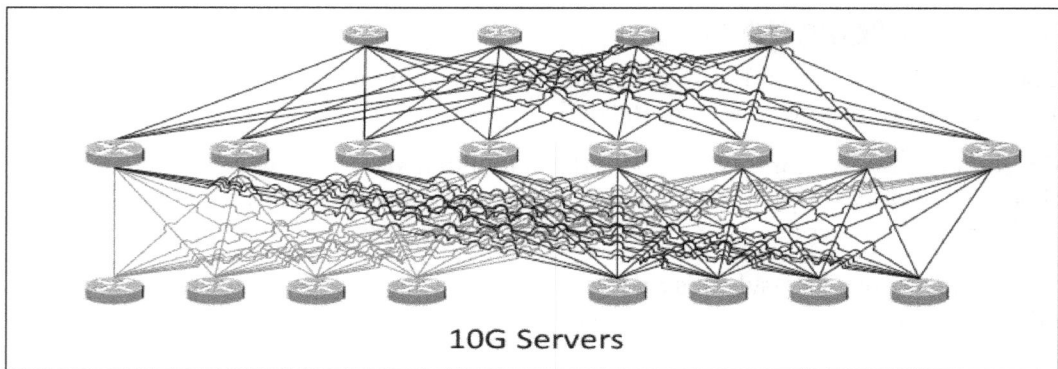

To provide customers with network connectivity between Azure and their on-premises network, virtual networks were introduced. This allows customers to use their own customer address space, and this also means that multiple customers can use the same address space.

Microsoft is using **Network Virtualization using Generic Routing Encapsulation (NVGRE)** to provide customers their own customer address space.

NVGRE is a technology that allows the IP configuration of a virtual machine to be unchanged when the virtual machine is moved between data centers.

It can be compared to the mobility of your mobile phone. When you travel abroad and take your mobile phone with you, you are still reachable on the same telephone number even though you're in another county and using a different telephone network provider.

NVGRE allows service providers that the IP address spaces used in the same datacenter to overlap. So, tenants can use their own IP address space.

In network virtualization, the IP address is abstracted from the service provider network. Not only that, Azure is massive; it has hundreds of thousands of nodes and millions of virtual machines. Networks are created and modified by customers more than a hundred times per day.

All those changes in the network need to be automated. The solution is **software-defined networking (SDN)**. Microsoft started developing a home-grown SDN in 2010 using about 100 developers. Since then, the Azure network architecture has changed completely.

SDN is a combination of software and hardware. Software is used to control components like virtual switches and routers. Most of the features offered by the network are in the software.

The SDN architecture of Azure has four main components:

- **Azure frontend**: The networks are created here by tenants using the API or the portal user interface
- **Load balancer**:
- **Controller**: This piece of software translates instructions and communicates with network devices to execute the instructions
- **VMswitch**: Each Azure node has a couple of Virtual Switches or VMswitches, and the virtual machines are connected to those switches

All four components are running as software in a virtual machine. This makes it very easy to add new features and distribute those using the same deployment tools as the virtual machines.

Load balancers

Microsoft Azure uses load balancers to be able to scale and provide performance and availability. The main purpose of a load balancer is to accept incoming network traffic sent to a virtual IP address and redirect it to a mapped internal IP address and port number.

In a massive infrastructure like Azure, it is impossible to use hardware load balancers. They cannot be provisioned automatically and do not fit in an agile infrastructure with lots of changes in configuration and performance.

Microsoft only uses software-based load balancers in Azure. All policies are software-based and are sent to the VMswitch using a protocol that is very similar to OpenFlow.

Three kinds of polices are used:

- **Access control lists**: This defines which virtual machine can talk to which virtual machine
- **Load balancing network address translation**: This defines which external IP address should be matched to which internal IP and port
- **Virtual network**: This is used for management of routing tables and virtual networking policies

Azure load balancers can only be reached from the public Internet. Traffic originating from an on-premises network connected over VPN cannot be load balanced using the Azure load balancers.

If network traffic increased, it is very well possible that the FC automatically adds more software load balancers.

It is, however, possible to use your own load balancing software and run it from your own virtual machine deployed in Azure.

When using Microsoft Azure IaaS, the load balancing features offered by the Azure load balancer are basic. It just redirects traffic based on the round robin technique.

When you're using the Microsoft Azure PaaS platform, more advanced rules are available.

The load balancing mechanism within the Microsoft Azure offering does not offer any Layer 7 functionality such as session affinity, content switching, compression, and any other application logic that can be applied if you are using a Layer 7 load balancer for your applications.

If you want these features, Kemp provides a free load balancer for Azure. It is installed as a virtual machine in a cloud service.

The components that have networking are as follows:

- Cloud service
- Virtual network
- Site-to-site network
- Point-to-site network

Cloud services

Cloud services are one of the main options shown in the left-hand side pane of the Azure Management Portal. It is very important to understand what the purpose of a cloud service actually is.

A cloud service can be seen as a container to group a set of virtual machines that are a part of the same application service.

Virtual machines part of the same cloud service share the same DNS domain name. These virtual machines are able to communicate with each other over the Azure internal network.

Each cloud service has a single public IP address. This is the virtual public IP address. Cloud services allow developers to use staging and are a requirement for autoscaling.

The main purpose of a cloud service is to manage applications. A cloud service is a group of one or more virtual machines. Each virtual machine can be accessed using the same public facing IP address.

A cloud service is linked to a production deployment. Virtual machines cannot be moved in or out a virtual network once they are created using a simple procedure. To perform such a movement, you will have to delete the virtual machine and recreate it using the virtual hard disk files of the original virtual machine.

If you select a cloud service for your virtual machine during provisioning, you will not be able to add the virtual machine to a virtual network.

You can secure connectivity for intra-tenant virtual machines via packet encapsulation.

> A very important point is that the virtual network *must* be created before any cloud services are created in it. Once a cloud service has been created, it is not possible to migrate it into a virtual network.

IP addressing of virtual machines

In the early days of Azure, it was not possible to assign a static IP address to a virtual machine. You could do it and it worked, but after a while the networking of the virtual machine would not be operational again. Customers could have some control over IP assignment to virtual machines by using virtual networks. The first virtual machine that would boot in a newly created virtual network would get the first available IP address in the IP range. However, this was not ideal.

In 2014, Microsoft enabled the ability to assign a static IP address to a virtual machine.

You cannot use your own DHCP server in an Azure network. For security and stability reasons, Microsoft Azure has its own managed DHCP mechanism. A virtual machine always receives an internal IP address, which is also referred to as a *DIP* from a pool of internal IP addresses. You can't change the DIP after it has been assigned. For this reason, if you plan to create a virtual network, create the virtual network before you deploy the virtual machine. Microsoft Azure will then assign the DIP from the pool of internal IP addresses that you designated when you created your virtual network.

The private IP address spaces available for use in Azure Virtual Networks are as follows:

- `10.0.0.0 - 10.255.255.255`
- `172.16.0.0. - 172.31.255.255`
- `192.168.0.0 - 192.168.255.255`

The public IP addresses assigned to Internet-facing devices depend on the region and datacenter.

Virtual network

A virtual network allows you to do the following tasks:

- Create a site-to-site VPN
- Use your own IP address space for virtual machines
- Set DNS servers of your choice
- Enable communications between different cloud services without having to expose services to the public Internet

The Microsoft Azure Virtual Network feature lets you provision and manage **virtual private networks (VPNs)** in Microsoft Azure, as well as securely link these with on-premises IT infrastructure. Companies can extend their on-premises networks into the cloud with control over network topology, including configuration of DNS and IP address ranges for virtual machines.

Virtual networks are very popular. Over 40 percent of the customers using the Azure Virtual Machines service are deploying virtual networks.

A virtual network subnet is related to the virtual network. You can divide the virtual networks into many smaller subnets.

Be aware of the fact a virtual network only lives in the data center it has been created. You cannot have a single virtual network span more than one datacenter/region.

There can be thousands of virtual machines connected to a virtual network.

A cloud service in a virtual network can directly access individual instances in a second cloud service contained in the virtual network without going through the load balancer hosting a public input endpoint for the second cloud service.

This means that once a traditional PaaS cloud service is added to a virtual network, the cloud service no longer forms a security boundary and any open port on its role instances can be accessed by any instance of any cloud service in the virtual network. This is regardless of whether the cloud service is IaaS or PaaS.

Site-to-site VPN

A VPN connection over the public Internet can be set up between an Azure virtual network and multiple on-premises sites. In the next chapter we will learn how to set up a site-to-site VPN.

Azure ExpressRoute

An alternative for a VPN connection is ExpressRoute. ExpressRoute enables a secure, reliable, high-speed direct connection from an on-premises datacenter or colocation environment into Microsoft Azure data centers. Private fiber connections can be set up by a growing number of providers. Currently supported are T&T, Equinix, Verizon, BT, Level3, TelecityGroup, SingTel, and Zadara.

ExpressRoute offers different tiers of bandwidth up to 10 Gbps and is covered by a **Service Level Agreement (SLA)**.

Virtual machine network interface

Each virtual machine deployed in Azure is limited to a single virtual network adapter. Users cannot add network adapters to a virtual machine yet. However, Microsoft is working on support for multiple network interfaces. Also, each network adapter is limited to a single IP address. This means you cannot use a virtual machine for routing or firewall-like features.

Endpoints

After a virtual machine has been deployed on Microsoft Azure, it is very likely services running in that virtual machine need to be accessed from the Internet. To be able to reach services, endpoints needs to be configured. An endpoint is a mapping between a public port number and a private port number over a specified protocol.

The number of endpoints per cloud service is limited. At the time of writing this book, the maximum number of incoming endpoints per cloud service was 150. Virtual machines that are a part of the same cloud service have no restriction on the number of ports.

When an endpoint is added to a virtual machine, an entry is made in one or more load balancers to allow network traffic originating from the Internet to reach the network port of the virtual machine.

NAME	PROTOCOL	PUBLIC PORT	PRIVATE PORT	LOAD-BALANCED SET NA...
HTTP	TCP	5555	5555	
PowerShell	TCP	63224	5986	-
Remote Desktop	TCP	57734	3389	-

Endpoints can have an ACL. By applying an ACL on an endpoint of a virtual machine, administrators can control which external IP address or range of IP addresses can access which virtual machine and its network ports.

This is another way to increase the security of the virtual machine. For example, an ACL can be set on virtual machine endpoints such that access is restricted to IP addresses used by workstations of software developers.

For each endpoint, multiple rules can be created. Each rule has an order number. The rules are evaluated in order starting with the first rule (the lowest order number) and ending with the last rule (the highest order number). This means that rules should be listed from least restrictive to most restrictive.

MANAGE ENDPOINT ACL

Specify ACL details for the Remote Desktop endpoint

You can create, manage, and delete rules that permit or deny access to the endpoints of a virtual machine through access control lists (ACLs).

ORDER	DESCRIPTION	ACTION	REMOTE SUBNET
1	allow developers	Permit	10.0.0.1/24
		Permit ⌄	REMOTE SUBNET

Summary

In this chapter, you've got a deep insight into the architecture of Microsoft Azure. You learned about the data centers and how processing, storage, and network is designed in Microsoft Azure.

You learned about the purpose of update and fault domains. In this chapter, you learned that Azure is managed as a software-defined network, which means intelligent software manages the network devices. You also learned how you can connect to Azure from on-premises using a VPN or a direct WAN connection using Azure ExpressRoute. Now, you can understand the terms used in Microsoft Azure and you are ready to deploy virtual machines.

4

Building an Infrastructure on Microsoft Azure

Now that we know what is running under the hood of Microsoft Azure, we can start building our infrastructure on Azure and connect to it from an on-premises environment. In this chapter, you will learn how to build virtual machines, enable two-way authentication, perform automation, and do a lot more.

This chapter covers the following topics:

- Purchasing Microsoft Azure
- Creating an account
- Understanding various IP configurations in Azure
- The current and new Azure Management Portal
- Creating storage, network, and virtual machines

Getting started with Microsoft Azure

In *Chapter 2*, *An Introduction to Microsoft Cloud Solutions*, you learned there are a couple of ways to try Microsoft Azure for free. Anyone with a valid credit card can try Azure for free for 1 month, including $200 credit.

A credit card is only used as proof of address. You will not be charged as long as you do not convert your trial to a paid subscription.

MSDN subscribers receive $75 free credit that renews each month. For the first month, you will even receive $150 credit.

For permanent subscription-based usage of Microsoft Azure, there are several ways to purchase:

- Pay using a credit card directory to Microsoft. This is a pay-as-you-go model as the customer pays exactly for the consumed resources.

- Alternatively, customers can use the invoice payment method. In some cases, payment by credit card is not possible. A spending cap on the credit card could limit the amount of Azure resources to be consumed. Instructions on using an invoice are available at `http://Azure.microsoft.com/en-us/pricing/invoicing/`.

- As part of an Enterprise Agreement, large enterprises can make an upfront monetary commitment. This means they pay a certain amount of money upfront. This allows the customer to use any Azure resource during a whole year. The credit is only valid for 1 year, and remaining credit does not roll over to the next year! If a customer's usage exceeds their commitment, they will be billed in-arrears for that usage, either quarterly or annually depending on whether that additional use is more than 50 percent beyond their original commitment.

- You can also purchase tokens from any Microsoft partner as part of Open Licensing. This license type is used by organizations that have 250 devices or less. They can purchase tokens worth $100 from a Microsoft Partner. This Microsoft Partner is then able to add the value of the token to the customer's Azure subscription.

This ability to purchase Azure in Open Licensing was added on 1st August, 2014 to offer Microsoft Partners a billing relationship between them and customers and develop new business models.

There is a big difference between purchasing resources from Amazon or from Microsoft. For Amazon, customers have to make a choice. For example, they purchase capacity upfront for compute resources. If the available compute capacity is not consumed 100 percent, the customer cannot consume a different resource like storage without having first to purchase storage resources.

This is different for Microsoft Azure. Customers purchase Azure resources upfront, but it is up to the customer on which service the credits are spent: compute, mobile services, disaster recovery, storage, and so on. This is much more flexible than the Amazon model.

Microsoft Azure is billed by Microsoft directly to its customers. There is no organization like a partner or a reseller between. However, this might change in the future. Microsoft does provide partners with a so-called kick-back free when a partner helps a customer to use Microsoft Azure.

Subscribing to Microsoft Azure is very simple and takes just a few minutes. Requirements are a credit card, a mobile phone for verification purposes, and an e-mail address. Then, perform the following steps:

1. Create a Microsoft account. A Microsoft account is a single-sign-on account that allows you to log on to many Microsoft sites. Previous names for Microsoft accounts were Microsoft Wallet, Microsoft Passport, .NET Passport, Microsoft Passport Network, and most recently Windows Live ID.

2. If your organization has a corporate account on Microsoft Office 365, you can use that account.

3. To create a Microsoft account, go to `https://signup.live.com/signup.aspx?lic=1`. The e-mail address that is chosen will be used as the account name to log in to Microsoft Azure.

4. After registering a Microsoft account, go to `www.microsoftazure.com` and select **Free trial**. The registration process is very simple. You will have to fill in a mobile phone number to receive a verification code through an SMS text message. You will also have to provide your credit card details. Microsoft will not charge your credit card during the trial period.

    When you have consumed the free $200 worth of credit, your services like virtual machines will be stopped. So you won't get any unwanted surprises when you forget to cancel your free trial or forget to stop virtual machines because of the spending limit, which is the standard in place. You can however choose to disable the spending limit. This ensures your Cloud Services will remain operational, but can incur certain costs to be charged to your credit card.

5. When the trial has ended and you want to continue using Azure, you can simply upgrade your subscription. Several options are possible, such as pay-as-you-go and plans in which you pay in advance.

6. After finishing the registration process, you will be presented with the Azure Management Portal. This is an HTML5-based portal that allows you to manage your Microsoft Azure environment.

The portal can be accessed using the URL `https://manage.windowsAzure.com`. The portal looks like the following screenshot:

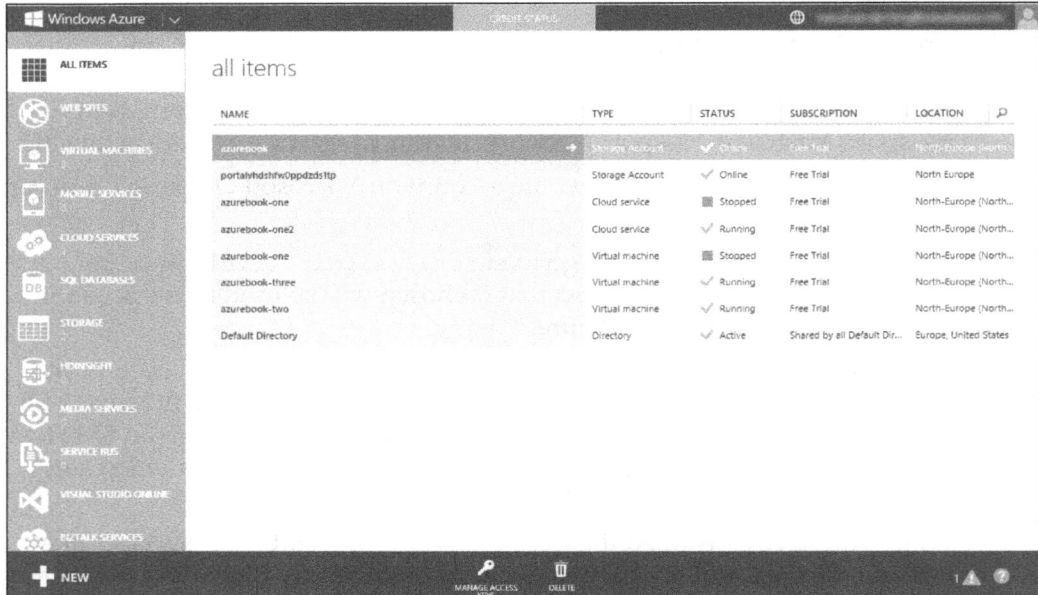

The new Azure Management Portal

Microsoft is working on a new Azure Management Portal. At the time of writing this book, the portal was available as a preview.

The new portal offers much more information and features and can look a bit busy compared to the old management portal. The main reason to create a new portal was to show the relationship between various Azure resources that are combined from a single application. Think about Azure Website, storage accounts, and virtual machines that are all used as components for an application.

Another reason for a new portal is DevOps. DevOps is a new way of working in IT which allows for much shorter development cycles. In DevOps, new versions of applications are deployed frequently. This requires close cooperation between the developers of the application and the operations team. The new dashboard enables this.

The new portal is accessed using `http://portal.azure.com`.

The new portal offers features not available in the current portal, like:

- **Customization of the interface**: You can size tiles and add windows to create your own dashboard with information like costs, performance, and health of services.

- **Cost overview**: The portal allows for a better overview of costs associated to your subscription. It allows you to get an estimate of the costs.

- **Deployment**: New features are available to deploy applications using resource groups.

- **Console access**: You can now access the console of a virtual machine using your browser while logged on to the Azure portal.

- **Role-Based Access Control (RBAC):** This allows much more granular control of which users have access to which resources. In the old Azure Management Portal, access control was very limited. RBAC was introduced in January 2015 available as a preview feature.

The following screenshot shows the new Azure Management Portal:

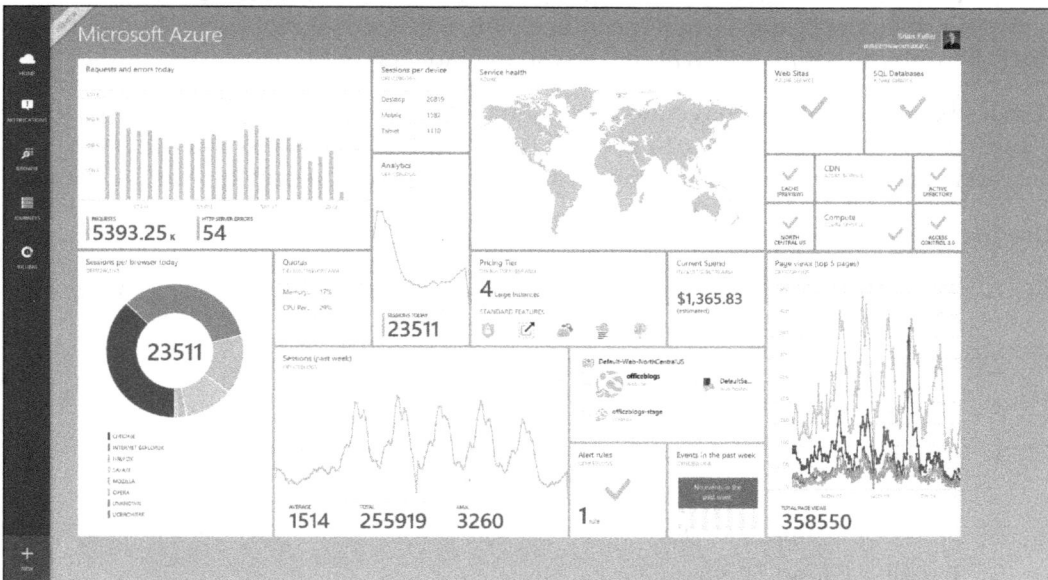

This book will focus on the current (January 2015) Azure Management Portal.

Creating a virtual machine

Now that we have access to the Microsoft Azure Management Portal, we are ready to create virtual machines to run our applications on.

It is very tempting to start creating virtual machines by selecting **VIRTUAL MACHINES** from the left pane and clicking on **New** in the bottom-left corner of the screen. This is a good way to explore Microsoft Azure. Within a few minutes, you will have your first virtual machine up and running.

You can access the virtual machine in Windows Azure using RDP for Windows Server or over SSH for Linux-based virtual machines. Be sure the connection at your office location allows you to connect through random ports to the Internet when you do not have a VPN into the Microsoft Azure cloud. By default, the RDP port number for virtual machines in Microsoft Azure is randomized, so you will not connect through the default port 3389.

However, if you are going to build an infrastructure that will run production workloads, it is very important to first create some supporting components for the infrastructure. Also, think about a naming convention for components like virtual networks, filenames, and virtual machines. This will save you lots of sorting out during troubleshooting and will make system management much easier.

Besides having a naming convention, you should know the restrictions of Microsoft Azure. When you have just starting building, it could be difficult to rollback some decisions you made in an earlier stage without nasty consequences such as downtime.

Use the following workflow to create a new virtual machine:

1. Determine your naming convention for components like affinity groups, virtual machines, and so on.
2. Determine which subscription to use.
3. Create an affinity group.
4. Create a storage account by selecting the affinity group created in the previous step.
5. Create a virtual network.
6. Create a Cloud Service.

If your application has several virtual machines, it will take some time to deploy these manually using the Azure Management Portal. Alternative methods are using PowerShell and Azure Automation.

The new Azure Management Portal allows for more advanced methods of deploying complete applications using application templates.

The portal offers some predefined application templates like one to deploy a complete SharePoint Server farm. With SharePoint Server Farm, the Microsoft Azure Preview Portal automatically creates a pre-configured SharePoint Server 2013 farm for you.

More information can be found at `http://azure.microsoft.com/en-us/documentation/articles/virtual-machines-sharepoint-farm-azure-preview/`.

Understanding the restrictions of Microsoft Azure

Currently, Microsoft Azure has a number of restrictions you should be aware of. Understanding these will save you a lot of time and annoyances later on. Note that these restrictions might be solved by Microsoft by the time this book has been published:

- Azure does not provide high availability for single instance virtual machines. If your application depends on the availability of a single virtual machine, you might experience unwanted downtime when Microsoft is updating Azure hosts. We discussed this in *Chapter 3, Understanding the Microsoft Azure Architecture*, in the section discussing update domains. You learned that Microsoft Azure is a so-called *best effort* type of cloud. If possible, always have at least two instances for applications that require maximum availability.

- It is not possible to add a virtual machine to a virtual network once created.

- It is not possible to move a virtual machine from one virtual network to another.

- It is not possible to renew the IP configuration (for example, by using `ipconfig/renew`) for a running virtual machine. To apply a new IP configuration assigned by a virtual network, restart the virtual machine. Best practice is to make sure your own managed DNS server is created first.

- It is not possible to use granular user rights in Microsoft Azure. Any user with access to a Microsoft Azure subscription has full administrative rights on all resources in that subscription.

- No support for remote console and `.VHDX` virtual disk format.

Some of these restrictions can be worked around by deleting the virtual machine and retaining the virtual disks. Then, create a new virtual machine and ensure that the required configuration is set.

Determining the naming convention for Azure components

One of the most important initial steps is to determine a naming convention for VMs, networks, and accounts to ensure a consistent usage of object naming, which will make management easier. Use this naming convention, for example, to differentiate between virtual machines in your on-premises data center and the virtual machines you have running in Azure.

Note that some components, such as a storage account, require a unique name for all of Azure. So, it is possible you might find out another Azure customer already claimed a name for a storage account.

I strongly advise you to first design a naming convention for the different components in Azure. By doing this before deploying virtual machines, you will have a much better understanding of location of virtual machines, storage account, disk types, and so on.

The following table shows all naming objects and restrictions in length and the allowed characters:

Object	Minimum length	Maximum length	Characters allowed	Uniqueness
Availability set	3	15	The name can contain only letters, numbers, hyphens, and underscores. The name must start with a letter and must end with a letter or a number.	Per subscription
Virtual machine DNS name	3	15	The name can contain letters, numbers, and hyphens. The name must start with a letter and end with a letter or number.	For Azure
VM endpoint	3	15	The name can contain only letters, numbers, hyphens, spaces, and underscores. The name must start with a letter and end with a letter or a number.	Per VM

Object	Minimum length	Maximum length	Characters allowed	Uniqueness
Cloud Service	1	63	The name can contain letters, numbers, and hyphens. The first and last character in the field must be a letter or number. Trademarks, reserved words, and offensive words are not allowed.	For Azure
Storage account	3	24	Only lowercase letters and numbers are allowed.	Per subscription
Virtual network	1	63	A name is required. The name can contain only letters, numbers, and hyphens. The name must start with a letter.	Per subscription
Local network	1	63	The name can contain only letters, numbers, and hyphens. The name must start with a letter.	Per subscription
Disk	1	100	The name can contain only letters, numbers, hyphens, and underscores. The name must start with a letter and end with a letter or a number.	Per storage account
VHD blob	1	1024	A blob name can contain any combination of characters, but reserved URL characters must be properly escaped.	Per container
Affinity group	1	63	The name must start with a letter or number. Name can contain letters, numbers, and dashes.	
Container	3	63	The name can contain letters, numbers, and the dash sign. It must start with a letter or number.	Per storage account
Image name	1	100	The name can contain only letters, numbers, periods, hyphens, and underscores. Start the name with a letter and end it with a letter or a number.	Per subscription
VHD filename	1	256	The name can contain only letters, numbers, periods, hyphens, and underscores.	Per storage container

Explaining Azure subscriptions

An Azure subscription is always attached to a Microsoft account or Organizational account. A subscription is a contract with Microsoft in which the consumption of cloud resources and optional support has been purchased.

Each account can manage up to 50 subscriptions. Each subscription can have a different so-called *plan*. A plan is an agreement about payment. It can be *pay as you go*, in which the customer pays at the end of the month for the consumed resources. Microsoft also has plans for customers committing themselves to Azure for a couple of months. Subscriptions can have one of the three available levels of support.

The person who creates the account is the account administrator for all subscriptions created in that account. That person is also the default service administrator for the subscription. The account administrator cannot be changed by the customer. A call to Microsoft support is needed to change the account administrator.

Each subscription has a service administrator. That person is able to change the name of the subscription, end the subscription, contact Microsoft support, change the payment method, and download billing details.

The service administrator is also authorized to purchase additional services from the Azure Store. The Store has services not offered natively by Microsoft but offers additional features such as sending e-mail or analyzing logfiles.

Each subscription is also connected to a user directory. This directory holds the user information for Azure.

Each subscription can have up to 200 co-administrators. This role has the same privileges as the service administrator. The only difference is the co-administrator is allowed to associate subscriptions to Windows Azure directories. It is recommended to add at least one co-administrator. This is for backup reasons in case the service administrator account is not useable anymore.

To add a co-administrator, open the Azure Management Portal. Go to **Settings**, select **Administrators**, and click on the **Add** button at the bottom of the screen. Then, fill in your e-mail address and select a subscription type.

Microsoft Azure offers an account center and a management portal. The account center is used for management of subscriptions while the management portal is used for technical management of Azure, such as provisioning of virtual machines and management of other Azure services.

Azure Resource Groups

A feature that is currently (January 2015) in preview is Azure Resource Groups.,

Resource Groups are used for the management of Azure resources. Previously it was very hard to understand how different Azure resources depend on each other. There could be a website that is using a particular storage account. Without a proper naming convention and documentation, there was no way to quickly understand how these two were related.

This is solved by using Azure Resource Groups. Resource Groups are managed using the Azure Resource Manager, which is part of the new Azure Management Portal.

Resource Groups can be used for lifecycle management. Groups of resources can be managed as a single entity. It is very easy to deploy, update, and delete a single Resource Group.

Resource Groups also allow you to set much more fine-grained access control than just the subscription level as is currently possible. Resource Groups are part of the new Azure Role-based Access Control feature.

Billing is made much more easy. Previously, when an Azure subscription was used by several departments, it was a lot of work to figure out which department had to be charged for costs associated to the consumption of Azure resources.

Now an Azure subscription can be organized in Resources Groups. Each department is assigned a different Resource Group. Consumption of resources in a Resource Group can be easily billed.

A single Azure subscription can have multiple Resource Groups. A single Resource Groups has multiple resources. Resources can be an Azure Website, an Azure SQL database, Azure Team Project, a MySQL database, storage accounts, virtual networks, and virtual machines.

A resource like a VM can only be part of a single Resource Group.

Not all Azure services can be added as a resource to a Resource Group. Service Bus and Cloud Services are examples of resources that today cannot be managed.

Another restriction in the preview is that you are not able to move resources to another Resource Group as well as not being able to rename Resource Groups.

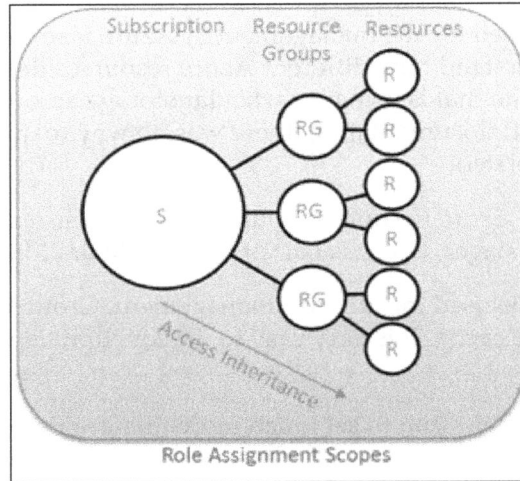

Role Assignment Scopes

Adjusting the subscription name

When you registered for Azure Microsoft Azure, you might have used the free trial offer or the MSDN offer.

In both cases, the Azure subscription has a generic name such as **Free trial**. Especially when using several subscriptions for different purposes, it makes sense to rename the subscription. The name of the subscription is used in billing. So, a name like `Project new Website` on your bill makes more sense than a name like `MSDN subscription`.

To change the name of the subscription, perform the following tasks:

1. In the Azure Management Portal, select the account name in the right upper corner of the screen.
2. Select **View my bill**.
3. Double-click on the subscription name you would like to change.
4. Scroll down and select **Edit subscription details**.
5. Fill in a new name and click on the checkmark.

Microsoft Azure accounts

To access Azure services, you obviously need an account. An account can be one of the following types:

- **An organizational account**: This can either be a Windows Azure Active Directory account or an Active Directory account used in your organization. Examples of accounts are `peter@contoso.onmicrosoft.com` or `peter@acme.com`.

- **A Microsoft account**: This is an account used to access Microsoft services like TechNet. A Microsoft account is the new name for what used to be called a Windows Live ID. You can use any e-mail address as an account name.

The preferred access to Microsoft Azure is by using organizational accounts. These are sourced from Microsoft Azure Active Directory, which means that the administrator has control over the accounts.

Also, organizational accounts can be configured to use multifactor authentication. This enables your users to require more than just a password but also an additional proof of identity. This can be a smart card, a pin code, or a smart phone.

Management of accounts can be pretty complex. Microsoft uses cookies to track whether you are logged in and which account you used. If you have issues with being authorized, one way to solve it is to delete all cookies in your browser or use another browser and try again.

Understanding Azure directories

Each Azure subscription has a directory associated to it. The directory stores information about users who have access to the Azure portal. The directory is part of **Windows Azure Active Directory (WAAD)**, which is a multitenant version of Active Directory available in Windows Server.

When a subscription is created, a directory named `Default Directory` is created. The directory has two default roles:

- Global administrator
- User

Other roles shown in the multifactor authentication window of the directory are as follows:

- Sign-in allowed users
- Billing administrators
- Password administrators
- Service administrators
- User management administrators
- Global administrator

In WAAD, only the global administrator role is used. The other roles in Microsoft Azure Active Directory are used by Office 365.

Windows Azure Active Directory Premium

Windows Azure Active Directory Premium is built on top of Windows Azure AD and provides a set of capabilities to facilitate companies with extended possibilities in the field of identity and access management.

It offers features that were formerly only available in an on-premises tool called **Forefront Identity Manager (FIM)**, similar to a user self-service portal for resetting passwords, group-based provisioning, and security reports.

It is expected that WAAD Premium will continue to grow and embrace a new identity and access management requirements of the cloud era.

Determining the Azure subscription to use

The usage of Azure resources is based on subscriptions. It makes sense to use different Azure subscriptions for different purposes.

Microsoft does billing per Azure subscription. It can be useful to create a unique Azure subscription for each software development project your company provides or for each department. This way, chargeback is much easier to process by the financial department, who receive the monthly credit card charge.

Another reason to use multiple subscriptions is to isolate Azure deployments. If you use one subscription for running multiple environments like test/dev and production, each user with access to that subscription has full administrator access to all virtual machines and virtual networks. This is particularly true when using App Controller.

Note that this isolation also means there is no network traffic possible between virtual machines that are a member of two different Azure subscriptions.

Subscriptions have some technical limitations you should be aware of (refer to the *Appendix, Configuration Maximums* for an overview of a lot more configuration limits):

- A single subscription has by default a maximum of 20 cores available. When all the cores are assigned to virtual machines, creation of additional virtual machines will fail. If you require more cores, you can fill in a support request using the Azure Management Portal. The maximum is 10,000 cores.
- A single subscription has a maximum of 200 Cloud Services.
- A single subscription has a maximum of 100 storage accounts.

A complete overview of configuration limits is listed at `http://azure.microsoft.com/nl-nl/documentation/articles/azure-subscription-service-limits/`.

Adding more administrators to a subscription

The Microsoft account that was used to register the subscription becomes the administrator by default. This user role is named *service administrator* or *service owner*.

It is likely that your Azure infrastructure needs more than just a single administrator who is able to use the Azure Management Portal. The next section will teach you how to add additional users to the co-administrators user role.

When adding administrators, make sure you add those users to the directory that has an Active Directory. If not, the added administrator might get an error after authentication like this: **We were unable to find any subscriptions associated with your account**.

Only users who are either the Service Administrator or a co-administrator on the subscription can sign in to the management portal.

Deciding the most appropriate Azure region for placement

As described in *Chapter 3, Understanding the Microsoft Azure Architecture*, Microsoft Azure is located in many regions spread out over the world.

You might be wondering what the best region is to create virtual machines and services in. There are many reasons to decide for a particular region like:

- **Compliance**: Some countries and organizations (like governments) put restrictions on the storage of data. They do not allow data to cross the national border or the border of, for instance, the European Union. This, in turn, restricts the choice of the datacenter.

- **Performance**: To have the best performance, it is best to be located as close as possible to the datacenter.

Note that the Western European region is housed in datacenters located in or near Amsterdam, the Netherlands. Dublin, which is further west than Amsterdam, houses the North Europe region. This can be a bit confusing.

There is a very useful website called Microsoft Azure Speed Test (`http://Azurespeedtest.Azure websites.net/`) that shows the latency between your web browser and the Microsoft Azure Blob Storage Service of all regions.

By using Azure Speed Test, you can determine the best location for running your application or storing your company data.

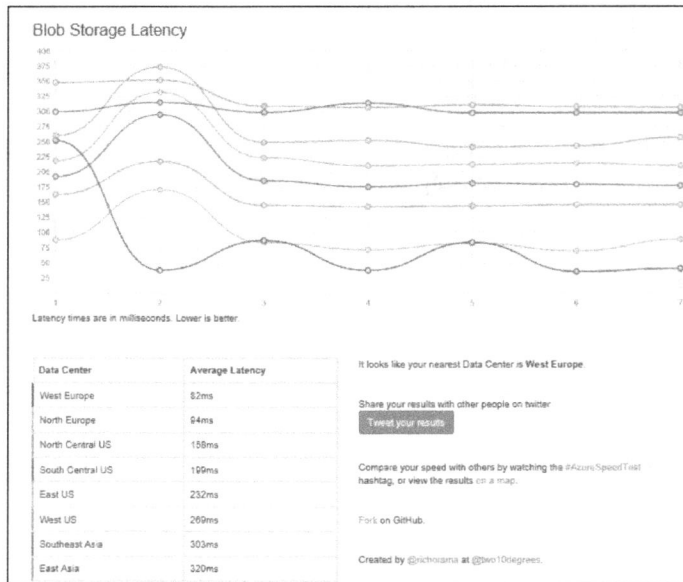

Data Center	Average Latency
West Europe	82ms
North Europe	94ms
North Central US	158ms
South Central US	199ms
East US	232ms
West US	269ms
Southeast Asia	303ms
East Asia	320ms

It looks like your nearest Data Center is West Europe.

Share your results with other people on twitter

Tweet your results

Compare your speed with others by watching the #AzureSpeedTest hashtag, or view the results on a map.

Fork on GitHub.

Created by @richorama at @two10degrees.

Creating an affinity group

In *Chapter 3, Understanding the Microsoft Azure Architecture,* you learned about **affinity groups**.

Using affinity groups, we can make sure compute and storage are close together to keep latency as low as possible. This is necessary because Azure datacenters are huge, and without these affinity groups, the virtual machines could reside on opposite sides of the datacenter. This could result in a performance penalty. With affinity groups, Microsoft promises to keep virtual machines as close together as possible.

Perform the following steps to create a virtual machine:

1. The first step in the process of creating a virtual machine is to create an affinity group.

2. To do so, go to the **Settings** menu item in the left window of **Azure Management Portal**. Then, select **Affinity Groups** in the menu bar.

3. Next, select **Add an affinity group**.

4. You will be presented with a window in which you give a name to the affinity group, a description, and select the region.

5. Fill in the fields and click on the checkmark.

Creating a storage account

The next step in creating a virtual machine for the first time is the creation of a storage account.

A storage account is automatically created when we create a virtual machine for the first time using the wizard. However, this automatically created storage account will get a randomly generated storage account name. This is not very useful for administration. It is better to use a storage account named `ContosoNorthEurope001` than `portalvhdfdfwedwd`.

To manually create a storage account and have control over its naming, perform the following steps:

1. Select the **Storage** menu in the left window of **Azure Management Portal**.

2. Then, select **Create a storage account**.

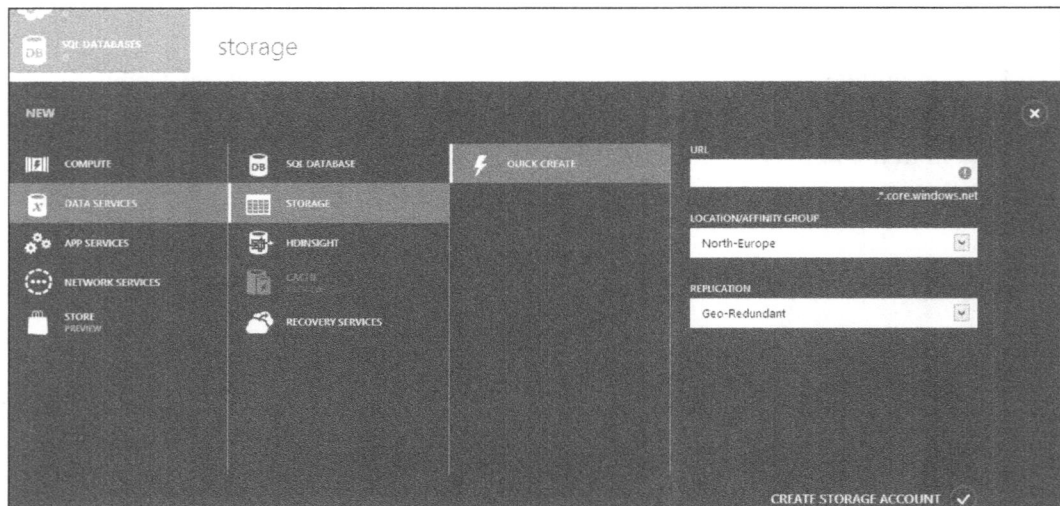

3. In the **URL** field, type in a descriptive name. This name has to be unique for all Microsoft Azure customers. It is highly advisable to use a naming convention for the URLs of your storage accounts.

4. Next, select the affinity group or the region you want to create your storage account in.

5. The last step is the selection of the replication type:

    ◦ **Locally Redundant** means that each block of data is stored on three different locations in the same region.

    ◦ **Geo-Redundant** is the default choice. It means the data is additionally replicated to the region paired to the one you selected in the previous step. The replicated data is stored in three different locations in the paired region. Costs for geo-redundant replication are higher than for locally redundant.

    ◦ The third option is **Read-Access Geo-redundant**. If the primary region is unavailable, read access to the data stored at the secondary region shall be available.

6. Select **Create storage account** as the final step for creating the storage account.

Creating Azure networks

The Microsoft Azure Management Portal allows you to create several components that are required for on-site connectivity with Microsoft Azure and for more control over intra-virtual machines networking traffic of Azure virtual machines.

The networks menu consists of the following components:

*   **Virtual networks**: This allows creation of IP subnets, site-to-site (S2S) VPN connections, and point-to-site (P2S) VPN connections

*   **Local networks**: This allows configuration of the public facing IP address of the on-site VPN device for P2S and S2S connections

*   **DNS servers**: This allows registration of non-Microsoft managed DNS servers

Creating a virtual network

Virtual networks, or VNets as Microsoft likes to call them, are an important component of Azure. The understanding of virtual networks in Microsoft Azure is very important. The purpose of a virtual network is as follows:

*   To connect to virtual machines over a site-to-site or P2S VPN connection, just as if the virtual machine was part of the internal network.

*   To be able to assign customer-defined IP addresses and DNS configuration to virtual machines. This way, the administrator has control over IP subnets and IP address allocation.

- To enable network connections between virtual machines in different Cloud Services.

[If you create an Azure Cloud Service first and a Virtual Network later, you will not be able to add a virtual machine to an existing Cloud Service.]

Only when a virtual machine is assigned to a virtual network during the creation of the virtual machine are you able to assign a specific IP subnet to the virtual machines.

Virtual Networks can be used to connect to other Virtual Networks located in a different region. Also, connections between Virtual Networks can cross Azure subscriptions.

This allows high availability and disaster recovery scenarios. Previously, without cross Virtual Network connectivity, network traffic between multiple Virtual Networks had to be routed via an on-premises network. Now, with cross Virtual Network connectivity, network traffic remains within the Azure network.

Customers can use cross Virtual Network connectivity to replicate databases to another region, for example. Think about SQL Always On with Availability Groups spreading across multiple Azure regions.

For Virtual Network to Virtual Network connectivity, dynamic routing VPNs are required.

Virtual networks are also used to apply DNS configuration to virtual machines. The virtual machine that is started first after creation of a new virtual network will always be assigned an IP address ending with .4. The first three numbers are assigned by the Azure fabric to Azure internal devices.

This assignment of x.x.x.4 to the first virtual machine in a virtual network is useful in situations where you want to be sure that a specific virtual machine always obtains the same fixed IP address. An Active Directory server is such an example.

Several methods are available to create a virtual network:

- Manual using the Azure Management Portal
- Importing an XML configuration file
- Using PowerShell
- Using the Azure Command-line Interface

When using a manual creation, two different options are available in the Azure Management Portal. Either Select **Networks** in the left pane and then select **create a virtual network** or select the plus sign in the bottom-left corner of the screen.

Understanding virtual network gateways

To connect a Virtual Network to an on-premises network or to another Azure Virtual Network, you need to configure a gateway.

The gateway is a virtual appliance which is automatically deployed and configured by Azure. Microsoft will make sure it is redundant.

A gateway comes in two flavors:

- The standard gateway, which is limited to 10 site-to-site connections
- The High Performance gateway, which is limited to 30 site-to-site connections

The High Performance gateway is a different SKU and has a different price tag.

To set up a gateway, PowerShell is used. The commandlet is `Get-AzureVNetGateway` and you need to use either `Default` or `HighPerformance` as the value for the `-GatewaySKU` parameter.

The following code shows how to create a High Performance gateway:

```
PS D:\> New-AzureVNetGateway -VNetName MyAzureVNet -GatewayType
DynamicRouting -GatewaySKU HighPerformance
```

The type of gateway can be changed using PowerShell as well.

This cmdlet example changes the gateway for MyAzureVNet from Default to High Performance. You also change the gateway SKU from High Performance back to Default:

```
PS D:\> Resize-AzureVNetGateway -VNetName MyAzureVNet -GatewaySKU
Default
```

Creating a local network

The purpose of a local network is to define the IP address of the VPN device that is located on-site. This allows cross-premises connectivity.

Using your own DNS servers

In many scenarios, it is required to have virtual machines assigned specific, customer-managed DNS servers. When a virtual machine is not part of a virtual network, it will receive a DNS server provided by Azure. DNS is managed by Microsoft staff.

If you are running your own DNS server, you will need to create a virtual network first. Follow this procedure to create your own DNS server:

1. Create a virtual network.
2. Create a subnet that the virtual machine that will have the DNS role will be part of. In this example, we call this `tier1`.
3. Create the virtual machine as the first virtual machine in subnet `tier1`.
4. As the first virtual machine in a subnet, it will receive x.x.x.4 as its IP address.
5. Register this IP address and the FQDN of this server in **Register DNS**.

> The command for a renewal of IP configuration in Windows Server, `ipconfig /renew`, will result in an error. For some reason, the client in Azure thinks that this request cannot reach the DHCP server.
>
> If you changed the IP address of the DNS server in the virtual network, you will need to restart the virtual machine to apply the new DNS server reference.

Deleting a virtual network

A virtual network can only be deleted when it is not in use. First, you need to delete all virtual machines that are a part of the virtual network. Microsoft Azure does not have a feature to move virtual machines to another virtual network at this moment.

If you want to keep the instance, delete the virtual machine and keep the virtual disks. Then, create a new virtual machine by using the existing virtual disks. If a gateway is part of the virtual network, delete this as well. Then, the virtual network itself can be deleted.

Creating a Cloud Service

In the previous chapter, you learned about Cloud Services. A Cloud Service is a collection of virtual machines that share the same public IP address and domain. All virtual machines that are part of the same Cloud Service are able to connect to each other over the internal Azure network. Network traffic is isolated inside a Cloud Service. This means that virtual machines part of a Cloud Service by default cannot communicate with virtual machines that are part of another Cloud Service.

However, when multiple Cloud Services are combined into a virtual network, all virtual machines in all Cloud Services can communicate to each other.

Cloud Service is a term used in the **Platform as a Service (PaaS)** offering of Microsoft Azure. Cloud Services in PaaS allow control over the guest operating system.

Cloud Services can have two versions: a staging deployment and a production deployment. Each deployment has a set of virtual machines which offer the same sort of application functionality as a web server or application server.

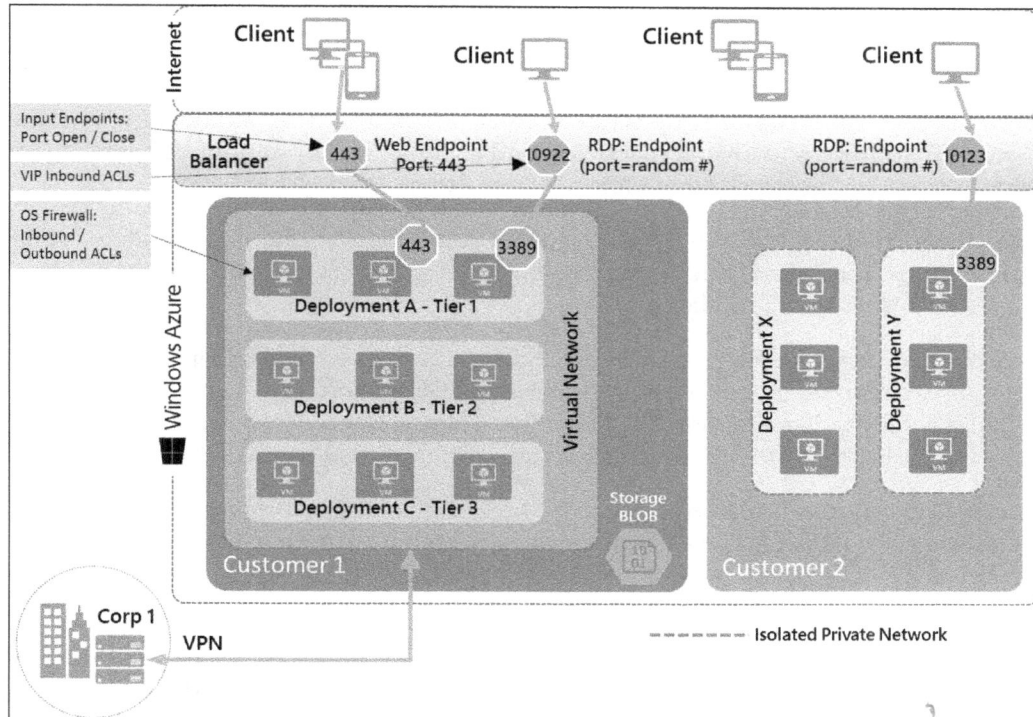

The main purpose of a Cloud Service is as follows:

- **Enable network connectivity between virtual machines part of the same Cloud Service**: Virtual machines part of the same Cloud Service can connect to each other over the network.

- **Enable scale-out**: When demand increases, additional virtual machines can automatically be started.

- **Enable high availability**: Virtual machines that are part of the same availability set in a Cloud Service are placed on different hosts.

- **Treat a set of virtual machines as one entity**: All virtual machines within a Cloud Service can be deleted with a few mouse clicks.

- **Enable release management**: A Cloud Service is mostly used in a PaaS environment. A Cloud Service serves applications and is particularly useful in multi-tier applications. A single Cloud Service can have two versions: staging or production. Staging is used in the development phase of an application. When the development stage is ready for production, it can easily be switched into production. This change will switch the Virtual IP Address of the Cloud Service.

A Cloud Service does not offer much administrative control over the network configuration. For instance, it does not allow us to control the IP subnet being used to allocate IP addresses to virtual machines, and a Cloud Service cannot be connected to your on-premises network over VPN.

Basically, virtual machines that are part of the same Cloud Service are treated as one. Scaling out is done at a Cloud Service level. All members of a Cloud Service can be deleted at once with a few clicks.

Once a virtual machine has been created, it cannot be moved to another Cloud Service easily. If you want to move a virtual machine to a Cloud Service, you should delete the virtual machine while retaining the VHD files. Then, create a new virtual machine and make it a part of a Cloud Service and use the existing virtual hard disks.

Availability sets can be created to ensure higher availability of virtual machines. An availability set is part of a Cloud Service, which means an availability set created in a Cloud Service cannot be used in another Cloud Service.

Now, let's create a Cloud Service by performing the following steps:

1. In **Azure Management Portal**, select **Cloud Services** in the left pane.

2. Press **NEW** in the bottom-left part of the screen.

3. Choose **Quick create**.

4. Fill in the URL. This URL is used to access services running on virtual machines in the Cloud Service.

5. Choose a region or affinity group.

6. Click on **Create Cloud Service**.

Deleting a Cloud Service

Cloud Services are deleted by selecting **Cloud Services** in the left pane of **Azure Management Portal**. You will be presented with three options:

- **Delete the Cloud Service and its deployments**: This action will completely remove the Cloud Service, its Virtual IP Address (also called VIP; it is a public IP address assigned to a Cloud Service), all virtual machines with attached disks, and associated VHDs.

- **Delete all virtual machines**: Virtual machines are deleted as well as the VIP of the Cloud Service. You'll keep the attached disks, their associated VHD files, and the Cloud Service.

- **Delete all virtual machines and attached disks**: All virtual machines, attached disks, and associated VHD files will be deleted. Also, the VIP will be deleted. The Cloud Service will not be deleted.

Creating a virtual machine

You have made it to the point where it really gets exciting. It is now time to create a virtual machine on Microsoft Azure.

Virtual machines in Azure can be created using several techniques:

- Using the Azure Management portal
- Using PowerShell
- Using the Azure Command-line Interface
- Using System Center App Controller
- Using third-party automation tooling like Puppet and Chef

Whatever method is chosen to create a virtual machine, the operation is performed by the **Red Dog Front End** (**RDFE**). You learned about the RDFE in the previous chapter. It comes into play after the image has been chosen and the administrator name, password, and so on have been set. This creates an ISO file that contains the bits to install Linux or Windows Server. Customization is added to the ISO. Then the RDFE instructs the Fabric Controller to select a host to deploy the virtual machine to. Then, a VHD is created, a virtual machine is created, the ISO is connected to the virtual machine, and the guest operating system boots from the ISO. The installation of Windows or Linux is performed, and after a couple of minutes, the virtual machine is ready to be used. To install a virtual machine using Azure Management Portal, perform the following steps:

1. Select **New** in the bottom-left corner of the screen. Then, go to **Compute | Virtual Machine | From Gallery**.

2. You are now presented with a long list of images. Make your choice. In this example, we are going to choose **Windows Server 2012 R2 Datacenter Edition**.

3. Select the release date. Microsoft offers various versions of Windows Server. The difference is the patch level. The most recent version has the most recent patches preinstalled by Microsoft. In some situations, you might need a version without some patches.

4. Type in a name for the virtual machine according to your naming convention, choose the size, define an account for administrative rights, and set the password.

5. Click on the right arrow.

6. In the next screen, select a Cloud Service or create a new one. Select the virtual network you created in the previous paragraph. Select a storage account you created earlier and select an availability set if that is applicable.

7. Click on the right arrow.

8. Configure the endpoints if you want. The default two endpoints are sufficient in our case.

9. Click on the checkmark button.

That's it! The virtual machine is being provisioned. This will take several minutes.

After the virtual machine is ready for use, you can select it. Click on the **Connect** button in the lower toolbar. This will present you with the .rdp file that can be used to initiate a remote desktop connection to the virtual machine.

Virtual machine extensions

In the first half of 2014, Microsoft added a very interesting new feature that allows better management of virtual machines. This is enabled by installing the VM agent. This agent, which is available on both Windows and Linux, is installed by default during provisioning. You can disable the installation if you want to.

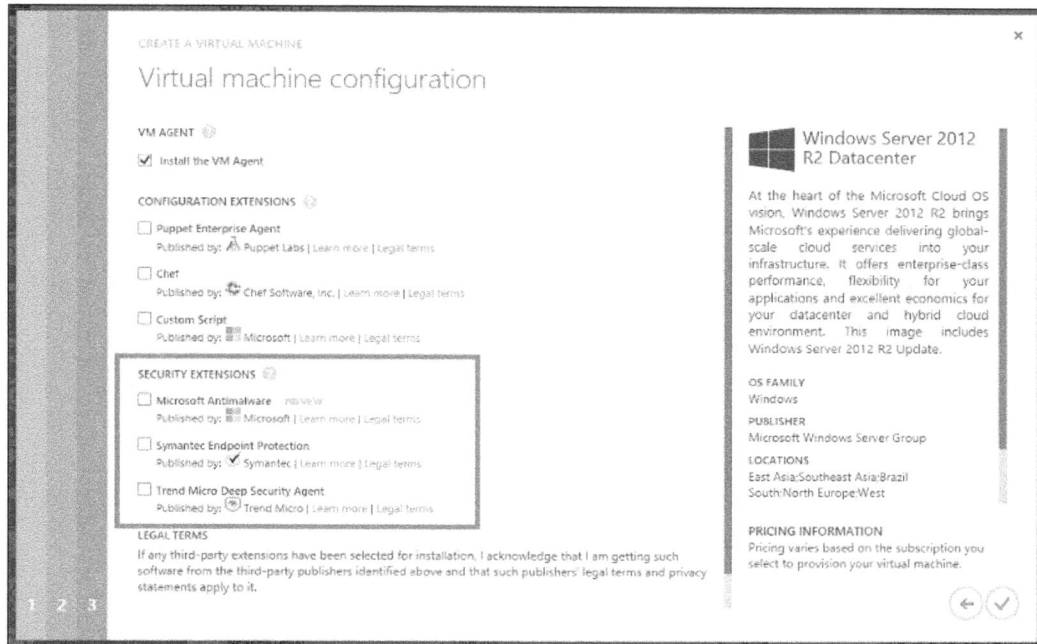

The agent uses extensions (software modules) that deliver all kinds of functionalities. Extensions can be added to instances of web roles, worker roles, and virtual machines. Extensions are made available by Microsoft and by third parties like Symantec.

Roughly, three types of extensions are available:

- VM access extensions
- Configuration extensions
- Security extensions

VM access extensions

The first available extension is BGinfo. This shows all kinds of useful configuration information of the virtual machine on the desktop once logged in.

A very useful extension is one which allows administrators to reset the password of an administrative account. This can be done using PowerShell scripting. This feature is not available yet in the Azure Management Console.

You might think, "Hey, that does not sound very secure!" Note that to be able to connect to Azure using PowerShell, you will need to upload a certificate. However, any administrator that has access to PowerShell will now be able to reset the administrator password.

Another useful use case is resetting the network configuration. If an administrator made a mistake in the IP configuration such that RDP connections are not possible anymore, remote access to the virtual machine is not possible anymore. The VM agent can be used as an out-of-band management port that allows constant access to the virtual machine in all circumstances.

If you have installed a virtual machine before the VM Agent feature was made available by Microsoft, you can download an MSI installer from Microsoft at `http://go.microsoft.com/fwlink/?LinkID=394789&clcid=0x409`.

Configuration extensions

Configuration extensions or agents allow us to configure the virtual machine after it has been provisioned. At the moment, there are three ways to configure the virtual machine:

- Using a PowerShell script
- Using Puppet
- Using Chef

We will discuss Puppet later in this chapter.

Security extensions

There are three security extensions available:

- **Microsoft Antimalware**: This is an agent that will identify, block, and remove malicious software.
- **Symantec Endpoint Protection**: This installs an Antivirus, Antispyware, and Proactive Threat Protection 60-day free trial version.
- **Trend Micro Deep Security Agent**: This provides anti-malware protection, a firewall, an intrusion prevention system, and integrity monitoring.

The agent is installed to `C:\WindowsAzure` and extensions are installed in `C:\Packages`.

When an extension needs to be added, you need to know some details about the extension, such as the name, version, and publisher of the extension. This can be obtained by using the PowerShell cmdlet `Get-Azure VMAvailableExtension`.

Deploying Linux images using VM Depot

Microsoft offers supported Windows Server and Linux images through the Azure image gallery. The selection of Linux-based images in which applications are preinstalled is limited.

However, VM Depot is a great library full of community-created Linux-based images. VM Depot is managed and offered by Microsoft Open Technologies. This is a separate organization that focuses solely on open source.

Note that most of the images are submitted by the open source community. There is no check on what kind of software is running in the operating system.

The home page for VM Depot is at `http://vmdepot.msopentech.com`. You can browse which images are available. You can also see what command to use for deployment of the image to Microsoft Azure. Examples of images available in VM Depot are as follows:

- WordPress on Ubuntu
- GitLab on Ubuntu
- Nagios on CentOS
- RubyStack on Ubuntu

Most of the images are based on Ubuntu.

There are two methods to create a virtual machine based on a VM Depot image:

- Using the Azure Management Portal
- Using the Azure command-line interface

Using the Azure Management Portal to deploy VM Depot images

Perform the following steps in order to use the Azure Management Portal to deploy VM depot images:

1. Open **Azure Management Portal**.
2. Select **Virtual Machines** in the left pane.
3. Select **Images** in the top menu.
4. Select **Browse VM Depot** in the lower menu bar.
5. Select the image you are interested in and click on the right arrow.
6. Now, select the Azure region where you want to store the image. If the region has an associated storage account, select the storage account. Otherwise, create a new storage account. ·
7. Click on the checkmark. Next, the image is copied from VM Depot to the selected Azure region. This can take a while.
8. The image is stored as a VHD file in a container named communityimages.
9. The image needs to be registered as an image. To do that, while in the **Virtual Machines** part of the portal, select the **Images** menu. Then, select the image you just downloaded and click on the **Register** button on the lower menu bar.

Change the name if appropriate. The URL name cannot be changed. Click on the checkmark when you are done.

To create a new virtual machine using the image we downloaded and registered, perform the following steps:

1. Click on the New button in the lower menu
2. Navigate to **Compute | Virtual machine | From gallery**
3. Then select **My images** screentext
4. Select the image you downloaded
5. Click on the right arrow
6. Fill in the required fields

Naming convention for VHD files

Now that the virtual machine is ready to use, let's have a closer look at the disks.

The filenames of the virtual disk files are not shown in the Azure Management Portal. For management of virtual machines, it can be very useful to have some sort of naming convention and know what .vhd belongs to which virtual machines.

When a virtual machine is created, Azure will use the following naming convention for VHD files:

```
<name of Cloud Service>-<name of the virtual machine>-<date of
creation>.vhd
```

When a virtual machine is created in the Azure Management Portal, there is no control over the naming of the VHD file that is used for the system disk (C:) and the temporary disk (D:).

Understanding IP addresses

Networking is a very important component to understand how Microsoft Azure works. This section will describe how IP addresses are assigned, and how we can access virtual machines from the Internet and from our own internal network.

You noticed that when deploying a virtual machine from the Azure Management Portal, there is no option to fill in an IP address. Each virtual machine in Microsoft Azure has its IP configuration assigned by DHCP. This DHCP server is managed by Microsoft. You should not change the IP configuration of the guest operating system. If you manually set IP addresses, this will work for a while, until the virtual machine is assigned a new host and the IP configuration is reset by the Fabric Controller.

Microsoft Azure uses software-defined networking. This means the logic of Azure responsible for networking needs to know which virtual machine has which IP configuration.

That is why the IP addresses are set by DHCP. A virtual machine gets an IP address assigned for its complete life cycle. So, you do not have to worry that the IP address changes after a while.

Virtual IP

Applications running on virtual machines that need to be accessed from the Internet are reachable using the **virtual IP address (VIP)** of the Cloud Service the virtual machine is part of. The VIP is a public IP address registered and owned by Microsoft.

The following image shows how virtual machines part of a Cloud Service are accessed using a VIP. The VIP in the following image is 1.2.3.4:

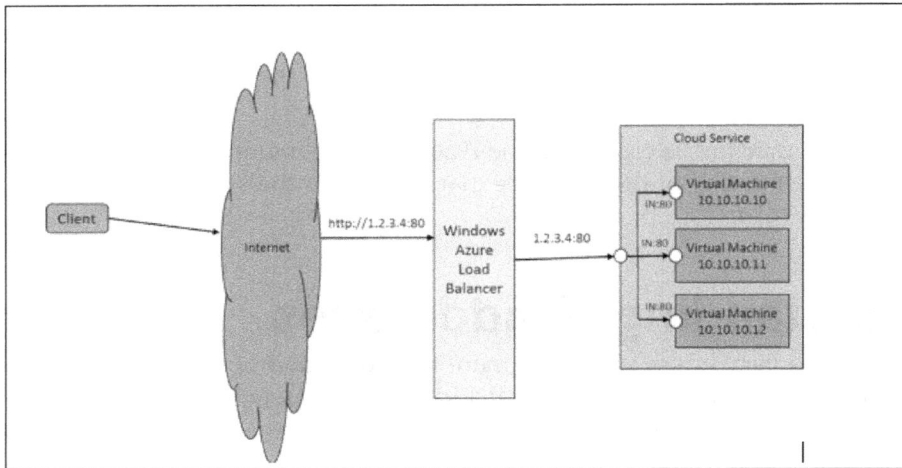

There are a couple of ways to determine the VIP. First, select a virtual machine, select **Dashboard** in the upper menu, and scroll down till you see **Public virtual IP (VIP) address** on the right-hand side of the screen.

Alternatively, select the Cloud Service, select **Dashboard** in the upper menu, and again scroll down till you see the VIP.

The VIP is glued to the Cloud Service as long as there is a minimum of one virtual machine running. If the one and only virtual machine is stopped, the VIP of the Cloud Service might change.

As all the VIP addresses are registered in the name of Microsoft, they are often registered as US-located IP addresses. Another example is that when some US datacenter IP addresses are looked up, you might see these are located in Brazil.

That is caused because US-located IPv4 address ranges are not available anymore. So Microsoft has to use IPv4 address space assigned to a non-US region to address services which may be in a US region. Microsoft is working with IP geo-location database companies to solve this issue.

This could raise issues when accessing certain websites. For example, when watching online movies or television programs, you might notice that you are not allowed to watch them because the website believes you are located in a different country.

You can also use this to your advantage, for example, to watch Netflix from regions that are not available for watching Netflix yet.

IPv6 will solve this issue. The official statement on IPv6 support of Azure is that foundational work to enable IPv6 in the Azure environment is well underway. However, Microsoft is unable to share a date when IPv6 support will be generally available at this time.

A complete list of IP address ranges that are used in Azure datacenters can be downloaded here:

```
http://www.microsoft.com/en-us/download/details.aspx?id=41653
```

Dynamic IP

Each virtual machine you deploy on Microsoft Azure gets an internal IPv4 address assigned by a Microsoft managed DHCP server. This dynamic IP address is known as the **Dynamic IP (DIP)**. Do not change the DHCP address assigned to manually set a static IP address.

Since May 2014, it is possible to set a static IP address on the network adapter of a virtual machine. This can be done using PowerShell. What happens is that a reservation is made in the DHCP server for that virtual machine. So, DHCP is still used to retrieve the IP address.

The DIP can only be used for communications between virtual machines inside the same Cloud Service. When a virtual network is used, a private IP subnet can be used. The first three IP addresses are reserved for inner workings within Azure and for that reason cannot be used. So, for example, when you select a private IP subnet of 192.168.0.x with a subnet mask of 255.255.255.0, the first server in this subnet will get 192.168.0.4 as its IP address.

Assign a static IP address to a virtual machine

In certain configurations, you really want to be able to set a static (fixed) IP address to a virtual machine. This is possible using PowerShell.

Four new commandlets were added in PowerShell for Azure 0.7.3

- Get-AzureStaticVNetIP
- Set-AzureStaticVNetIP
- Remove-AzureStaticVNetIP
- Test-AzureStaticVNetIP

The guest operating system still has to be set to use DHCP. However, there is some sort of permanent reservation made in the Azure fabric when Set-AzureStaticVNetIP is used.

Some things to consider are:

- Setting a fixed IP address to a VM can only be done using PowerShell. It is not possible using the Azure Management Portal.
- It is required that the VM is part of an Azure Virtual Network.

To specify a static IP upon the creation of the virtual machine, use the following PowerShell code:

```
New-AzureVMConfig -Name $vmname -ImageName $img -InstanceSize Small |
Set-AzureSubnet -SubnetNames $sub | Set-AzureStaticVNetIP -IPAddress
192.168.4.7 | New-AzureVM -ServiceName $vmsvc1 -VNetName TestVNet
```

It is also possible to set a static IP to a previously created virtual machine. To apply the static IP, the virtual machine will have to be rebooted:

```
Get-AzureVM -ServiceName StaticDemo -Name VM2 | Set-AzureStaticVNetIP
-IPAddress 192.168.4.7 | Update-AzureVM
```

Assign a static public IP address to a virtual machine

Virtual machines that are part of a Cloud Service can be accessed using the public IP address of that Cloud Service. However, sometimes it is desired that an individual virtual machine is directly accessible over the Internet without using a load balancer, for example, when using passive FTP. Another example is when access to external resources originating from an Azure virtual machine is based on the originating source IP address.

Microsoft offers public facing IP addresses in a feature called instance-level public IP (PIP). Instance-level public IP addresses cost around € 3/ $ 3.36 per month. You can assign up to 5 instance-level IP addresses per subscription.

The following image shows two virtual machines. These are accessible using the VIP: port number as well as using the public IP address (PIP) assigned to each VM.

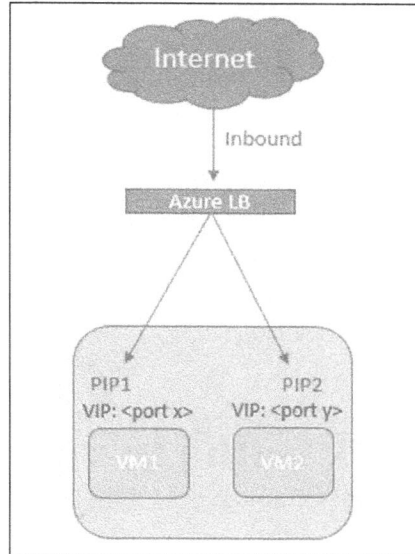

Just like with many other features of Azure, you need to configure PIP using PowerShell.

As of January 2015, a PIP is not supported for multi-NIC virtual machines.

To request a PIP for a new virtual machine, use the PowerShell code shown as follows:

```
New-AzureVMConfig -Name "FTPInstance" -InstanceSize Small -ImageName
$images[50].ImageName | Add-AzureProvisioningConfig -Windows
-AdminUsername narayan -Password abcd123 | Set-AzurePublicIP
-PublicIPName "ftpip" | New-AzureVM -ServiceName "FTPinAzure"
-Location "North Central US"
```

Using Reserved IP addresses for a Cloud Service

In this chapter, we explained the virtual IP address of a Cloud Service. If you want to keep the public IP address of a Cloud Service, you can use a Reserved IP address. The advantage of a Reserved IP address is:

- The IP address will be available in your Azure subscription even if you have deleted all Cloud Services

- The IP address will be available even when all virtual machines of a Cloud Service have been stopped or deallocated
- To make sure all outgoing traffic has a static IP address

Each subscription gets 5 Reserved Public IP addresses for free. Each additional IP address costs about € 3 per month.

You can use PowerShell or REST APIs to request Reserved IP from a particular region. To create a Reserved IP, use the PowerShell code shown as follows:

```
New-AzureReservedIP - ReservedIPName "MyReservedIP" -Label
"ReservedLabel" -Location "Japan West"
```

To get an overview of all Reserved IP's in your subscription, use the following code:

```
Get-AzureReservedIP
```

Managing network traffic to virtual machines

Azure offers two methods to control which type of network traffic is allowed to enter or exit a virtual machine:

- Network Security Groups
- Endpoints

Managing Network Security Groups

Network Security Groups (NSG) allow for the segmentation of a Virtual Network and control of the inbound and outbound traffic of a virtual machine. Previously, when NSGs were not available, administrators had to use either the firewall of the operating system or endpoints to control inbound and outbound traffic. Both are managed on the VM level, which means a change on network inbound or outbound traffic had to be configured at each individual virtual machine.

However, an NSG cannot be used to control network traffic from the Internet to Virtual Networks. NSGs are used to control traffic inside Virtual Networks, between Virtual Networks, and between on-premises networks and Azure Virtual Networks.

One of the use cases for NSG is where customers who are using Office 365 require single sign-on for user accounts located in Microsoft Active Directory running in Azure. In this configuration, several server roles are required like ADFS, Web Application Proxy servers (WAP), AAD Sync, and AD domain controllers. It is not wise to make Active Directory domain controllers accessible over the Internet. Using NSGs, network traffic can be segmented.

Using NSGs also enables you to deploy multi-tier applications in Azure. Such an application has multiple frontend servers (like Webservers) that are accessible over the Internet. Application servers and backend servers like databases require a more strict security, which means those servers are not accessible directly from the Internet. To control network traffic, NSGs can be used.

A Network Security Group consists of rules. A single rule has 5 tuples (source IP, source port, destination IP, destination port, protocol). Rules have a number applied. The lower the number, the high its priority.

Each NSG has a couple of default rules which cannot be deleted. The first default rule is 'deny all outbound traffic' and 'deny all inbound traffic' with a number of 65500. All default rules have a number in the 65xxx range.

Some characteristics of Network Security Groups are as follows:

- Each Azure subscription can be a maximum of 100 Network Security Groups.
- Each Network Security Group can have as many as 200 rules. This is a soft limit. On request, Microsoft can increase this limit.
- Management of Network Security Groups is limited to using PowerShell and RESTapi only.
- Any change made on the Network Security Group is immediately applied to all VMs in the subnet.
- Can be applied to regional virtual networks only.
- Can be applied to a virtual machine or to a subnet.
- Can only be applied to the primary NIC of a virtual machine. In the future, Microsoft will support Network Security Groups for multiple NICS.

An alternative way to control inbound and outbound traffic per Virtual Machine is using endpoints. You can either use Endpoints or a Network Security Group for a VM, not both.

Managing endpoints

To enable network connections between the virtual machine and the Internet, Microsoft Azure uses endpoints. Endpoints are basically mappings or Network Address Translations in Azure firewalls that connect the Virtual IP port number to the DIP port number.

When a Windows Server virtual machine has been created, only a port allowing RDP traffic and a port for PowerShell are opened; this means port 3389 and port 5986 on the inside of a virtual machine. For security reasons, these ports are randomized on the VIP side. This means when you want to make a remote desktop connection to the virtual machine from the Internet, you must be able to connect to a large number of ports, which can prove to cause difficulties in the field because of closed outgoing ports on firewalls.

If additional ports need to be mapped, you will need to manually add endpoints. Endpoints can easily be created in the Azure Management Portal as well as by using PowerShell.

To create or modify endpoints, perform the following steps:

1. Select the virtual machine you would like to modify the endpoint for.
2. Select the **Endpoints** menu item at the top of the screen.
3. Either press **Add** or **Edit** in the lower screen.

To add some security and be able to define which computers have access to Azure virtual machines, you can set access control lists to endpoints.

Access control lists (**ACLs**) can be used to permit or allow certain ranges of IP addresses for connections to an endpoint of a virtual machine. By default, each system connected to the Internet is able to connect to a virtual machine's endpoint. ACLs are an additional layer of security. You can allow for instance only developers pcs access to virtual machines. All other traffic is denied access.

ACLs are created using rules. Each rule denies or allows a subnet access to an endpoint of a virtual machine. You can specify a maximum of 50 rules per endpoint.

When an ACL is created using one or more rules, what happens is that the host in the Azure datacenter that is running the virtual machine will filter packets bound for the virtual machine. A *lowest takes precedence* rule is used, which means a lower listed rule shown in the GUI (or the lower rule number) will take precedence over a higher listed rule (or higher rule number).

Using ACLs, you are able to deny or permit network traffic to a virtual machine endpoint. You will not be able to control network traffic to the Azure Management Portal. To enable ACLs, perform the following steps:

1. Select the virtual machine for which you would like to set an ACL on the endpoint.
2. Select **Endpoints** from the top menu.
3. Select the endpoint you would like to set an ACL on.

4. Click on the **Manage ACL** button in the lower menu bar.

5. You will see the following screenshot. It shows two rules:

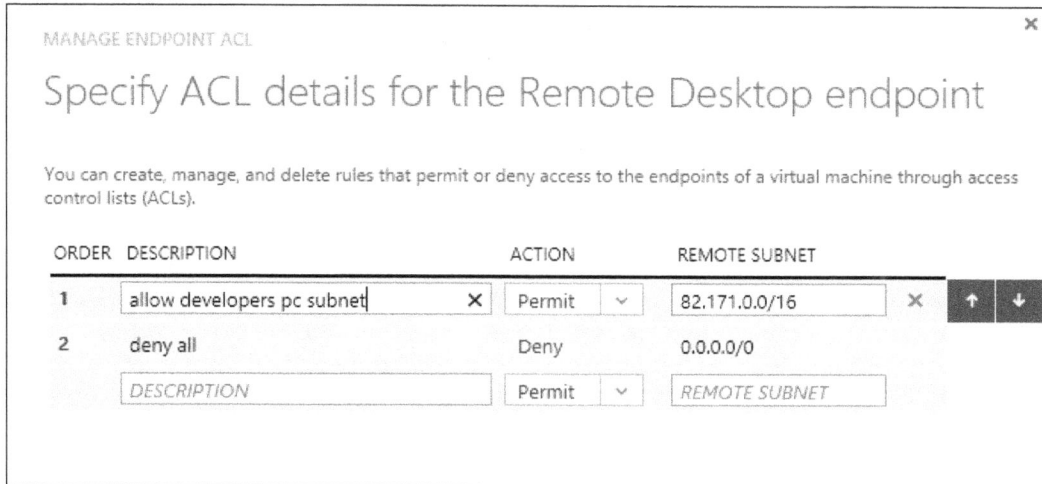

MANAGE ENDPOINT ACL

Specify ACL details for the Remote Desktop endpoint

You can create, manage, and delete rules that permit or deny access to the endpoints of a virtual machine through access control lists (ACLs).

ORDER	DESCRIPTION		ACTION		REMOTE SUBNET			
1	allow developers pc subnet	×	Permit	⌄	82.171.0.0/16	×	↑	↓
2	deny all		Deny		0.0.0.0/0			
	DESCRIPTION		Permit	⌄	*REMOTE SUBNET*			

The second **deny all** rule denies all network traffic on the RDP endpoint of a virtual machine. The first rule allows clients with an IP in subnet 82.171.x.x/16 to connect to the RDP endpoint. By using this rule, we are sure only clients in a subnet managed and owned by our organization can access virtual machines.

Testing virtual machine endpoints

After having added one or more endpoints, you might want to test whether a network connection to your service is possible. Obviously, this can be done by trying to reach the application.

If you are running a web server on port 80, you can test it by using a browser and type in the URL of your web server. You might get an error. If you are unsure what causes the error, try to probe the network port that is used by the application.

This can be done by using the Telnet command. Suppose you have an application running on an Azure virtual machine that uses port 8080. You, in your role as an IT professional, want to make sure that network connection to the application is functional.

Take any client with an Internet connection and execute the following command:

```
telnet <dns name of Azure service> 8080
```

If there is a response, you are sure network connectivity is possible and the problem is caused by the application.

Setting DNS server configuration

When using your own DNS servers in Microsoft Azure, you should make sure servers and clients are querying your managed DNS servers. As you learned earlier, static IP addresses and IP configuration is not supported. We are required to set IP addresses and DNS for our virtual machines dynamically via the Microsoft managed DHCP services.

If we cannot manually set the DNS server addresses and have no control over DHCP, how are we able to define DNS servers? The answer is Azure Virtual Networks. When configuring virtual networks, we can set one or more DNS server names and IP addresses. Any virtual machine part of that virtual network will automatically have those DNS servers set in its IP configuration.

Deployment and configuration using Puppet

In the first half of 2014, Microsoft made it very easy to install either a Puppet Enterprise agent or a Chef agent during provisioning of a new virtual machine.

If you are used to managing Windows Server, you might not have heard of a tool called Puppet. This is becoming an increasingly popular tool especially because of interest in DevOps.

Puppet is an open source deployment and configuration management tool used mainly in Linux environments. It allows you to automatically deploy servers and configure them using a set of policies. Using this method, servers can be configured in a uniform manner.

Puppet uses a Puppet Master Server that holds a set of tasks to be performed by Puppet nodes. Each node has an agent installed. This agent has a configuration file that gets its input from so-called "Puppet manifests."

Puppet manifests contain instructions on what should be done on a server. The instructions are written in a very easy-to-read language called domain-specific language. This is a so-called declarative language. Puppet language does not say *how to do* something, but only instructs the computer *what to do*.

Puppet is available as a free Standard edition and a commercial Enterprise edition. The latter is free for a maximum of 10 nodes. Both versions are functionally equal. The only difference is that Puppet Enterprise has the possibility for commercial support.

Agents contact the Puppet Master over HTTPS and ask what to do. The master creates a so-called "Catalog" that has instructions. This is sent to the agent.

There are Puppet agents available for Linux and Windows Server operating systems. The Puppet Master Server can only run on Unix or Linux.

Microsoft Open Technologies released an Azure Puppet Module that allows provisioning of Linux and Windows Server virtual machines as well as virtual networks. The module is available in the Puppet Labs Forge at `http://forge.puppetlabs.com/msopentech/windowsAzure`.

Service healing

Service Healing is an important Azure characteristic.

Microsoft Azure constantly checks the health of the nodes and virtual machines (instances). Both the software and the hardware of nodes are monitored by the Fabric Controller. If a problem occurs, for instance, a cooling fan malfunction, the host agent will inform the Fabric Controller about this. The Fabric Controller will then move virtual machine from the problematic node to other nodes. As Microsoft Azure does not have the ability of Live Migration like in Hyper-V, the virtual machines will be shut down, reallocated to a different node, and then restarted. The fault node is marked "out for repair" so that Microsoft staff can replace the node. This process is called *service healing*.

When a virtual machine is restarted, the IP configuration will be reset. As you learned earlier, it is not wise to manually set the IP address of virtual machines. This will work until the virtual machine is reallocated to a different node.

The result of service healing is:

- The virtual network adapter in the virtual machine will change
- The MAC address of the virtual network adapter will change
- The processor/CPU ID of the virtual machine will change
- The IP configuration of the virtual network adapter will not change as long as the virtual machine is attached to a virtual network and the virtual machine's IP configuration is defined as part of the virtual network or the virtual machine itself (not the guest operating system)

Installing additional software

The advantage of the Azure Virtual Machines services is the ability to have control over the virtual machine operating system. Also, the persistent state means that after reboot and service healing, the state remains the same as before the reboot. This is very useful. When a virtual machine restarts, software installed on it will remain available. The only exception is the content of the temporary drive D:, which will be lost after service healing.

It is likely that you want to install your own software on an Azure virtual machine. Microsoft offers a lot of software out of the box like SQL Server, SharePoint, and even Oracle software. These are available as images from the Azure Management Portal.

There are several options to upload and install your own software:

- Download from within the guest operating system using a browser
- Upload using FTP or file shares
- Upload a VHD disk which includes the application installation software

In the next section, you will learn how to create a VHD locally, upload the VHD, and attach it to a virtual machine running in Azure.

Creating a VHD to upload installation files

The first step for being able to upload installation software to Azure is to create an empty VHD file locally. This VHD will be used as the storage media for our installation files. Keep in mind that currently only uploading of VHD files to Azure is supported. The newer VHDX file types are not supported.

Creation of a VHD file can be done in several ways, for example, using Hyper-V Manager on Windows 8. It is a little easier to create an empty VHD using Disk Management in Windows 7, Windows 8, and Windows Server 2008 R2 and later:

1. Go to **Disk Management** under **Computer Management**.
2. From the **Action** menu, select **Create VHD**.
3. Select a location to store the VHD.

> Give the VHD file a descriptive name, for example, WindowsServer2012R2UK.vhd.
>
> It is possible that you would want to reuse this VHD for future installation, so a descriptive filename will help to remember the content of the VHD.

4. Set the size of the VHD. The size of the VHD file is not important as long as it is large enough to hold your installation files. The upload mechanism will skip unwritten disk space in the VHD.

5. Make sure **Virtual disk format** is **VHD** as VHDX is not yet supported by Microsoft Azure.

6. Also, make sure **Virtual hard disk type** is set to **Fixed size**.

7. Click on **OK**.

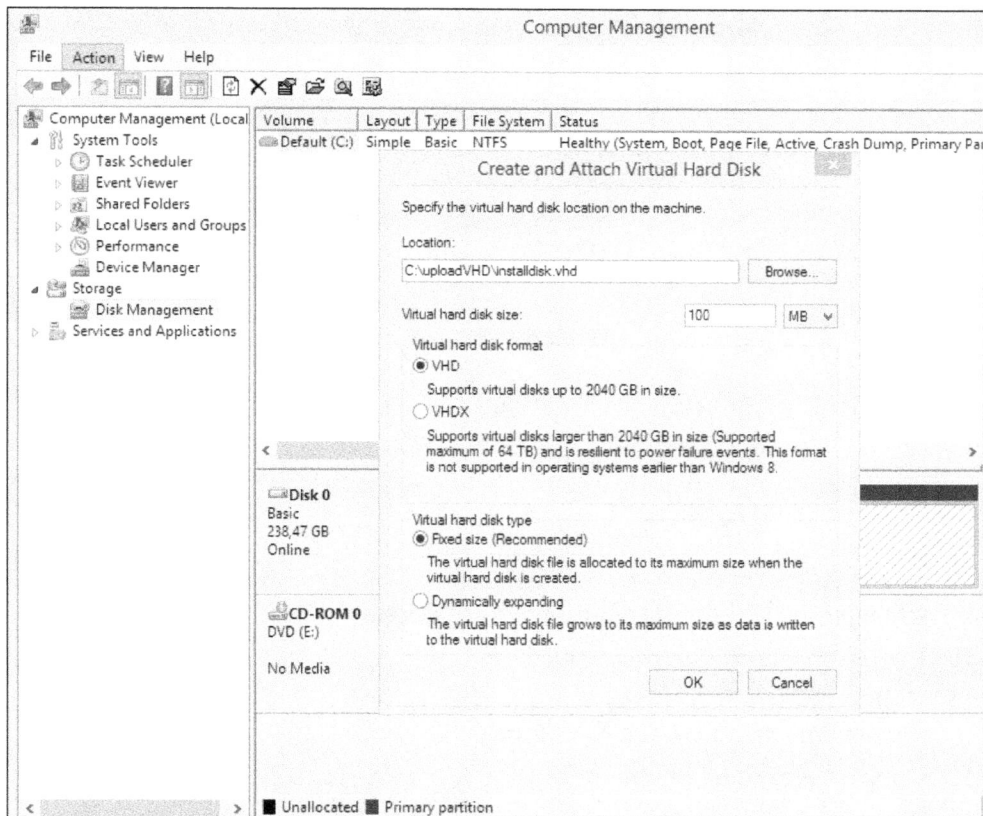

8. Position the mouse cursor over the newly created disk. Depending on the number of the disk, the disk number will be different than the one shown in the following screenshot:

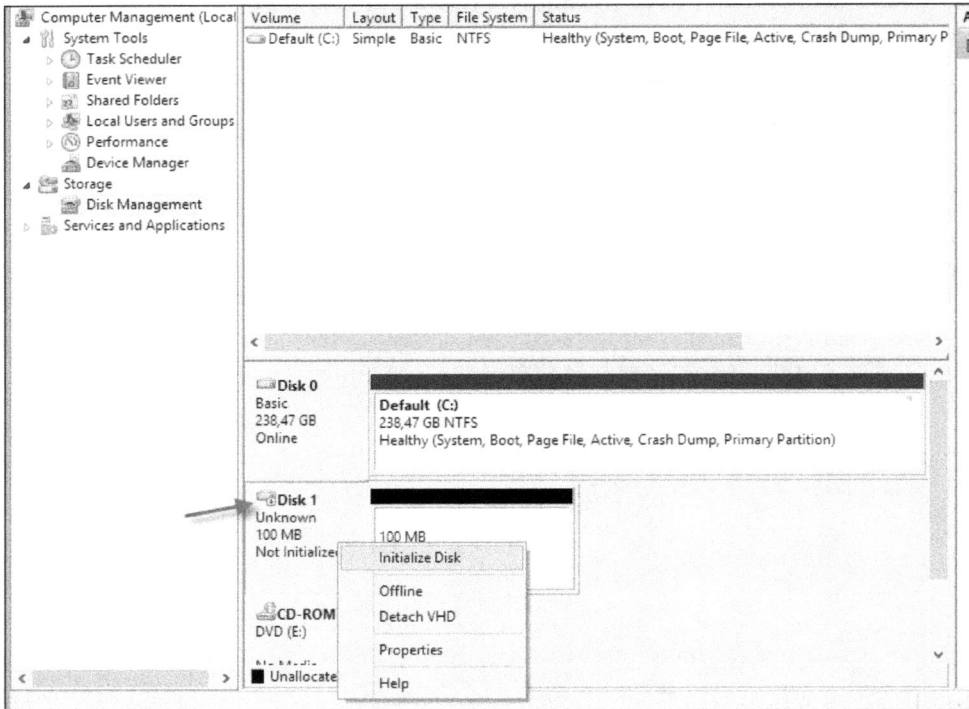

9. Click on the right mouse button and select **Initialize Disk**.

10. Keep the default values and click on **OK**.

11. Position the mouse cursor over the newly created disk, click on the right mouse button, and select **New simple volume**.

12. Click on **Next**, change the settings if you want, and click on **Finish**.

13. You now have a new drive displayed in Windows Explorer. Copy the required installation software to this new drive.

14. When finished copying, go to **Computer Management | Disk management**.

15. Position the mouse cursor over the disk containing the installation software. Click on the right mouse button and select **Detach VHD**.

16. Now, we are ready to upload the VHD to Microsoft Azure and attach the VHD to a virtual machine.

Uploading files to Microsoft Azure

In this section, you will learn how to upload virtual disk files and other files to Microsoft Azure. The main reasons behind uploading VHD files are:

- You created a customized virtual machine on-site and want to upload this to Azure
- You created a VHD containing software to be used in Microsoft Azure

Several tools are available for uploading files to Microsoft Azure:

- Use System Center App Controller
- Use PowerShell
- Use third-party solutions

I prefer using Cerebrata Azure Explorer to upload files to Microsoft Azure. The software is free to use and not limited by time. Cerebrata is very useful if you are not using System Center App Controller on-site. To use App Controller to upload files, you need to install SQL Server and SCVMM first. To upload files into a demo environment, a tool such as Cerebrata is much easier.

Let's get started with installing Azure Explorer and start learning how to use it.

The software can be downloaded from `http://www.cerebrata.com/labs/Azure -explorer`.

Installation is very simple and requires just a few clicks. After starting Azure Explorer, you need to configure an Azure storage account. This allows use access to the Azure blob storage.

The account name and access key is required. To find out these, perform the following steps:

1. Go to **Azure Management Portal**.
2. Select **Storage** in the left pane.
3. Select the storage account you want to use.
4. Click on **Manage access Keys** in the bottom bar.
5. You will be presented with a screen showing the storage account name, primary key, and secondary key.
6. Now, select **Cerebrate Azure Explorer**.
7. Select **Azure Storage Accounts** in the left pane.
8. Click on the right mouse button and select **Add Account**.

9. Copy and paste the account name and primary key into the respective fields.

10. Click on **Test connection**. You should get a window saying FS: ST.

11. Click on **OK**.

12. In the left pane, select the newly created storage account and open the folder named vhds.

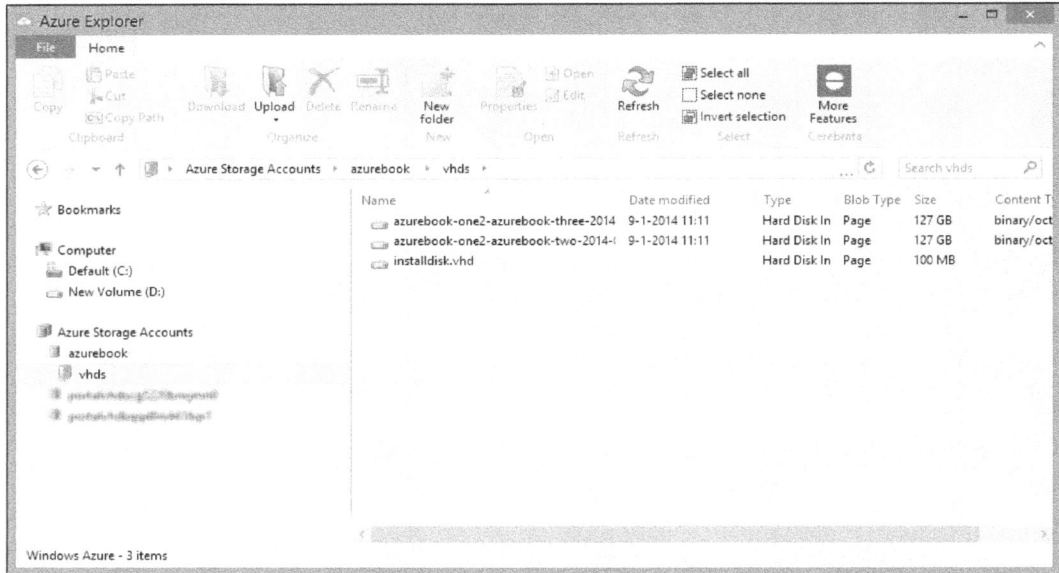

13. Place the mouse cursor over the right window, click on the right mouse button, and select **Upload**.

14. Select **Page blob**.

15. Browse to the folder on your on-site system where you created the VHD file that contains the installation software.

16. Click on **Open**.

17. The .vhd file will now be sent to Microsoft Azure Storage.

Another way of uploading a VHD to Azure is by using PowerShell. However, there are some prerequisites you need to upload a VHD with PowerShell. These prerequisites are:

* The Azure PowerShell module
* A management certificate (can be self-signed)
* A VHD file

The next thing to do is to create a storage account in Azure, which you will target with your PowerShell command. After creating the storage account and writing down the URL of this service, you will need to prepare the connection to Azure from PowerShell.

You can accomplish this with the `Get-AzurePublishSettingsFile` command and importing this into the local store of your computer. The last step is to upload the VHD file to Azure with the `Add-AzureVHD powershell` command. This command will perform a check of the checksum of the VHD, after which the file is uploaded to the previously defined storage account.

For more information, please visit `http://www.windowsazure.com/en-us/documentation/articles/virtual-machines-create-upload-vhd-windows-server/`.

Connecting the VHD to a virtual machine

The last step is to connect the VHD file to a virtual machine:

1. Open **Azure Management Portal** using a web browser.
2. Select **VIRTUAL MACHINES** in the left pane.
3. Select the virtual machine you want to attach the uploaded VHD to. Do not to select the name of the virtual machine in the **NAME** column.
4. Click on **Disks** in the upper menu.

5. Then, click on **CREATE** in the lower menu:

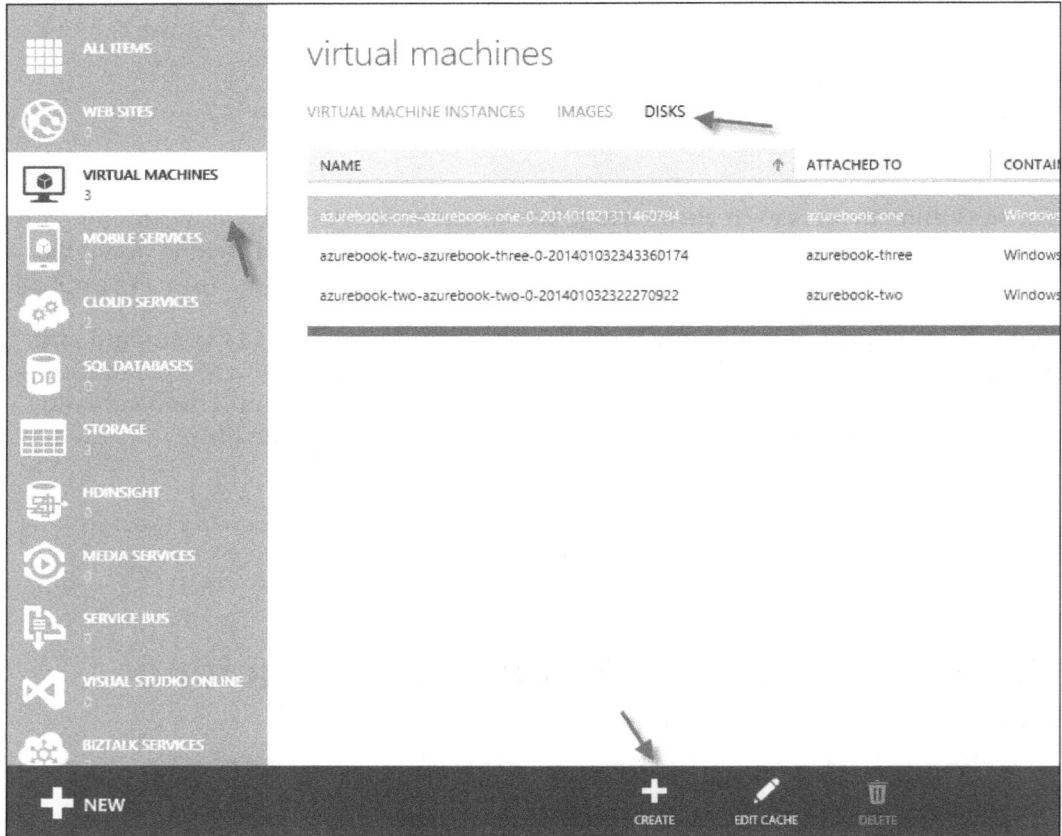

6. In the **Name** field, type in a descriptive name.
7. Click on the VHD URL button, select the Azure storage account in the left pane, browse to the VHD folder, and select the VHD you just uploaded.
8. Click on **OPEN**. Do *not* select **The VHD contains an operating system**.

9. Click on the checkmark button.

Create a disk from a VHD

NAME

installdisk

VHD URL

☐ The VHD contains an operating system.

OPERATING SYSTEM FAMILY

Windows

10. After the disk has been created, make sure the correct virtual machine is selected.

11. Click on **Attach** in the lower menu.

12. Select **Attach disk**.

13. Select the correct available disk.

14. Leave the default **Host cache preference** as **NONE**.

15. Click on the checkmark button.

Attach a disk to the virtual machine

VIRTUAL MACHINE NAME

azurebook-one

AVAILABLE DISKS

installdisk

HOST CACHE PREFERENCE

NONE READ ONLY READ/WRITE

16. Now, start a remote session to your virtual machine. In Windows Server 2012 R2, the disk is automatically connected. If not, go to **Computer Management | Disk Management** and select **Refresh disks** in the **Actions** menu.

    You now have an extra disk containing the installation software you prepared in the previous steps.

17. If you do not want to use the disk, simply select the virtual machine in Azure Management Portal and select **Detach Disk** in the lower menu bar.

Summary

In this chapter, you learned how to purchase a Microsoft Azure subscription and how to create an account. You also learned how to create your first virtual machine in Microsoft Azure. The importance of understanding the function of Virtual Networks is clear now. Apart from being created manually, virtual machines can be created by PowerShell or even by using a command-line interface. PowerShell is a very powerful tool for managing large numbers of virtual machines.

In the next chapter, you are going to learn how to connect our on-premises infrastructure to Microsoft Azure using a VPN connection. To provide non-IT staff access to clouds running on-premises, in Azure, or in a service provider environment, we use System Center App Controller.

5
Connecting to Microsoft Azure

Now that we have built some virtual machines, we are ready to connect our on-premises infrastructure to Microsoft Azure. This chapter is all about connections and will cover the following topics:

- Connecting to Azure using a VPN connection over the Internet
- Connecting to Azure using ExpressRoute as a dedicated connection
- Securing connections using two-way authentication
- Managing virtual machines using App Controller

Connection options

To be able to connect your own managed data centers with Azure, you have three options:

- A **site-to-site** (**S2S**) VPN connection using public Internet.
- A multisite VPN.
- Azure ExpressRoute using a private network. This option is available if your data center is located in a facility like a co-location that offers Azure ExpressRoute. Alternatively a customer site can be connected directly to Azure using network service providers.

For a S2S VPN, a connection is made between a VPN gateway running in Azure and an on-premises VPN endpoint. Initially, when S2S VPN became available, only a single S2S VPN connection could be created. As of May 2014, this has been extended to a maximum of 10 S2S VPN connections. This enables to connect, for example, multiple offices or data centers to the same Azure Virtual Network. Note that a maximum of 10 connections share a maximum of 80 to 100 Mbps throughput.

A multisite VPN connection at the time of writing this book cannot be created using Azure Management Portal. The network configuration file needs to be used instead.

Azure ExpressRoute

ExpressRoute is a new service that became publically available in May 2014. It allows customers to use dedicated connections from on-premises or colocation data centers to Azure without having to use public Internet.

The advantage of ExpressRoute over VPN connections is more bandwidth, lower latencies, more reliable because of redundancy, and more secure. This service is charged by Microsoft and backed by a SLA. Depending on the bandwidth, a fixed price has to be paid. When outgoing network traffic exceeds a certain threshold cost per GB is charged.

Microsoft partners with cloud exchange service providers such as Equinix and TeleCity Group who offer data center and infrastructure facilities for their customers. For connections between on-premises and Azure, Microsoft partners with **point-to-site (P2S)** connectivity service providers like level 3.

ExpressRoute is configured using the PowerShell ExpressRoute module or using REST API.

Most Microsoft Azure services can be accessed over an ExpressRoute connection. However some services such as RemoteApp and Multifactor Authentication are not supported over ExpressRoute. Also Office 365 can be used over ExpressRoute connections.

A single ExpressRoute connection can be shared by up to 10 other Azure subscriptions. Up to 10 virtual networks can be connected to an ExpressRoute connection.

The following figure shows the two deployment scenarios for ExpressRoute. Either via a facility that offers an ExpressRoute entry or directly via a WAN connection from customer on-premises sites to Azure.

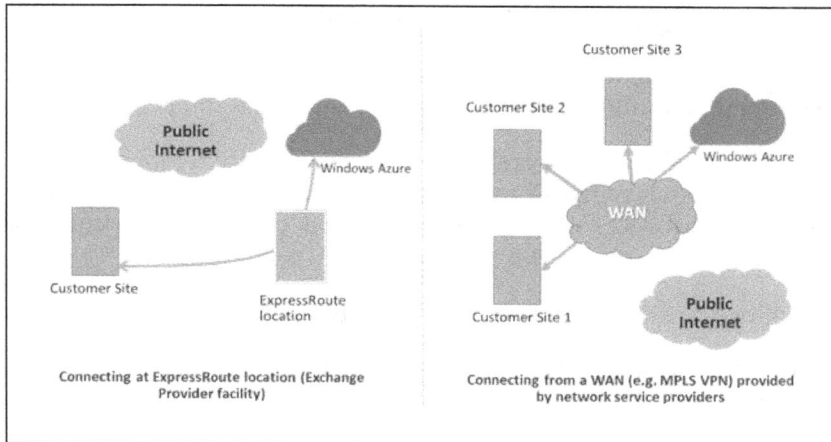

Connecting at ExpressRoute location (Exchange Provider facility)

Connecting from a WAN (e.g. MPLS VPN) provided by network service providers

Connecting to Azure using a point-to-site VPN

When a connection to Azure is made over the Internet, two types of connections can be made:

- **An S2S VPN connection**: This connects the Microsoft Azure virtual network to an on-premises network over VPN
- **A P2S VPN connection**: This allows a secure VPN connection between a client device and Microsoft Azure

To set up a P2S connection, these high-level steps need to be performed:

1. Create a virtual network in Azure.
2. Define the address block for the clients.
3. Create a dynamic routing gateway.
4. Create certificates.
5. Export certificates and upload them to Microsoft Azure.
6. Download and install the VPN client software.

> At the time of writing this book, it is not possible to disable VPN access for a certain user. This is required, for example, when an employee leaves the company he or she works for. The only way to disable VPN access is by recreating certificates.

Creating a virtual network

Virtual networks are an essential component in Azure. They allow control over IP address assignment and allow connectivity to on-premises data centers.

Since May 2014, virtual networks created in different Azure regions can be connected to each other. This allows network traffic to travel over dedicated Microsoft connections instead over S2S VPN connections. Also, virtual networks that are part of different Azure subscriptions can be connected to each other.

Perform the following steps to create a virtual network in Azure:

1. In the Azure Management Portal, select **Networks** in the left pane and click on **New**.
2. Select **Quick Create**.
3. Fill in a name using your naming convention.
4. Select an address space.
5. Select the appropriate affinity group.
6. Click on **Create a virtual network**.

   The following screenshot shows the Quick Create window of a virtual network:

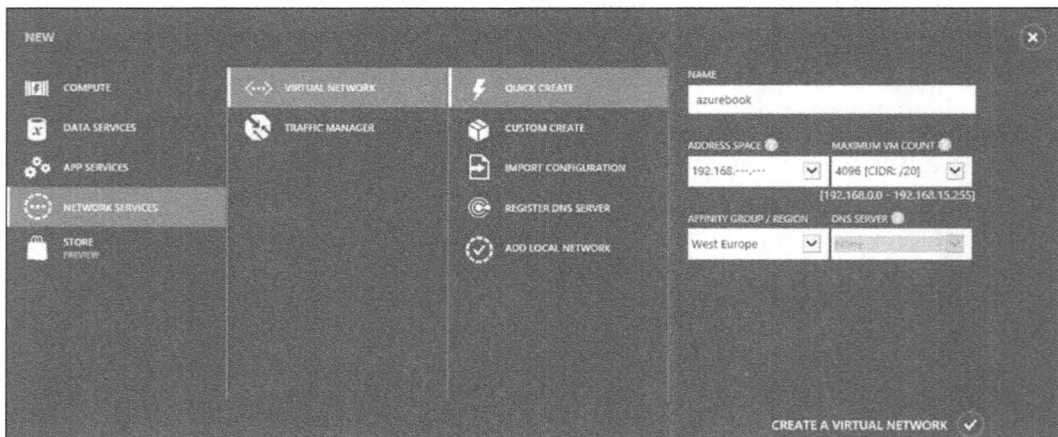

7. Once the virtual network is created, select the virtual network (called **azurebook** in our example) and then click on **Configure**.

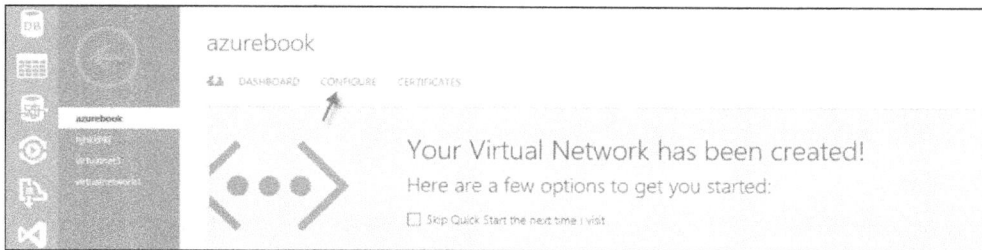

8. Once you click on **Configure**, the screen shown in the following screenshot will appear:

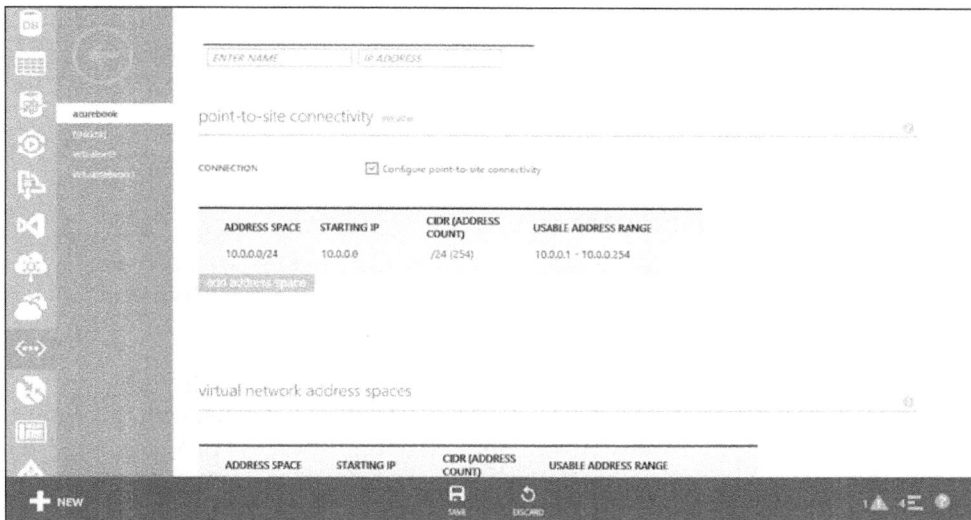

9. Enable **Configure point-to-site connectivity**.
10. Click on **SAVE** at the bottom of the screen.

11. The next step is to create a virtual gateway. Select the **Dashboard** menu option at the top of the screen.

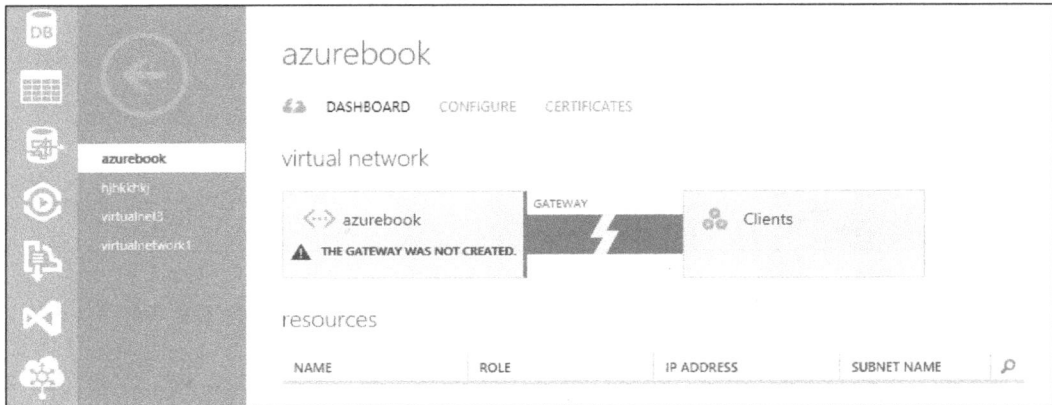

12. Select the **Create Gateway** button located at the bottom of the screen.
13. Select **Yes** for the question **Do you want to create a virtual gateway?**

Creating certificates

The next steps describe how to create certificates. Certificates are used as a way to authenticate clients to Microsoft Azure and are an alternative to account-based authentication.

Certificates can be created using **Public Key Infrastructure (PKI)**. If your organization does not use PKI, you can use the **makecert** tool. This tool is part of the Windows SDK, which can be downloaded for free. It is also part of Visual Studio. Alternatively, it could also be downloaded separately.

If you use the Windows SDK, installation of the Windows Software Development Kit feature is sufficient. Uncheck the other features during setup to keep the installation base as small as possible.

First, we create a self-signed root certificate by performing the following steps:

1. Start a command prompt as administrator and enter the following command:

```
makecert-sky exchange -r -n "CN = <RootCertificateName>"-pe -sk
<NameofCertificate> -a sha1 -len 2048 -ss MyStore
```

```
C:\Program Files\Microsoft Message Analyzer>makecert -sky exchange -r -n "CN=azu
rebook" -pe -sk azurebook -a sha1 -len 2048 -ss MyStore
Succeeded
```

2. The next step is to generate a client certificate with the following command:

```
makecert.exe -n "CN=CertificateName" -pe -sk Name -sky exchange -m 96 -ss
Mystore -in "RootCertificateName" -is MyStore -a sha1
```

```
C:\Program Files\Microsoft Message Analyzer>makecert.exe -n "CN=azurebook-client
cert-client" -pe -sk azurebook -sky exchange -m 96 -ss MyStore  -in "azurebook"
-is MyStore -a sha1
Succeeded
```

3. Then, export the root certificate. Start the Microsoft Management Console on the client machine you used to create the certificates.

4. Add the certificates add-on and select the current user.

5. Then, go to the **MyStore** folder.

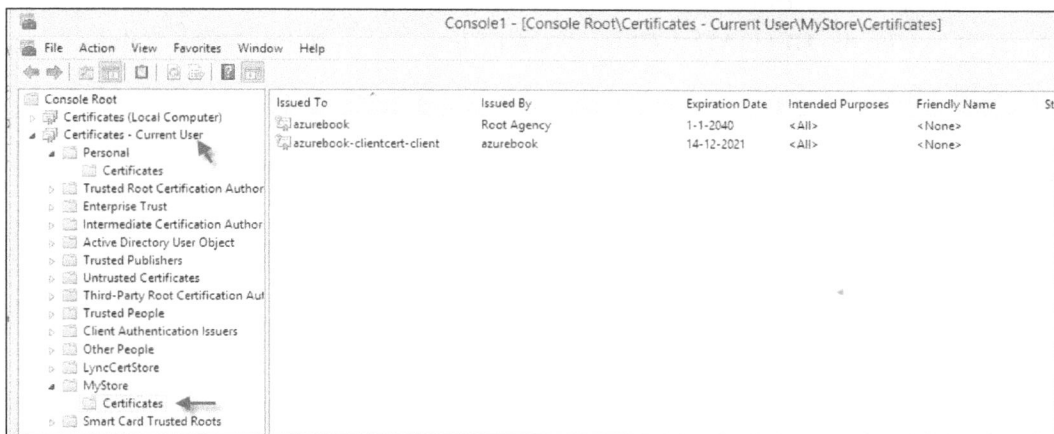

6. Select the root certificate (in our example this is named **azurebook**).

7. Click on the right mouse button, go to **All tasks**, and choose **Export**.

8. Click on **Next.**

9. Choose not to export the private key.

10. Select **DER encoded binary X.509 CER file**.

11. Select a folder and give the certificate a name.

The next step is to export the client certificate:

1. While still in the MMC, select the client certificate.

2. Click on the right mouse button, select **All tasks**, and choose **Export**.

3. Click on **Next**.

4. **Yes**, export the private key.
5. Accept options and click on **Next**.
6. Enable the password option and set the password.
7. Click on **Next**.
8. Select a folder and type in a filename.

The next step is to upload the root certificate to Azure:

1. Open the Azure Management Portal.
2. Select **Networks** in the left pane.
3. Select the network we created in the previous step.
4. Select the **Certificates** menu option.
5. Click on the **UPLOAD A CERTIFICATE** link shown at the bottom of the screen.

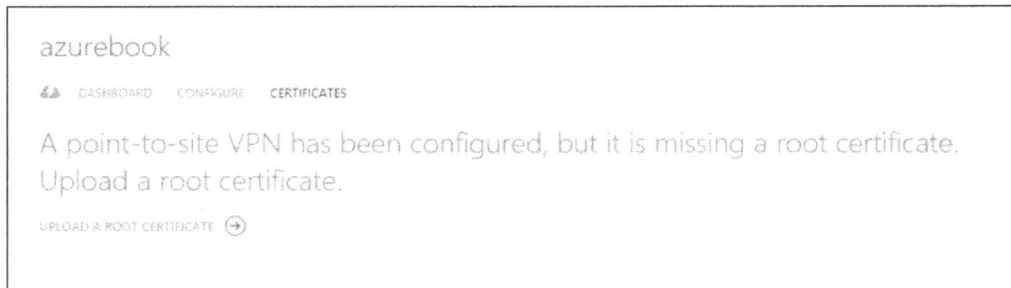

azurebook

DASHBOARD CONFIGURE **CERTIFICATES**

A point-to-site VPN has been configured, but it is missing a root certificate. Upload a root certificate.

UPLOAD A ROOT CERTIFICATE →

We're done with certificates. The only thing we need to do is to download and install the VPN client software from Azure on the clients from which we'd want to set up our P2S VPN connection.

Installing the client certificate and downloading the VPN client

In this section, we will install the client certificate and the VPN client software.

1. Navigate to the folder on your client PC where the client certificate is stored, and double-click on the `.pfx` file.
2. This will start the import wizard. Select all the default options. Do not modify the installation location.

3. We need to download and install the VPN client software. Select the **Dashboard** menu option in the **Network** section of **Azure Management Portal**.

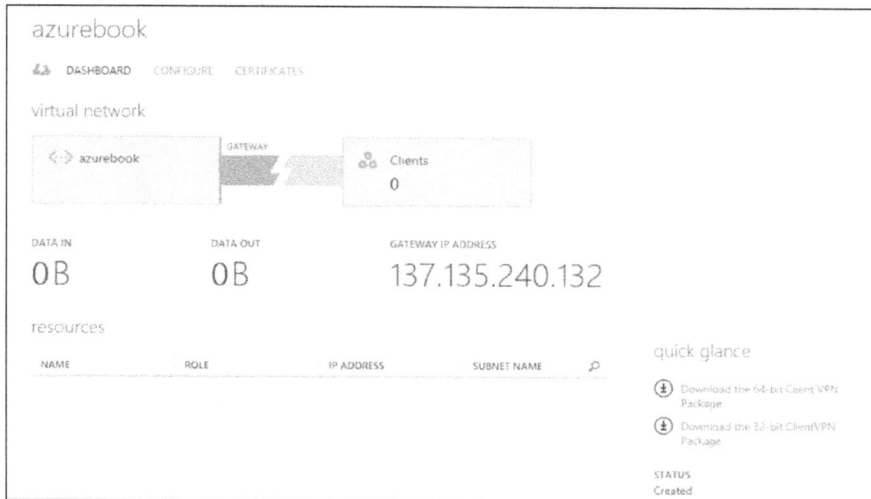

4. Select the download link for your client operating system. The supported operating systems are:

    ° Windows 7 (32-bit and 64-bit)
    ° Windows Server 2008 (64-bit only)
    ° Windows 8 (32-bit and 64-bit)
    ° Windows Server 2012 (64-bit only)

5. Next, we make a P2S connection to Microsoft Azure. In Windows 8, you can do that by clicking on the connections icon in the bottom-right corner.

6. Select the connection we created. In our example, it should be named **azurebook**:

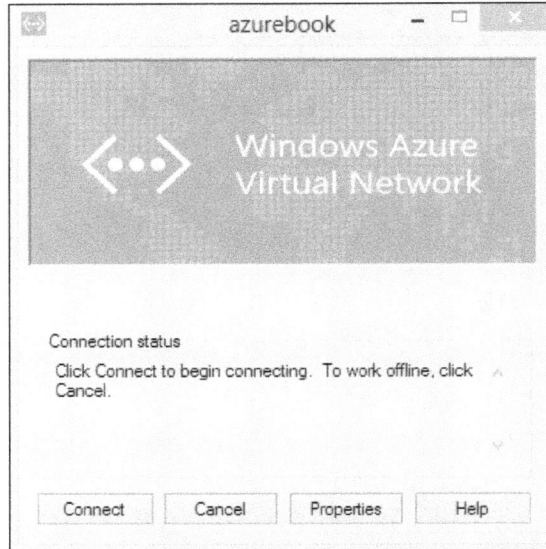

7. Click on **Connect**.

We now have an operational VPN connection from a client into Microsoft Azure. This scenario is often used for developers who need access to their development environment in Azure without a S2S VPN in place.

Support on Microsoft Azure

You might have technical questions or run into issues related to Microsoft Azure. When using your own managed infrastructure, you just walk to your co-worker who is responsible for managing storage, application, or network. When using Microsoft Azure, the customer is not able to manage networking, storage, and compute. So, you will have to request Microsoft for assistance.

Microsoft offers several levels of support:

*   Free (included in the free trial period)
*   Developer
*   Standard
*   Professional direct
*   Premier

The free support is available for MSDN and evaluation-based subscriptions. However, the support is limited to questions on billing. Also, requests to increase the quote on the number of cores per subscription are also handled.

To solve technical issues that you can't solve, you will need a paid support subscription. Microsoft has outsourced the customer and technical support on Microsoft Azure to several companies, mostly located in India. One of them is Spectrum Consultants.

Also, operations and troubleshooting, including incident response, service updates, and security investigations, are being subcontracted. Here, most of the work is done by a contractor in India called Mindtree Consulting. Operations and troubleshooting on Microsoft Azure Active Directory is mostly done by US companies.

Set up Multi-factor Authentication in Microsoft Azure Management Portal

In the previous chapter, you learned that Microsoft Azure Management Portal is one of the ways to manage virtual machines, networks, and more. As the portal is accessible from the Internet, we want to make sure only those who are authorized have access to the portal.

The default authentication to access the management portal is by typing in an account name and password. In specific cases, this is not enough and two-way authentication is required. Think about security-sensitive information. A combination of just an account name and password could be not secure enough as hackers can make guesses or execute social hacking to get the credentials.

Two-way authentication works by requiring any two or more of the following verification methods:

- Something you know (typically a password)
- Something you have (a trusted device that is not easily duplicated, such as a phone)
- Something you are (biometrics)

Microsoft Azure has several options to supply a token required for two-way authentication:

- Using an app on a mobile phone
- Using a mobile phone
- Using a smart card

Microsoft calls this service **Multi-Factor Authentication (MFA)**, and it is additionally charged. For customers of Azure Active Directory Premium MFA is free both for on-premises as well as for cloud-based users.

Multi-Factor Authentication can be used for both Azure-based services as well as for on-premises resources. Customers can, for example, add an additional layer of security to their Microsoft Desktop Services by using MFA. To do so an Azure Multi-Factor Authentication Server needs to be installed on-premises. Authentication will then be redirected to Azure. Azure MFA will request the user to enter a secret code or enter the # sign on a mobile phone.

One of the advantages of using this cloud-based MFA over traditional solutions such as RSA is costs. Azure MFA is considerately cheaper than RSA and scales much better with the organization. If the organization grows, additional users can easily be enabled for MFA with a single click of the mouse. There's need to purchase additional licenses and hardware tokens.

Lets have a look how multi-factor authentication is enabled.

Configuring Multi-factor Authentication using a phone

Multi-Factor Authentication using a phone involves the following steps:

1. A user is authenticated on Microsoft Azure using a username and password. Then, the user is automatically called by Microsoft Azure. The user answers the phone, presses the # sign, and is then authenticated.
2. Multi-Factor Authentication is not free. Microsoft offers two billing options:
   ° The first is charged per enabled user. Each unique user can authenticate an unlimited number of times per month.
   ° The other billing option charges on per authentication. In this, a number of authentications can be performed that are user-independent.

Multi-Factor Authentication is free for Microsoft Azure Active Directory Global Administrators. To configure Multi-Factor Authentication, perform the following steps:

1. In Azure Management Portal, select **Active Directory** in the left pane.
2. Then select **Multi-factor auth providers**.

3. Create a new Multi-Factor Authentication provider. Fill in your name in the **NAME** field and set the **USAGE MODEL** as **Per Enabled User** or **Per Authentication User**. Then, select the Microsoft Azure Active Directory for which you like to enable Multi-Factor Authentication.

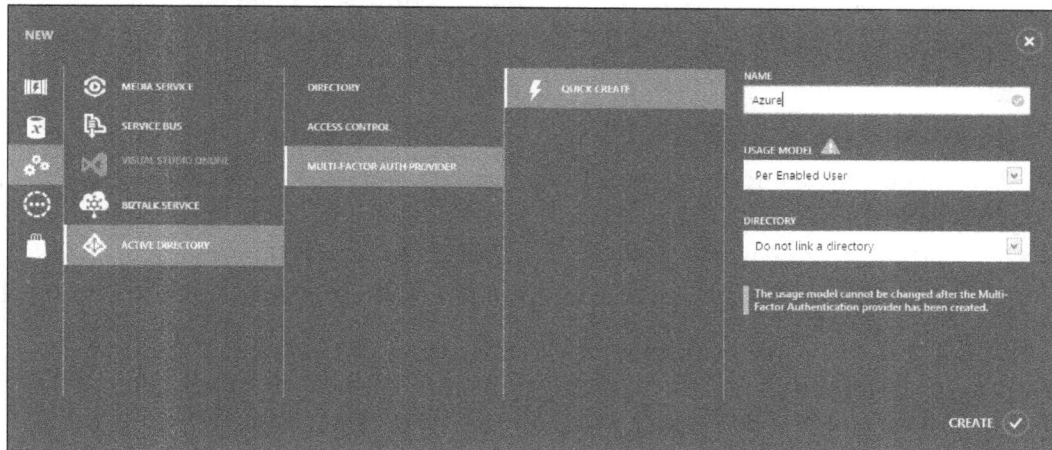

4. Click on **Create**.
5. After creation, make sure the correct authentication provider is selected and click on the **Manage** button at the bottom of the screen.
6. The Azure Multi-Factor Authentication management screen is displayed. Close this window.

Enable a user for Multi-factor Authentication

In this section, we will discuss how to enable Multi-Factor Authentication for a user account. This will enable an additional challenge during authentication. This can either be filling in a passcode or pressing the # sign on a mobile phone.

> Keep in mind that it can take a couple of hours before a user account created in Microsoft Azure Active Directory shows up in the Multi-Factor Authentication window!

The procedure to enable Multi-Factor Authentication is as follows:

1. The administrator enables Multi-Factor Authentication.
2. The user logs in and completes the registration process.
3. Select **Active Directory** in the left pane of **Azure Management Portal**.
4. Select the default directory.
5. Select **User**.
6. Click on the **Manage Multi Factor Auth** button at the bottom of the screen.
7. Select the user accounts you like to enable and click on **Enable** in the right pane.
8. Click on **Enable multi-factor auth**. The user account is now enabled.
9. Now, the user has to sign in to **Azure Management Portal**.

The administrator can set the user account to have the user enforce configuring Multi-Factor Authentication. This is done from a different portal which is available at `https://account.activedirectory.windowsazure.com/`.

When the account has been set to enforce, the next time the user logs in, they have to set an additional authentication method. This can be done by either of these two methods:

- Using a mobile phone
- Using an app

When choosing a mobile phone, the user can select whether the code has to be sent by SMS or by phone. The user needs to fill in the phone number. When the option of SMS has been selected, the user receives a verification code of six digits. The user fills in this code in the browser. If the code is filled in correctly, the account has been enabled for Multi-Factor Authentication.

Each time the user wants to log in to Azure Management Portal, they will need to supply a password as well as a six-digit code that is sent by SMS to authenticate to Azure.

Enabling IP Whitelist

In specific situations, it can be inconvenient for users to perform Multi-Factor Authentication. When a request originates from your internal network, for example, there is no need for additional authentication. Azure allows to Whitelist ranges of IP addresses. Requests with such an IP address as source will be excluded from Multi-Factor Authentication.

To enable IP whitelist, log in to Azure Management Portal as an administrator and then perform the following steps:

1. Select **Active Directory** in the left pane.
2. Choose the directory for which IP Whitelist should be enabled.
3. Select **Configure** at the top of the window.
4. Select **Manage service settings** listed under **Multi-factor authentication**.
5. Under **ip whitelist**, enter the IP addresses in the boxes provided using CIDR notation. For example: xxx.xxx.xxx.0/24 for IP addresses in the range xxx.xxx.xxx.1 to xxx.xxx.xxx.254, or xxx.xxx.xxx.xxx/32 for a single IP address. You can enter up to 12 IP address ranges:

Multi-factor apps

Users can select to perform the multi-factor authentication using an app on their mobile phone. Apps for iOS, Android, and Windows mobile are available. Examples of apps are:

- Multi-factor authentication by PhoneFactor (free) for iOS and Android
- Google Authenticator app

In certain situations, for example, when no mobile phone coverage exists or the mobile phone is lost, the administrator can enable One-Time Bypass. This allows the user to only use the user account and password for authentication.

Introduction to System Center App Controller

One of the essential characteristics of cloud computing is that it provides a self-service portal. A self-service portal enables persons without or with minor IT knowledge to deploy virtual machines and services running on it.

The on-premises self-service portal of Microsoft System Center is called **App Controller**. App Controller is a web-based tool that allows developers and non-IT staff to manage virtual machines on both private and public clouds.

App Controller is not a replacement for System Center Virtual Machine Manager or Azure Management Portal. It is limited to provisioning new virtual machines and the target audience is certainly not system administrators.

The target audience for App Controller is application developers, application owners, and other roles that require to roll out applications but cannot be given full control to Virtual Machine Manager.

In the R2 release, App Controller misses some features that are available when using SCVMM or Azure Management Portal. There is no indication of costs and App Controller does not suggest which cloud is most appropriate for the placement of virtual machines. Also, an approval workflow is missing. It can be used to have a manager or administrator approve the creation on an object such as a cloud or virtual machine. When you need this kind of functionality, you need to explore more products within the System Center Suite, such as Service Manager and Orchestrator.

The main purpose of App Controller is to provide a common Windows Graphical User Interface delivering a single and consistent pane of glass for management of both public and private clouds.

Also, it provides the possibility to copy virtual machines from your on-premises private cloud to Microsoft Azure or a service provider. At the moment, this copy involves downtime.

For access to Azure, App Controller communicates with the Microsoft Azure REST API. To be able to access SCVMM, App Controller needs to have a local installation of the SCVMM console on the server where you are running App Controller.

To access System Center managed clouds hosted by service providers, the **Service Provider Foundation (SPF)** software is accessed. SPF is a component of System Center and is installed by service providers to empower their tenants with self service capabilities.

To be able to install App Controller we first need to install System Center Virtual Machine Manager. Virtual Machine Manager requires a SQL database. As SQL is required in almost any Active Directory we need to make sure this is available as well.

App Controller is a web-based application that uses Microsoft SilverLight. This automatically means App Controller cannot be used for instance using the Safari browser on iPad and iPhone as Safari do not support Microsoft SilverLight.

In this section, you will learn about the following tasks:

- Installing App Controller
- Connecting App Controller to Virtual Machine Manager
- Connecting App Controller to Microsoft Azure

Prerequisites

The installation prerequisites for App Controller 2012 R2 are:

- Virtual Machine Manager console installed on the App Controller server
- WCF Data Services 5.0
- Web Server IIS Role and Role Services

Log in using your domain user account that is a member of the SCVMMAdmins group (this is a group you created when you installed SCVMM and will ensure you have rights to SCVMM) and then perform the following steps:

1. Click on **Install**.

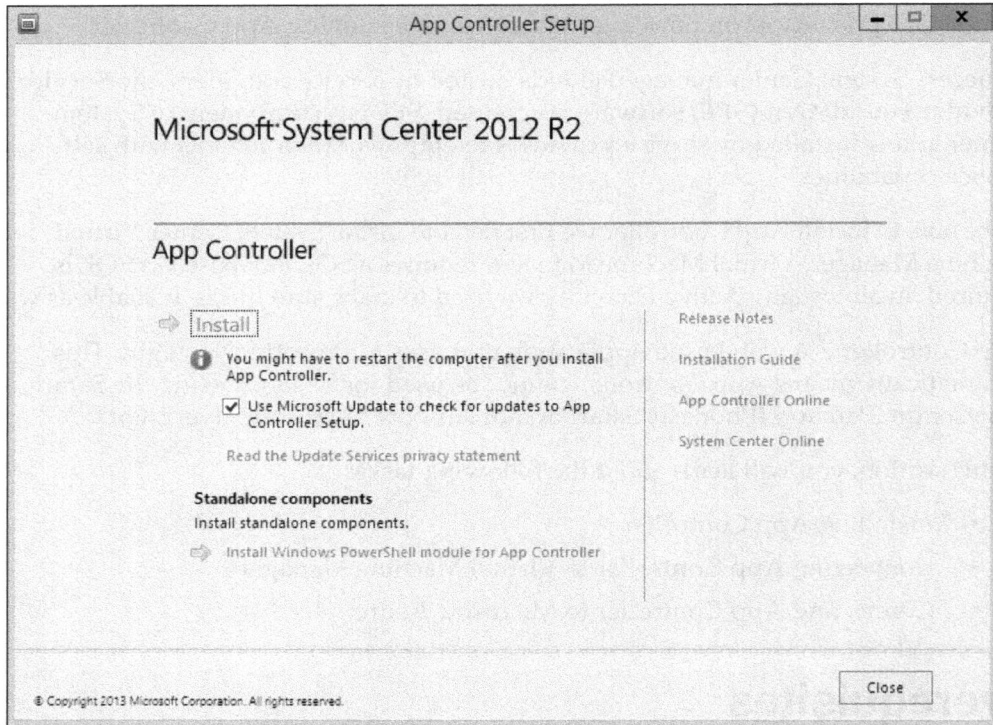

2. On the next screen, type in the product key. You can skip this if you are evaluating App Controller.

3. On the next screen, make sure that you have read and agree with the terms of the license agreement.

4. The installation wizard will check whether the server has the Web Server role and Role Services installed. If not, it will be installed automatically. The installer also checks whether WCF Data Services are installed. If not, it they will be installed automatically as well.

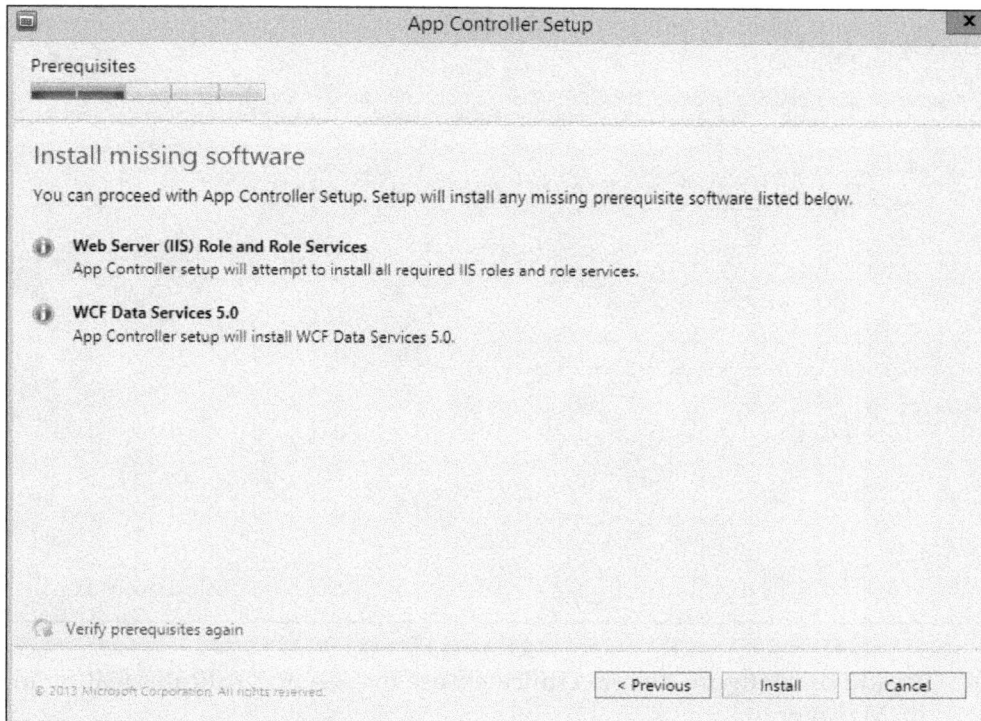

App Controller Setup

Prerequisites

Install missing software

You can proceed with App Controller Setup. Setup will install any missing prerequisite software listed below.

ⓘ **Web Server (IIS) Role and Role Services**
App Controller setup will attempt to install all required IIS roles and role services.

ⓘ **WCF Data Services 5.0**
App Controller setup will install WCF Data Services 5.0.

↻ Verify prerequisites again

© 2013 Microsoft Corporation. All rights reserved.   < Previous   Install   Cancel

---

5. Next select the installation path.

6. Now, choose the account that is used for the App Controller service.

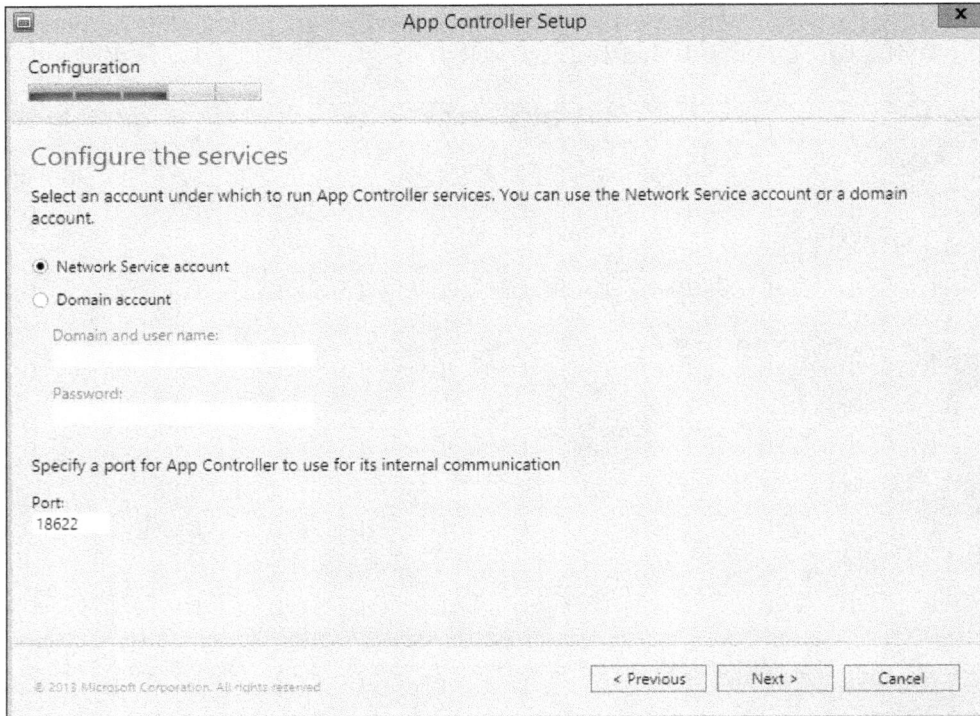

To add or configure server certificates, use the server certificates feature in IIS Manager.

If you use a self-signed certificate, the certificate must be added to the Trusted Root Certification Authorities store of all computers that will access the App Controller website. Some browsers will fail to display App Controller if the certificate is not trusted.

> It is highly recommended that you use a certificate from a trusted certification authority instead of using a self-signed certificate in production environments.

App Controller Setup

Configuration

Configure the website

Specify the binding settings you want to use for the App Controller website.

Type:	IP address:		Port:
HTTPS	10.0.0.2	▼	443

◉ Generate self-signed certificate

○ Use existing certificate:

| | ▼ | View... | Refresh |

© 2013 Microsoft Corporation. All rights reserved.

< Previous   Next >   Cancel

7. Next, configure the SQL database. Select the server where the SQL server is running for your App Controller installation, or set localhost when the SQL server is running on the same server as App Controller will be installed on. Leave the **Port** field empty.

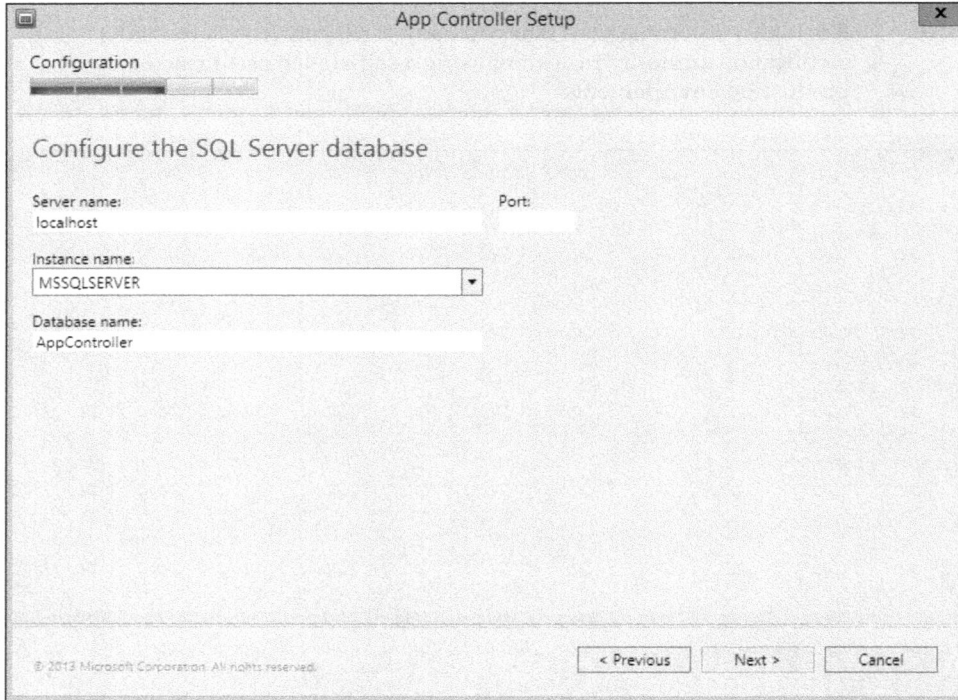

8. Choose if you want to participate in the Customer Experience Improvement Program or not, and select whether you want to use Microsoft Update to update App Controller.

9. Confirm the settings and click on the **Install** button.

Using App Controller

After the installation is done, we are ready to start exploring App Controller. The following software must be installed before installing the App Controller web console:

- Windows 7, Windows 8, Windows Vista, Windows Server 2008, Windows Server 2008 R2, and Windows Server 2012 R2

- A 32-bit browser that supports Silverlight 5

- Internet Explorer 8, Internet Explorer 9, or Internet Explorer 10

In your browser, type the **Fully Qualified Domain Name (FQDN)**, which is associated to the IP address you typed in during the installation of App Controller. Be sure to use https for the URL.

Any user account that has the administrator role in SCVMM has access to App Controller.

User roles in App Controller

There are two types of user roles in App Controller:

- **Administrator**: Members of the administrators user role can perform all administrative actions on all App Controller objects. This is a built-in group and cannot be deleted or renamed. Virtual Machine Manager administrators in connected Virtual Machine Manager servers are not automatically added to the App Controller administrators user role. During setup, this role is automatically populated with all supported users and groups in the local administrators group of the computer on which App Controller is installed.

- **Self-service user**: Administrators can create one or more self-service user roles in which to delegate user access to Windows Azure subscriptions or hosting service providers. Self-service users can deploy and manage services only to Windows Azure subscriptions or hosting service providers to which they have access. Additionally, Self-service user roles can be designated as read-only for the specified scope.

As App Controller is meant to be used by non-system administrators you will have to create some dedicated Active Directory security groups. In this section, we will show you how to do that. The names used in this example are just that, examples. When other naming conventions are used within your environment, be sure to adhere to those policies.

To be able to use user roles in App Controller we perform the following steps:

1. Create a global security group in your Active Directory named appcontroller-users.

2. Create a user account named appcontroller-user1 and make this a member of the appcontroller-users group.

3. Start the SCVMM console and log in with a user account that has the administrator role in SCVMM.

4. Select **Settings** in the left pane, and then **Security** in the left pane.

5. Select **Create User role** from the top menu.

6. Provide a name, for example, `appcontroller-users`.

7. Provide a description, for example, `allow use of App Controller and manage VMs of cloud name 'testcloud'`.

8. Click on **Next**.

9. Select **Application Administrators** as the user role profile.

10. Click on **Next**.

11. Select the global security group `appcontroller-users` created in the first step.

12. Click on **Next**.

13. Select the scope of the user role. The scope is the clouds the user role should be allowed to consume resources from.

14. Click on **Next**.

15. Optionally, set quotas.

16. Select the allowed networks.

17. Click on **Next**.

18. Set which resources can be used and press **Next**.

19. Set the allowed action for this user role.

20. Click on **Next**.

21. Set **Run As** to **Accounts**.

22. Click on **Next**.

23. Click on **Finish**.

Now when the user with account `appcontroller-user1` authenticates to App Controller, they will be able to perform all the actions you allowed them for on the private cloud managed by SCVMM. However, to be able to use the Azure cloud we first need to connect to Azure.

Connecting App Controller to Virtual Machine Manager

After we connect to the App Controller website, we can connect to System Center Virtual Machine Manager by performing the following steps:

1. In App Controller, click on **Connect to a Virtual Machine** under **Private Clouds**.
2. Fill in a connection name. Make sure this name makes sense as it is used at several places in App Controller, for example, `private cloud New York` or something similar.
3. Fill in a description.
4. Fill in the FQDN of the SCVMM server.
5. Click on **OK**.

The following screenshot shows the input mentioned in the preceding steps:

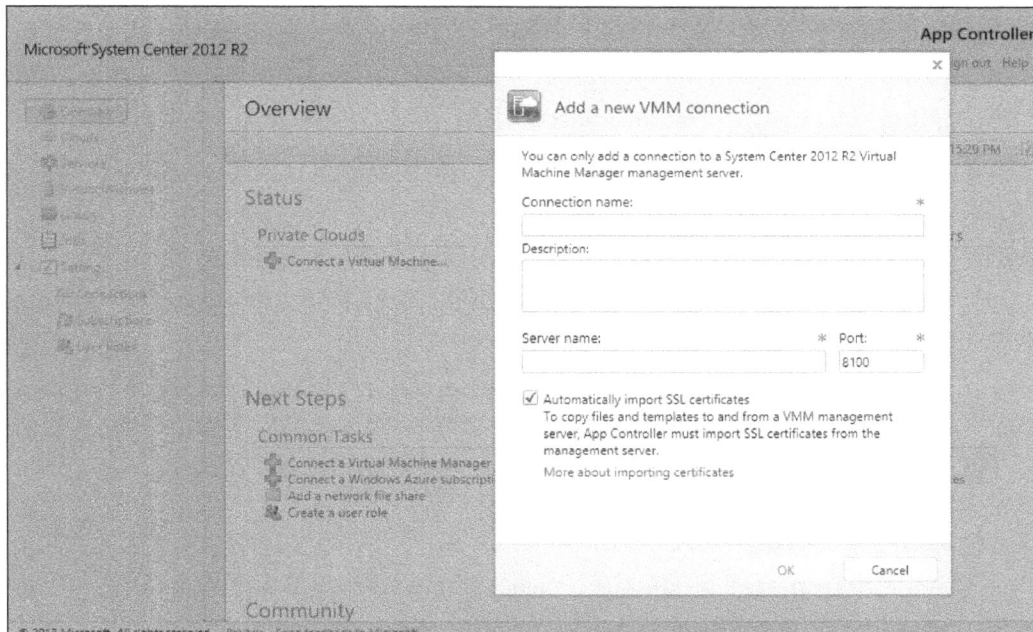

There's a checkbox in the connection screen. The **Automatically import SSL certificates** option that should be selected allows you to copy needed files and templates to and from a Virtual Machine Manager server. This also enables you to copy resources between different Virtual Machine Manager server environments / libraries easily — something that enables the IT process of moving a service from development to test to production, for instance.

Today, you can't define a service in Virtual Machine Manager or Windows Azure that spans both clouds, so you can't define a service template in Virtual Machine Manager that also creates VMs in Azure at the time of deployment. The Virtual Machine Manager server and App Controller server needs to be in the same domain or in domains with two-way trust established. It's also strongly recommended, although not required, that a Virtual Machine Manager administrator is also an App Controller administrator.

If all goes well you will be able to see virtual machines managed by your SCVMM server.

Connecting App Controller to Microsoft Azure

To connect App Controller to Microsoft Azure, you need a self-signed certificate. These certificates are required for many scenarios such as when using Azure as a storage location for offsite Windows backups.

There are two ways to create self-signed certificates:

- Using the Microsoft makecert tool
- Using **Internet Information Server (IIS)**

In this section, you will learn how to use IIS to create self-signed certificates.

Using IIS to create self-signed certificates

In this section, you will learn how to create self-signed certificates using IIS. To do so, please perform the following steps:

1. Install the IIS Management console feature on a Windows server or Windows 8 system. IIS Manager has already been installed on the server where you installed App Controller.

2. Once it is installed, open **IIS Manager**.

3. Double-click on **Server Certificates**.

4. In the **Action** pane on the right, select **create self-signed certificate**.

5. Specify a friendly name.

6. Make sure the **Personal** certificate store is selected.

7. Click on **OK**.

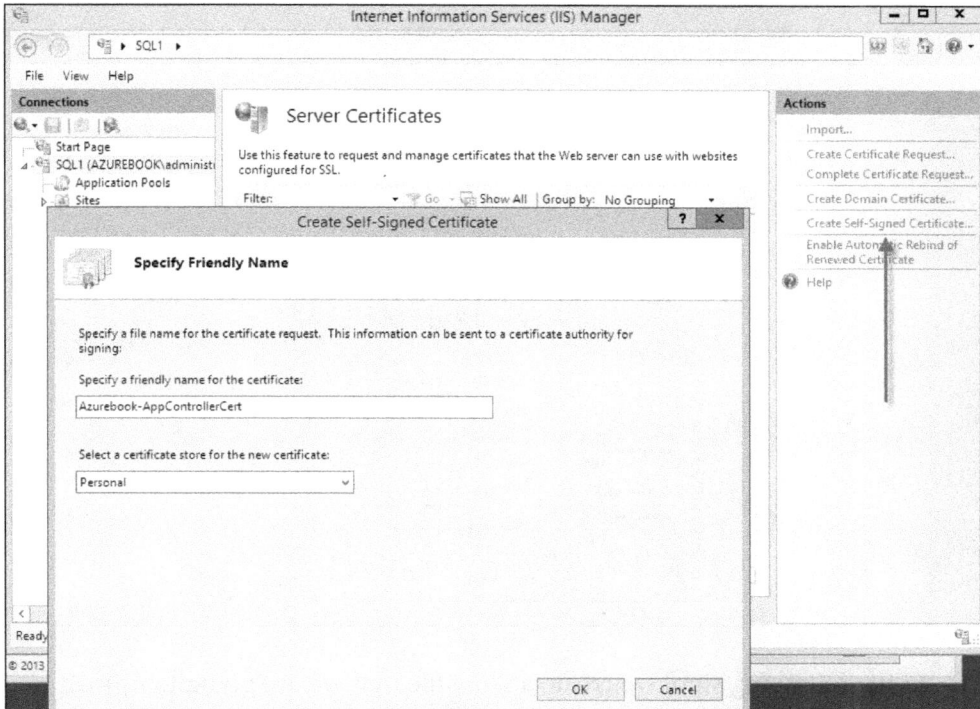

Next we need to export the certificate to a `.pfx` file. To do so, perform the following steps:

1. Select the certificate created in the previous step.
2. Select **Export** in the right pane.

3. Select a folder to store the exported certificate in and type in a password.

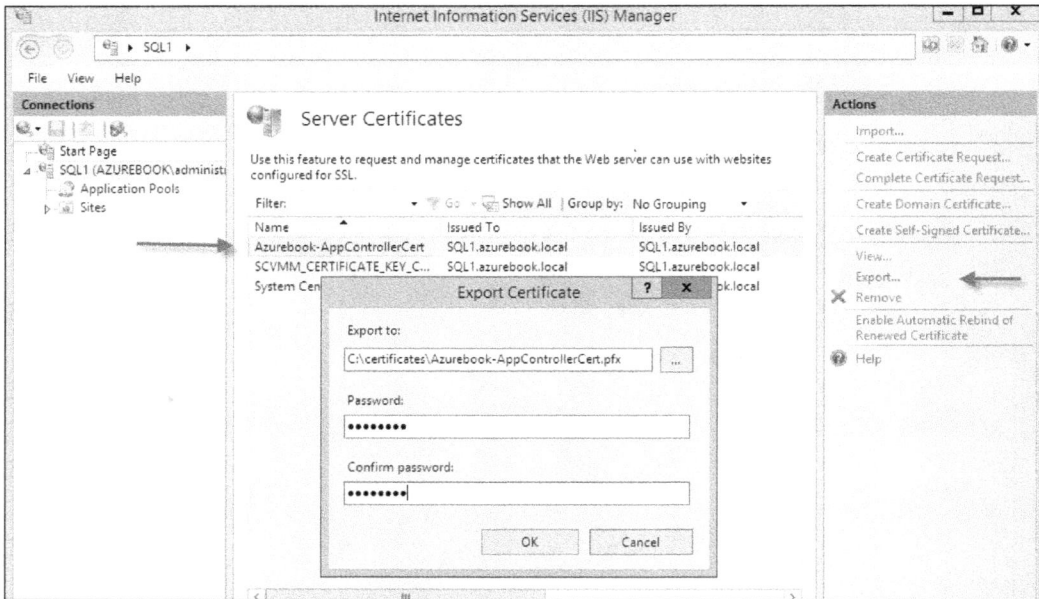

In the following step, we create a `.cer` file that we are going to upload to Microsoft Azure.

4. Run `certmgr.msc` and select the folder named `Personal`.

5. Right-click on the folder name, and select **Import** under **All tasks**.

6. The certificate import wizard starts. Select **Next**.

7. Navigate to the folder in which you stored the certificate, and make sure that the file type is set to **Personal Information Exchange**.

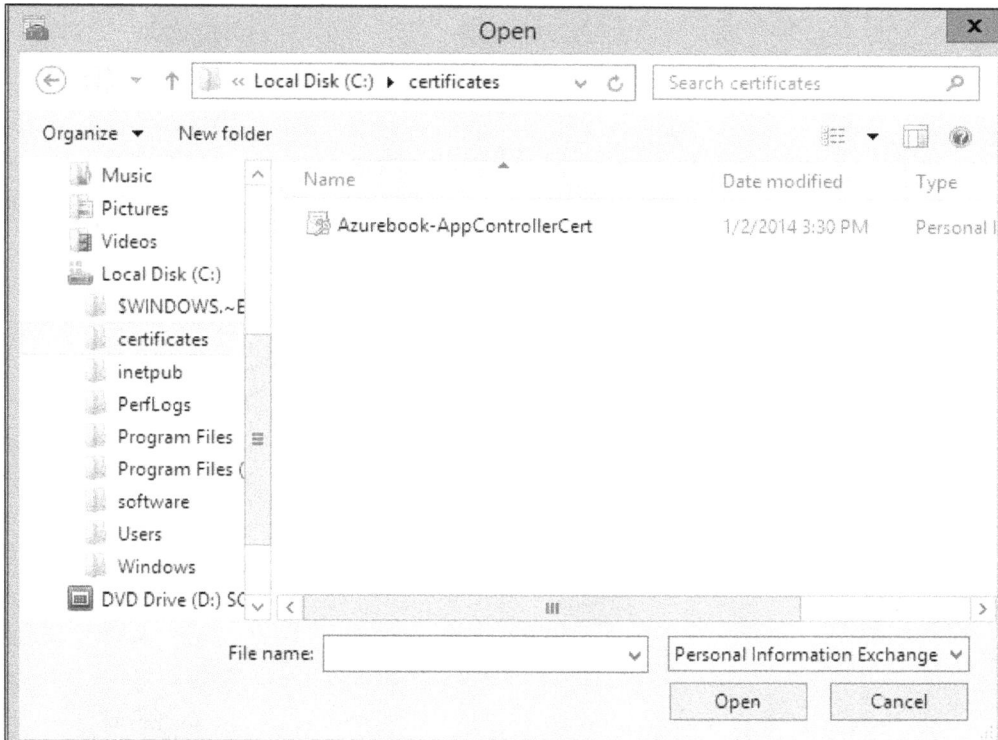

8. Type in the password for the certificate and click on.

9. Save the certificate in the **Personal** store. Click on **Next**.

10. Click on **Finish**.

11. Now, select the certificate we just imported. It is under the **Personal** store. The **Friendly** name is displayed as typed in at step 4.

12. Right-click on this certificate and select **Export** under **All tasks**.

13. Keep all the default values ('such as'? DER Encoded), and store the exported certificate in a folder.

Uploading the certificate to Microsoft Azure

Now we need to upload the certificate we just created to Microsoft Azure; the steps are as follows:

1. Open Azure Management Portal and select **Settings** in the left pane.

2. Then, select **MANAGEMENT CERTIFICATES** in the upper menu.

3. Then press **UPLOAD** in the lower menu.

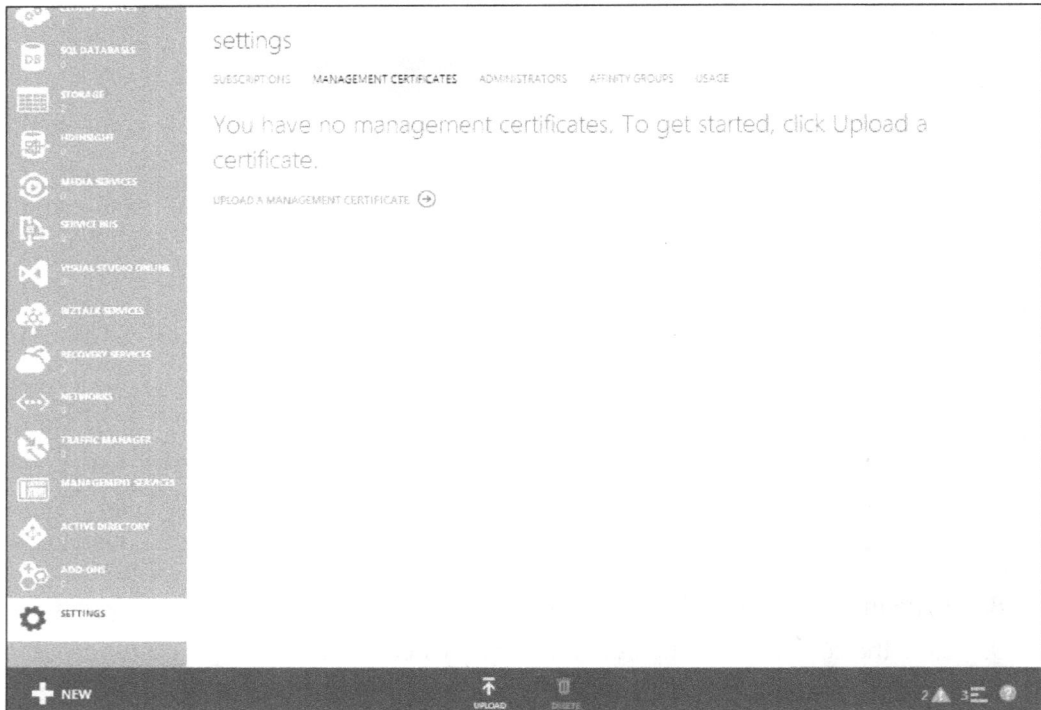

4. Select the `.cer` file and click on the **OK** button.

If the upload succeeds, you will see a certificate listed in Management Portal.

Configure App Controller to connect to Microsoft Azure

The final step is configuring App Controller to connect to Microsoft Azure. To do so, we need the subscription ID. There are various ways to get the subscription ID, for instance:

1. In Azure Management Portal, navigate to **Settings | Subscriptions**.

2. Copy the subscription ID.

3. Now, open App Controller and select **Connect a Windows Azure Subscription**.

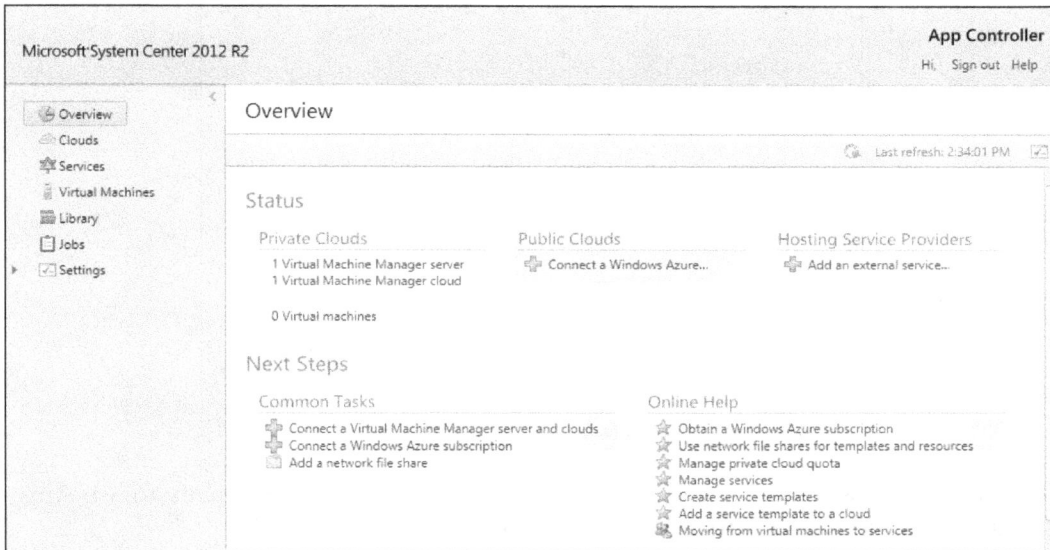

4. Fill in the name and description of the connection. The name will we shown in App Controller when a cloud is selected.

5. Then, paste the subscription ID taken from Azure Management Portal.

6. Select the .PFX certificate we created in the previous steps and fill in the password associated to this certificate.

7. Click on **OK**.

If all went well, we now have a connection with Azure and we are ready to use App Controller to manage Azure resources such as virtual machines.

Authenticating a user to use Microsoft Azure

If a user account that does not have the SCVMM administrator user role, authenticates to Azure, it will not be able to access resources in Microsoft Azure.

App Controller will display **No access to public clouds**. What we need to do is add Active Directory users to User Roles in App Controller by performing the following steps:

1. In App Controller, go to **Settings | User Roles.**
2. Click on **New**.
3. Fill in the user role name.
4. Fill in the description.

5. Select the Active Directory users who should be part of this user role. We take the same AD group as in the previous sections: `appcontroller-users`.

6. Scroll down, select the scope, and click on **OK**.

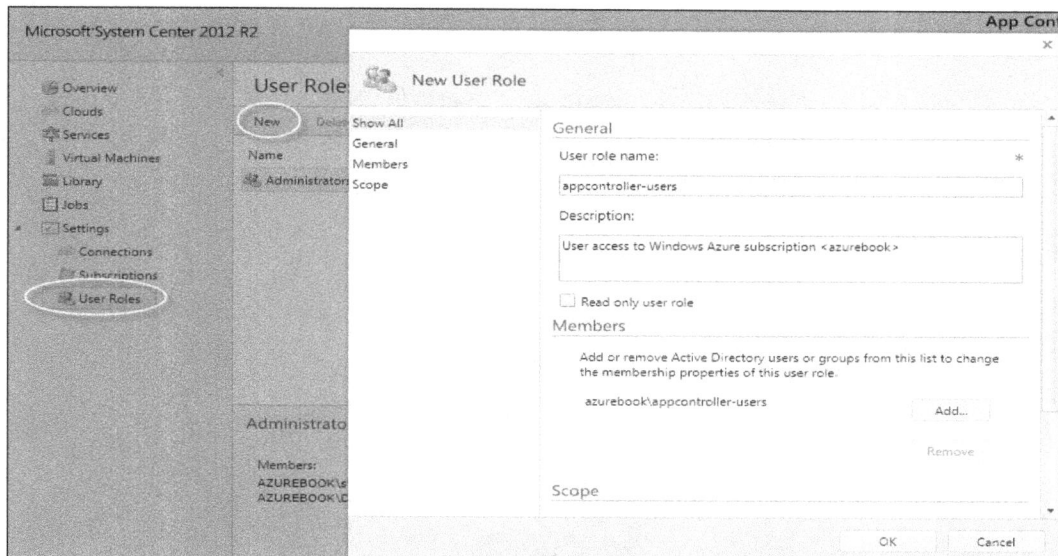

Users are now able to create, modify, and manage virtual machines in Microsoft Azure.

Note that Microsoft Azure does not have multiple user roles. Each user with access to Management Portal has administrative rights, which means full control.

This means if a single Azure subscription contains virtual machines for which different departments in an organization are responsible for management, you might want to create a subscription for each environment.

Using App Controller

In this section, I will give a quick tour of using App Controller. In the left pane, you will see the menu items shown in the following screenshot:

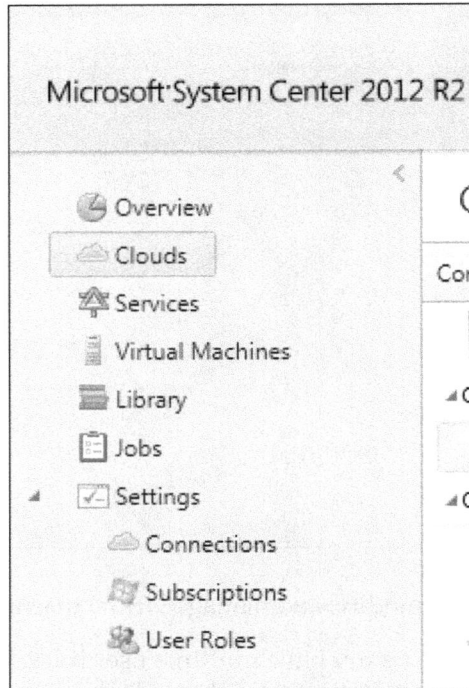

```
Microsoft·System Center 2012 R2

                            <        (

    Overview
    Clouds                           Con
    Services
    Virtual Machines
    Library                          ◢C
    Jobs
◢   Settings                         ◢C
        Connections
        Subscriptions
        User Roles
```

The various menu items are described as follows:

- The **Overview** menu item has a dashboard function. It shows the clouds that App Controller is connected to.

- The **Clouds** menu item allows connecting to SCVMM, Microsoft Azure, or to clouds running the Microsoft Azure Pack. It is also used to create cloud services in Microsoft Azure.

- The **Services** menu item allows deploying services. A service is a collection of one or multiple virtual machines that provide an application. When creating a service you will be presented with a diagram. The diagram guides you in the process of creating the service. It will request which cloud to use, which images/disks, which cloud service, and which virtual network, and it will present a wizard to create a new virtual machine.

- The **Virtual Machines** menu item allows virtual machines to be started or stopped. Also, properties such as size, availability set, and disks can be modified. You can also edit the endpoints. Unlike the Azure Management Portal, App Controller does not have the ability to edit Access Control Lists of endpoints.

- The **Library** menu item allows the management of disks and images.

- The **Jobs** menu shows an overview of jobs submitted in App Controller and the status of these jobs.

- The **Settings** menu item allows creating new connections to clouds, managing Azure subscriptions and managing user roles.

Deploying a virtual machine using App Controller

The deployment of a virtual machine using App Controller is very easy. Follow these steps:

1. Select **Virtual Machines** in the left pane.
2. Select **Deploy**.
3. You will be presented with a deployment diagram. Click on the blue link and select/fill in the requested items.

4. When ready, click on **Deploy**.

Have a look at the following deployment diagram:

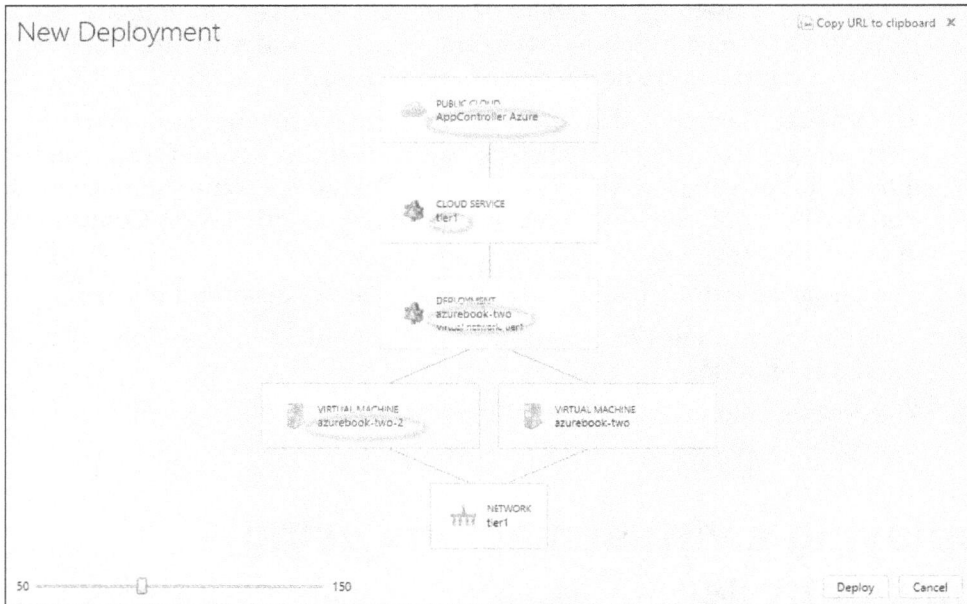

Uploading files to Microsoft Azure

App Controller can be used to upload and download files between data centers on-premises, Azure, and service providers. To do this, select the **Library** menu item in the left pane. You can browse the various locations for storage of templates, images, disks, and VHD files.

Suppose you created a VHD file on your local system, you can upload that VHD to Azure by performing the following steps:

1. Create a new file share on the system containing the .vhd file.
2. After creating the share, select it and navigate to the folder that holds the .vhd file.
3. Select the .vhd file, right-click on it, and select **Copy**.
4. Browse to the destination of the .vhd. This could be a vhd folder on Azure.
5. Right-click somewhere in the destination folder and select **Paste**.
6. Now the .vhd file will be uploaded to Microsoft Azure or a service provider.

Installing the Windows PowerShell module for App Controller

The procedures in this section will describe how to install the Windows PowerShell Module for App Controller.

Before you begin the installation of the Windows PowerShell module for App Controller, ensure that you have a computer with a supported version of Windows PowerShell installed or enabled.

Membership in the local administrators group, or equivalent, on the computer that you are configuring is the minimum requirement to complete this procedure.

Installing the Windows PowerShell module for App Controller

To install the Windows PowerShell module for App Controller, perform the following steps:

1. On your installation media, right-click on **setup.exe** and then click on **Run as administrator**.

2. On the main setup page, click on **Install Windows PowerShell module for App Controller**.

3. On the **End-User License Agreement** page, review the license terms, select the **I accept the terms in the License Agreement** checkbox, and then click on **Next**.

4. Click on **Install** to install the Windows PowerShell Module for App Controller.

5. Verify the installation results and then click on **Finish**.

The Windows PowerShell module allows automated tasks to be performed on App Controller. The module contains about two dozen commandlets. The PowerShell module is, at the time of writing, quite limited in use. It is likely Microsoft will extend the functionality.

PowerShell for App Controller can be started in two ways:

1. On the server on which App Controller is installed, navigate to **Start | All Programs | Microsoft System Center 2012 R2 | App Controller | App Controller PowerShell.**

2. You can import the App Controller module into an open Windows PowerShell session using the `Import-Module -Name AppController` command.

To get an overview of available commandlets, execute the following command:

```
Get-command -module Appcontroller
```

```
PS C:\Users\administrator.AZUREBOOK> import-module -Name AppController
PS C:\Users\administrator.AZUREBOOK> get-command -module Appcontroller

CommandType     Name                              ModuleName
-----------     ----                              ----------
Cmdlet          Add-SCACAzureDisk                 AppController
Cmdlet          Add-SCACAzureImage                AppController
Cmdlet          Add-SCACAzureSubscription         AppController
Cmdlet          Add-SCACCloudSystem               AppController
Cmdlet          Add-SCACShare                     AppController
Cmdlet          Export-SCACAesKey                 AppController
Cmdlet          Get-SCACAdminSetting              AppController
Cmdlet          Get-SCACAzureHostedService        AppController
Cmdlet          Get-SCACAzureRoleInstance         AppController
Cmdlet          Get-SCACAzureServiceDeployment    AppController
Cmdlet          Get-SCACAzureSubscription         AppController
Cmdlet          Get-SCACCloudSystem               AppController
Cmdlet          Get-SCACJob                       AppController
Cmdlet          Get-SCACServer                    AppController
Cmdlet          Get-SCACShare                     AppController
Cmdlet          Get-SCACTemporaryStorage          AppController
Cmdlet          Get-SCACUserRole                  AppController
Cmdlet          New-SCACUserRole                  AppController
Cmdlet          New-SCACUserRoleScope             AppController
Cmdlet          Remove-SCACAzureSubscription      AppController
Cmdlet          Remove-SCACCloudSystem            AppController
Cmdlet          Remove-SCACShare                  AppController
Cmdlet          Remove-SCACUserRole               AppController
Cmdlet          Resume-SCACServiceDeployment      AppController
Cmdlet          Set-SCACAdminSetting              AppController
Cmdlet          Set-SCACCloudSystem               AppController
Cmdlet          Set-SCACTemporaryStorage          AppController
Cmdlet          Set-SCACUserRole                  AppController
Cmdlet          Suspend-SCACServiceDeployment     AppController
```

Summary

In this chapter, you learned how to connect Azure to the on-premises infrastructure. You also learned how to install System Center App Controller to enable users to use resources in various clouds.

In the next chapter, we will focus on the operational aspects of virtual machines. You will learn how to manage virtual machines, cost management, and automation using PowerShell.

6
Managing the Microsoft Hybrid Cloud

In the previous chapter, you learned about the preparations required for the deployment of a virtual machine. You also learned about virtual networks and how to connect from on-premises infrastructures to Azure using a VPN connection.

In this chapter, we will go a bit deeper into managing Microsoft Azure. You will learn about making our virtual machines highly available and perform daily operations such as monitoring the Azure infrastructure. As automation using PowerShell has become a must for administrators, we will spend some time on the basics of using this powerful tool.

In this chapter, we will cover the following topics:

- Understanding Azure Active Directory
- Using Active Directory for authentication to Azure
- Importing and exporting data into Azure using offline media
- Managing disks
- Monitoring your Azure infrastructure
- Automation
- License mobility

Understanding Azure Active Directory

Microsoft offers many online services which run in the cloud. To sign into services such as Office 365 and Microsoft Azure, a multitenant identity management service is used.

This service is called Azure **Active Directory (AD)**. It is a comprehensive identity and access management cloud solution. It combines core directory services, advanced identity governance, security, and application access management. Azure AD also offers developers an identity management platform to deliver access control to their applications, based on a centralized policy and rules.

Azure AD, which was known as Windows Azure Active Directory, was developed by Microsoft and is based on the Active Directory available in Windows Server. Each Azure AD directory is distinct and separate from other Azure AD directories. Just as a corporate office building is a secure asset specific to only your organization, an Azure AD was also designed to be a secure asset for use by your organization only. The Azure AD architecture isolates customer data and identity information from commingling. This means that users and administrators of one Azure AD cannot accidentally or maliciously access data in another directory.

Just as in **Software as a Service (SaaS)**, customers are restricted in adjusting Azure AD to their needs. For example, customers cannot change the schema, groups are limited, additional third-party tooling is nonexistent, and so on.

User accounts in Azure AD are organized in containers that are called directories and are similar to Active Directory domains.

A typical use case for multiple directories is for management reasons. Cloud services such as Office 365 can be used by a single organization that has multiple IT departments or multiple business units; another example is using one directory for production and one for test.

When an Azure subscription is created, a directory is created automatically. This directory is named `default directory`. The directory is used to store user accounts and groups. It is also used to connect Internet-based SaaS applications to user accounts in a particular directory.

Each directory comes with a domain name that is constructed like this:

```
<customer supplied domain name>. onmicrosoft.com
```

You can add a so-called **custom domain**. This should be a domain your organization owns. Adding a custom domain allows users to authenticate using their local Active Directory account and password.

To be able to use the local user account and password, we need to synchronize those accounts and passwords.

Each directory has a domain that is labeled **primary domain**. This is the domain name that is displayed by default when you add a new user.

In Azure Management Portal, there are no features for changing or disabling user passwords, or deleting user accounts. All this can be done using the on-premises AD when it is synchronized with a directory hosted by Azure AD.

Azure AD is available in three offerings:

- **Azure Active Directory Free**: This has options for the management of user accounts and directory synchronization. It is limited to 500,000 objects.

- **Azure Active Directory Premium**: This has all the features of Active Directory Free, along with an unrestricted number of objects, free Multi-Factor Authentication, usage of groups for application access, synchronization with on-premises directories, machine-learning-based security, and usage reports. Azure Active Directory Premium also empowers end users with, delegated group management, customizable environment for launching enterprise and consumer applications, Microsoft Identity Manager (MIM) server licenses, and many more features.

- **Azure Active Directory Basic**: There are no limits in the number of objects. Microsoft offers a SLA. There is a self-service password reset for cloud users

Azure Active Directory Premium will be available for purchase through Microsoft's Enterprise Agreement volume licensing program.

Now that we understand what the role of Azure AD is, we are ready for a more detailed look into Azure AD.

Authentication models in Azure AD

For authentication on Microsoft Azure and Office 365, three authentication models are available:

- **Cloud Identity**: This is also known as the standard authentication and uses a cloud-based username and password stored in Microsoft Azure Active Directory. A typical example of a username is `useraccount@<organization>.onmicrosoft.com`.

- **Synchronized Identity**: This is also known as managed authentication, and this allows synced usernames and passwords with on-premises AD as the source.

- **Federated identity**: This is also known as federated authentication. This allows single sign-on to Microsoft Office 365 and Azure because of a federation with an on-premise Microsoft Active Directory. Azure kind of trusts the Active Directory a user was authenticated on and does not require additional authentication, making live for users easier.

Cloud Identity is the simplest way to authenticate users. Administrators manage user accounts in Azure AD. There is no connection between Azure and any other external directory (like Active Directory). Accounts are managed using Azure Management Portal.

While this works for smaller organizations, it is not preferred for larger organizations. It is not easy to efficiently manage both an on-premises directory as well as an Azure AD. Also, users cannot use their on-premises Active Directory credentials for access to Azure and Office 365.

Synchronized Identity allows administrator access to Azure Management Portal using their on-premises user credentials stored in AD. In the next sections, you will learn how to synchronize user accounts and passwords using AD as a source and Azure AD as a target.

Federated Identity allows authentication on Microsoft cloud services using on-premises AD as source for authentication. This allows for single sign-on so users already signed( )in to AD are not presented with another request for credentials while signing in to Office 365, Azure, and so on.

To enable Federated Identity, several servers are required on-premises. Also, public IP addresses and certificates and required. One of the services to be installed is **Active Directory Federation Services (ADFS)**. Availability of ADFS is essential for users to be able to sign in to Office 365 and Azure. So, in many cases, ADFS needs to be made redundant using load balancers and multiple installations of ADFS. This makes it a complex configuration.

It is recommended that you use the simplest identity model that meets your needs. If your needs change, you can switch between these models easily.

Connecting an on-premises Active Directory to Microsoft Azure

When using a hybrid cloud, you obviously want a single directory service. Most organizations use Microsoft AD for identity management.

It is very easy to extend your on-premises AD to Microsoft Azure. This extension has many advantages:

- Single identity source for both on-premises and Azure
- Users can authenticate to Microsoft Azure using their corporate credentials
- No dependency on availability of on-premises AD and the VPN or ExpressRoute connection with Azure.
- Ability to authenticate to third-party SaaS solutions using AD
- Allow single sign-on access to the Azure Management Portal using on-premises AD credentials

The following are possible ways to extend your on-premises AD:

- Synchronize AD objects using DirSync to Microsoft Azure AD
- Replicate Active Directory to a virtual machine running in Azure

The first option is best suited to organizations that want users to be authenticated on Microsoft and third-party hosted SaaS applications using their corporate credentials.

The advantages of synchronizing AD objects using DirSync to Microsoft Azure AD are:

- No costs for running virtual machines and storage. Azure AD is free to use for up to 500,000 objects. Note that Microsoft has a default quota of 150,000 objects. You can contact Microsoft support to increase this quota.
- The ability of Azure AD to provide single sign-on to Microsoft-hosted applications plus to a growing number of third-party SaaS services such as Salesforce.com.
- No need to set( )up a VPN connection. Syncing with Azure Active Directory uses port 443.
- Azure AD is very scalable.
- Azure AD is very robust and highly available.

- The simplicity of setting up Azure AD. It requires just a few mouse clicks.
- Outsourcing a part of the management AD. You only manage objects, not servers and replication.
- Azure AD is also used by Office 365. If your organization is using Office 365, there is only one identity management solution.

If your organization is already using Office 365, it is quite simple to activate Azure AD for Azure authentication.

In scenario 1, a one-way synchronization is used. Accounts and groups in on-premises AD are synchronized to Azure AD. Synchronization from Azure AD towards on-premises AD (so in reverse) is not possible.

When using Azure AD, you are still in control over policies such as password length and complexity. There will always be a requirement for an on-premises AD server, which is a master for both AD and Azure AD.

The second option is best suited to running a hybrid cloud with your own managed application, which needs AD authentication. This scenario is also suited to securing your AD.

If you are looking for a replica of your AD for disaster recovery purposes, then this scenario is the best option.

The advantage of the second option is two-way replication. Even if your on-premise site is lost, the AD running in Azure is still operational.

The replication of on-premises AD to Azure AD is performed by a tool named **Microsoft Azure Active Directory Sync Tool** or **DirSync** for short. DirSync is a free version of the Microsoft **Forefront Identity Management** (**FIM**) server.

DirSync is installed on a Windows server on-premises. The supported versions are as follows:

- Windows Server 2008 SP1 or higher
- Windows Server 2008 R2 SP1 or higher
- Windows Server 2012 or higher

DirSync can be installed on a domain controller or on a member server.

> Microsoft uses cookies for authentication to Microsoft Azure and other online services. You might encounter issues with signing in to Azure. If you are sure you used the correct username and password but are still denied access, it is advised to delete cookies or use another browser. In many cases, you will be able to sign in successfully afterwards.

Synchronizing an on-premises AD with Azure Active Directory

In this section, we are going to synchronize our on-premises AD user accounts and passwords to Azure AD. To do so, perform the following steps:

1. In Azure Management Portal, select **Active Directory** in the left pane. You will see a directory named **Default Directory**.

2. Click on the **Add** button in the lower menu bar.

> Since May 2014, it is possible to delete directories that you do not need anymore.

3. Fill in a descriptive name for the field titled **Name**.

4. Fill in a domain name. The default AD will be named <organization name>.onmicrosoft.com. This can be adjusted later. Do not worry if the domain is not unique. Just type something that is descriptive.

5. Next, select the country. This choice determines the Azure datacenter that your Azure AD will be active in.

6. Click on the tick mark.

Add directory

DIRECTORY

Create new directory

NAME

Azurebook

DOMAIN NAME

azurebooklab   .onmicrosoft.com

COUNTRY OR REGION

Select country or region

7. Next, we are going to verify our domain name. Select the AD we just created and click on the name.

8. Select the **Domains** menu item at the top.

9. We are ready to add a custom domain. Select **Add** in the lower menu.

10. Type in the domain name you are an owner of. I used `azurebook.nl` for this example. Do not select **I plan to configure this domain for single sign-on with my Local Active Directory**.

11. Click on **add**.

12. Click on the right arrow.

13. Now we need to verify that the domain name typed in is actually owned by us. We do this by adding either a TXT or MX record in our DNS settings. As this procedure depends on the domain registrar, we are not going to explain this step.

14. After adding the record in your DNS, click on the **Verify** button. It may take a while (around 15 minutes), but when Azure has verified that you actually own the domain, a status bar should appear to show that the domain has been verified. The status of the verification process is also shown in the main window. For some unknown reason, sometimes it can be hard to get your domain verified by Azure. You can check the domain record by using a domain query tool such as `http://dnsquery.org/`.

15. Select the newly created domain, and select **Domains** from the top menu.

16. Select the **Change primary** button on the lower menu bar.

17. Make sure your domain is listed under **NEW PRIMARY DOMAIN** and click on the tick mark.

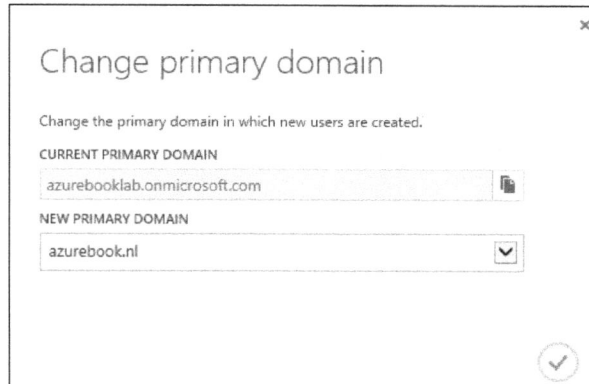

Change primary domain

×

Change the primary domain in which new users are created.

CURRENT PRIMARY DOMAIN

azurebooklab.onmicrosoft.com

NEW PRIMARY DOMAIN

azurebook.nl

✓

We now need to create a global administrator in our Microsoft Azure AD:

1. Select the AD we made primary in the previous step. Then, click on the **Users** menu time in the top menu.

2. Click on the **Add User** button in the lower menu bar.

3. Fill in a user name. Admin, and click on the right arrow.

4. Fill in first name, for example last name, and display name.

5. Make sure to select **global administrator** as the role.

6. Fill in the alternate e-mail address.

7. Click on the right arrow.

8. Click on the **Create** button. A temporary password will be shown.

9. Click on the check mark.

10. Now, log out of Azure Management Portal by clicking on the account displayed in the upper-right corner. Select **Sign out**.

11. Next, sign in to Azure using the organizational account you just created. In the example, this is admin@azurebook.nl.

12. After a successful login, you are requested to change the password.

13. You will see a message showing **We were unable to find any subscriptions associated with your account**. This is correct as the Azure subscription we used was originally initiated by a Microsoft account we used.

Next, we are going to set up the directory synchronization:

1. Sign in to Azure Management Portal with the account that is associated with a subscription containing the directory we created.

2. Select **Active Directory** in the left pane, then select the directory we created.

3. Select **Directory Integration** in the top menu.

4. Set **Directory Sync** to **Activated**.

5. At the bottom of the screen, click on **Save**.

6. Click on **Yes** for the question **Are you sure you want to activate directory sync**.

Next, we are going to prepare the on-premises AD controller for the directory synchronization. The first step is to install .NET 3.5 on the Domain Controller:

1. Select the **Add roles and features** on the DC you like to use for DirSync.

2. Check the **.NET 3.5 Framework 3.5 Features** checkbox.

3. Click on **Next**.

4. On the confirmation screen, click on **Specify an alternate source path**.

5. Set the path to `d:\sources\SxS`. This is the media on which the Windows Server 2012 R2 install files are located.

6. Click on **Install** and then click on **Close**.

Next, we are going to install DirSync. It uses TCP port 443 for communication with Microsoft Azure. Make sure this port is open at the server DirSync is installed on as well as on your firewall.

1. Download DirSync from the Azure Management Portal.

2. Log in to a server on-premises with an administrator account. This server can be a member server or a domain controller.

3. Run the DirSync installation. This will take around 10 minutes.

4. Click on **Next**.

5. Make sure that you remove the check mark on **Start configuration wizard**.

6. Click on **Finish**.

7. If you installed DirSync, you need to log off from the domain controller and log in again using the account you used to install DirSync. The logoff is required as DirSync added the installation account to a newly created security group.

8. If you installed DirSync on a member server, sign out, and then the login is not required.

The next step is the configuration of the DirSync tool.

1. You will find a shortcut on the desktop named `Directory Sync configuration`. Double-click on this shortcut.

2. Click on **Next**.

3. Type in the credentials of the global administrator account of the Azure AD domain and click on **Next**.

4. Fill in the credentials of an account with administrator rights of the on-premises AD.

5. Click on **Next**.

6. Click on the checkbox for **Enable Hybrid Deployment** and click on **Next**.

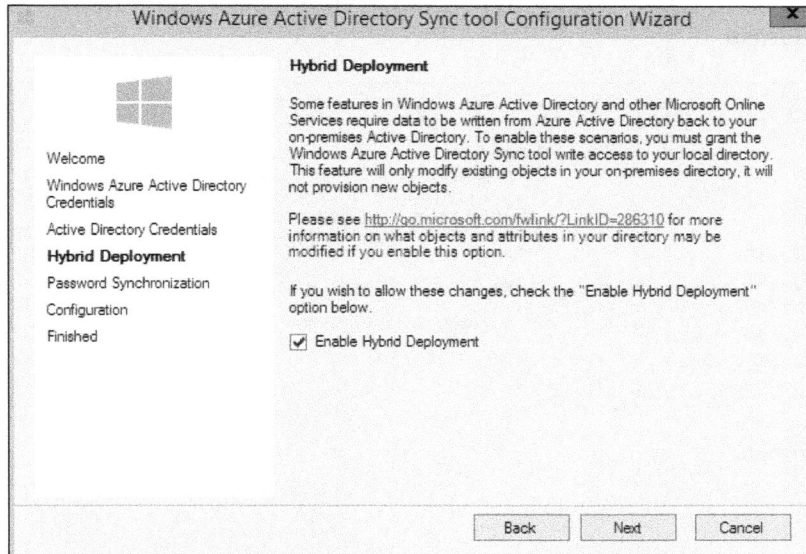

7. Click on the checkbox for **Enable Password Sync** and click on **Next**.

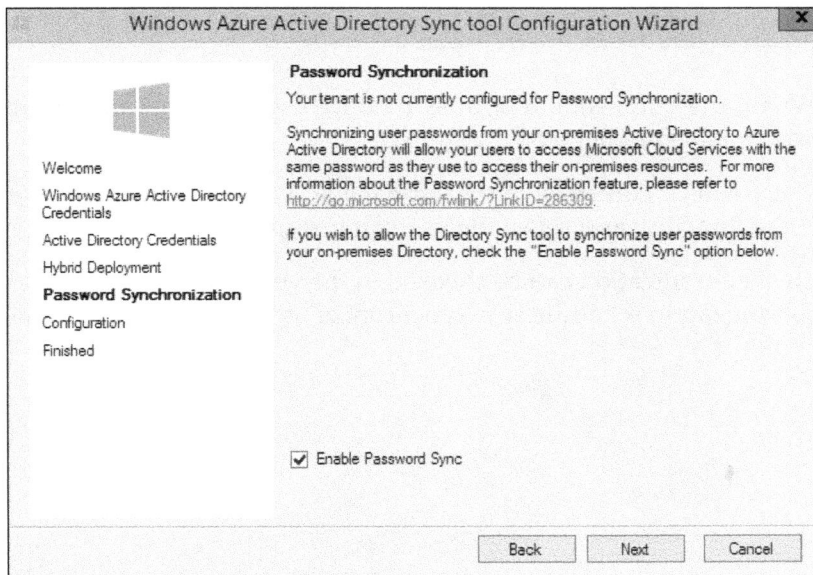

8. After the configuration has finished, click on **Next**.

9. Click on the checkbox for **Synchronize your directories now** and click on **Finish**.

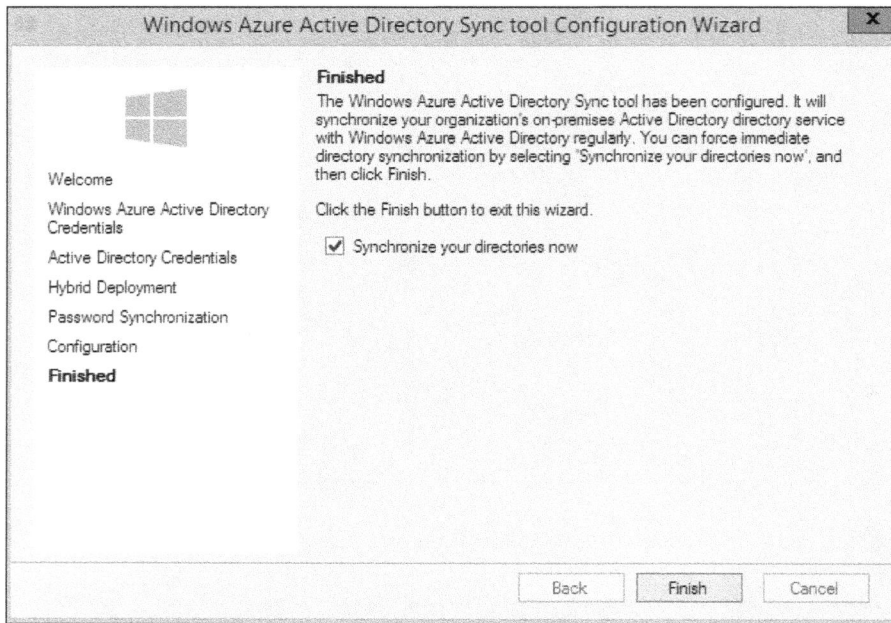

Within a few minutes, you should be able to notice user accounts and groups from your AD are available in Microsoft Azure AD.

To check, select **Active Directory** in the left pane of Azure Management Portal. Then, select the directory and select the users or groups.

The status of synchronization can be checked in the Windows Event Viewer. The default synchronization schedule is to synchronize user accounts and passwords once every 3 hours.

To force a synchronization, perform the following steps:

1. Double-click on C:\Program Files\Microsoft Azure Active Directory Sync\DirSyncConfigShell.psc1, and it will launch the DirSync PowerShell.

2. In the PowerShell, run Start-OnlineCoexistenceSync.

Synchronizing partially

It is possible that you do not want to synchronize all of your local AD accounts to Microsoft Azure.

One of the reasons to synchronize is that you want to have administrators sign in to Azure using their local AD credentials.

If your applications do not support authentication to Azure AD and you are interested in single sign-on with SaaS applications, there is no direct need to synchronize.

It is possible to configure DirSync to synchronize just a single or multiple organizational units instead of the complete directory. The following steps show how to configure a partial synchronization:

1. To select which OUs to synchronize, start miisclient.exe. This is located in the folder C:\Program Files\Microsoft Azure Active Directory Sync\SYNCBUS\Synchronization Service\UIShell.

2. Select the **M**anagement agents tab and double-click on **Active Directory Connector**.

3. Select **Configure directory partitions**.

4. Click on the **Container** button.

5. Reset the password of the account name listed and fill it in.

6. Select the OUs (containers) you would like to synchronize.

7.   Click on **OK**.

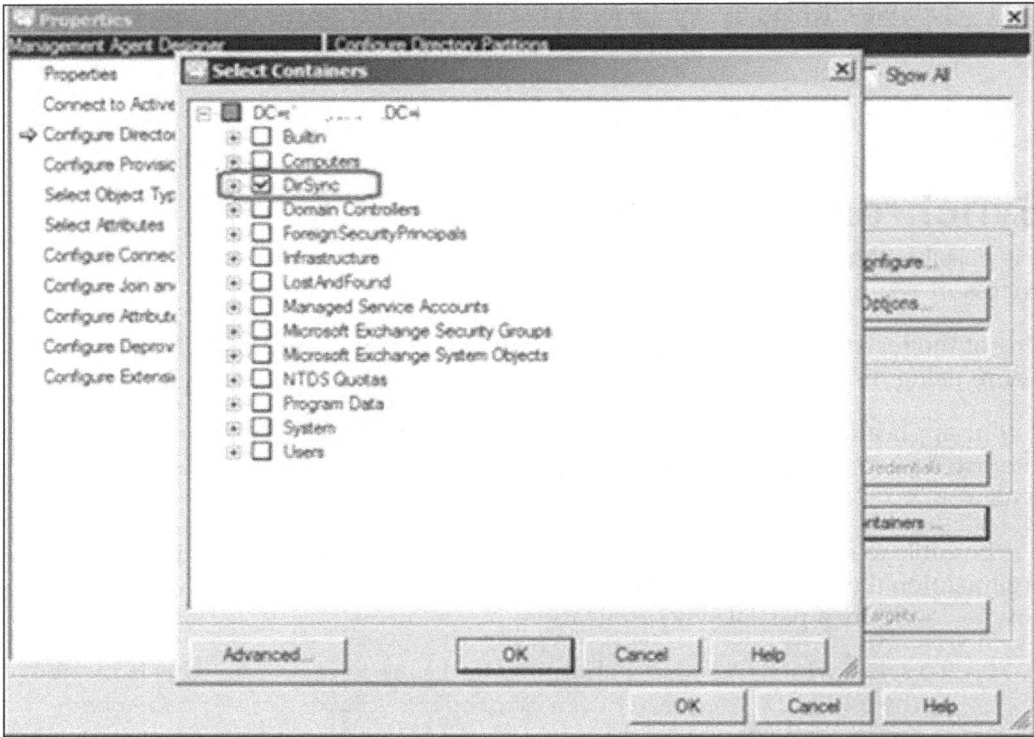

Deleting a domain

If for some reason you wish to delete a domain, you need to follow the steps described here:

1.   Disable the directory synchronization.

2.   Make sure the domain you want to delete is not the primary domain.

3.   Delete all user accounts member of the domain. This can be done manually or by using a PowerShell script. Use the PowerShell module for Microsoft Azure AD.

4.   Finally, delete the domain itself.

The domain being deleted must be empty; that is, there cannot be any users or groups with e-mail addresses in this domain.

Adding an AD account as a co-administrator

It is advised not to use Microsoft accounts for management tasks in Azure Management Portal. There is no control over user accounts by IT.

What you want is to use accounts from your on-premises AD and assign them the co-administrator role. In this section, we are going to discuss how to do this. If you are signed in to the Azure Management Portal using a Microsoft account you will not be able to add an organizational account as a co-administrator or service administrator for security reasons. Someone could be trying to find out if a corporate account exists, for example, `supervisor@contoso.com`.

If you are signed in with an organizational account, you will be able to add both organizational accounts as well as Microsoft accounts.

The co-administrator must be either a Microsoft account or a user account homed in the directory named `Default Directory`.

The procedure to add a co-administrator from an AD not being the default AD is as follows:

1. Log in using the Microsoft account.
2. Navigate to **Settings | Administrator** and add the administrative account from the default directory.
3. Assign it the co-administrator role.
4. Log in using this account to the Azure Management Portal.
5. Add the on-premises directory.
6. Add an administrator from the on-premises replicated directory.

Importing and exporting data

If we are going to move our on-premises virtual machine to Azure, we might run into capacity issues when transferring especially when we are connected to Azure using a VPN. If the VPN has a low bandwidth, it might take an unacceptable amount of time to transfer the data. Azure ExpressRoute could be used but might not be an option in your scenario because of availability or costs.

To overcome this, Microsoft offers an Import/Export service that allows us to transfer large amounts of data to or from an Azure datacenter using external hard drives. For security reasons, all data needs to be encrypted using BitLocker. The service is currently only available when the hard disks sent to Azure originate from a US location. Exported data is limited to shipments to US locations only. An import job is free of charge. When data is exported from an Azure location, Microsoft will charge for data leaving the datacenter.

Import and export jobs can be created using the Azure Management Portal. Microsoft charges a fee for the Import/Export service itself.

Managing Azure disks and images

In the previous chapter, you learned how to use the Microsoft supplied operating system images. You learned how to upload application software so we can customize servers.

The next step is creating our own images. An image is a reference guest operating system that can be used to deploy operating systems. By using images, we will be sure that each server is configured and installed according to our standards.

Creating an image from a virtual machine

It is very likely the images supplied by Microsoft as listed in Azure Management Portal are not sufficient for your goal. You might want to include your own software to the image or change the time zone and so on.

This can be accomplished by creating your own image. Configure the guest operating system and applications the way you want, capture the image, and use it for deployment.

In this section, you are going to learn how to create an image for a Windows Server virtual machine. During the image capture, the virtual machine including the virtual hard disks will be deleted. If you want to be able to reuse the virtual machine if something goes wrong, make sure you make a backup of the disks (by exporting data) as described in the previous section.

Note that a virtual machine deployed from an image use the same storage account as the virtual machine that was used as a baseline. During deployment of an image there is no option to select a storage account!

The following steps describe how to create an image from a virtual machine:

1. Start an RDP session to the Windows server that is going to be used as a baseline for other servers.

2. Open a Command Prompt as an administrator.

3. Start `%windir%\system32\sysprep\sysprep.exe`.

4. Select **Enter System Out-of-Box Experience (OOBE)**.

5. Make sure that you select the **Generalize** checkbox.

6. Select **Shutdown**.

7. Click on **OK**.

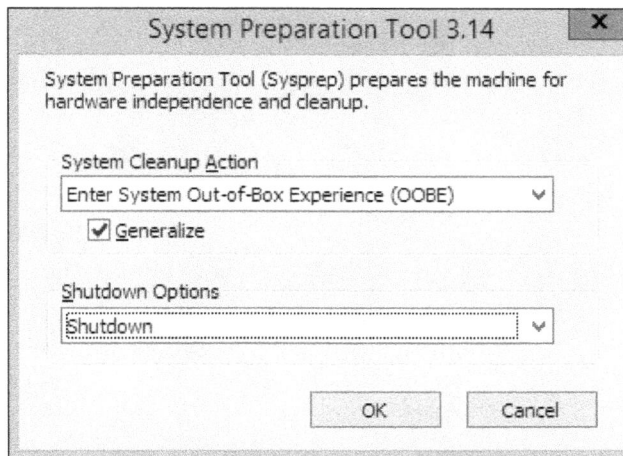

Sysprep will now generalize Windows by removing the computer name, IP settings, and so on. When the process is ready, the virtual machine will shut down. This will take about 5 minutes.

Make sure that the virtual machine you want to create an image from is shown as **Stopped** in the **Management Portal**. You might have to refresh the browser window to get an update on the status.

×

Capture an image from a virtual machine

The operating system disk of the virtual machine is used to create an image that can be used to create new virtual machines. The virtual machine will be deleted after the image has been captured.

VIRTUAL MACHINE NAME

azurebook-2008

IMAGE NAME

windows-server-2008-r2-27012014

☑ I have run Sysprep on the virtual machine 🕜

⚠ **IMPORTANT NOTE**

The virtual machine will be deleted when the image is captured.

✓

---

8. Select the virtual machine and click on the **Capture** button in the lower menu.

9. Type in a name for the image. Make sure you enable **I have run Sysprep on the virtual machine**.

10. Click on the check mark in the bottom-right corner.

11. When the capture has completed, you can deploy a new virtual machine. Click on the **NEW** button and the virtual machine from the gallery. Select **My Images** and select the image you just created.

Converting dynamically expanding disks to a fixed size VHD

Microsoft Azure does not support dynamically expanding disks. A dynamically expanding disk consumes as much storage as the amount of data stored in the disk file (.vhd). However, the guest operating system to which a dynamic disk is attached sees the maximum size of the disk. Using a dynamic disk is a way to overprovision your storage to keep storage costs low. However, when using dynamic disks, you should constantly monitor the disk usage to prevent a situation when the underlying storage runs out of disk space. This will result in stopped or crashed virtual machines.

If you want to upload a dynamic disk from on-premises to Microsoft Azure, you first need to convert that disk to a fixed size. Actually, there is no conversion. The process creates a new fixed disk and copies the data of the dynamically expanding disk on to it.

Note that you need the amount of free disk space available equal to the maximum size of the dynamic disk. If your dynamic disk has 3 GB of data but has a maximum disk size of 50 GB, the conversion requires 50 GB of free disk space.

> When converting a disk, make sure the file size of the virtual disk is a whole number in MB. So, 500 MB is accepted by Azure. If the VHD file is 500.5 MB in size, Azure will present an error when the VHD is registered as a disk in Azure Management Portal:
> ```
> The VHD http://<path>/<filename>.VHD has an unsupported
> virtual size of <number> bytes. The size must be a
> whole number (in MBs).
> ```

Several methods are available for conversion to a fixed-sized disk:

- PowerShell
- Third-party tools
- Hyper-V manager

Perform the following steps to convert a dynamically expanding disk to a fixed-size disk:

1. In Hyper-V Manager, select the virtual machine to which the to-be converted disk is attached.
2. Select the virtual disk and click on the **Edit** button.
3. In the **Choose action** part, select **Convert**.
4. Make sure that the disk format is VHD.
5. Set **Fixed size** for the **Disk type**.

Managing disks and VHD files

When a virtual machine is created using Azure Management Portal, the disks and VHD files are named according to a naming convention designed by Microsoft. You cannot change the names of disks and VHD files.

VHD files in Azure have a fixed format, so they do not grow dynamically. Azure does not support the VHDX format that is supported by Windows Server 2012 Hyper-V.

To see the names of the disks and VHD files that are attached to a virtual machine, select that virtual machine in the management portal and click on the name. Then select the **Dashboard** menu item and scroll down.

An alternative method to find out the naming of VHD files is by selecting **Storage** in the left pane, selecting the storage account, selecting containers, and double-clicking on the folder named VHD. You will not be able to see the D: disk as this disk is stored locally on the host.

The naming convention for the OS disk is as follows:

```
<name of cloud service>-<name of virtual machine>-0-
<year><month><day><time-of-creation><sequence number>
```

If you add an additional disk to the virtual machine, the naming convention by default is as follows:

```
<name of cloud service>-<name of virtual machine>-<month><day>-
sequence number starting with 1>
```

You are able to change the naming of additional disks. It is advised to use your own naming convention. You could, for example, add the drive letter of the Windows server guest in the filename. This makes troubleshooting and maintenance a lot easier.

The naming convention for the VHD files is as follows:

```
<name of cloud service>-<name of virtual machine>--<year>-<month>-
<day>.VHD
```

If you add an additional disk to the virtual machine, the naming convention by default for the VHD is the same as for the disk:

```
<name of cloud service>-<name of virtual machine>-<month><day>-
sequence number
```

Disks and VHDs

Microsoft Azure uses two terms for the same object. Microsoft Azure stores virtual hard disk files or .vhd on disks. These .vhd files are registered as an object, which is called a disk.

A virtual machine object is linked to a disk object. A disk object is linked to a VHD. An image can be linked to a VHD as well. This means you can delete a disk object while the linked VHD is not physically removed from the blob storage.

Azure TRIM support

Costs are clearly visible when using cloud. The Azure portal allows a download of a CSV file that clearly shows costs of consumption of, for example, disk storage.

So, you might think about how large a virtual disk should be. It should not be too large, because then you will pay for using disk capacity which is not used by data. Also, it cannot be too small or you might run out of data space.

You shouldn't worry when using Microsoft Azure. Microsoft actually charges for the data written to Microsoft Azure Storage. Microsoft does not charge for reserved capacity.

So, when you store a 127 GB disk on Azure and only 50 GB is used, you will pay for 50 GB of data.

In 2013, Microsoft introduced TRIM support. Without TRIM support, data that has been written on a Blob but has been deleted later is still being accounted for in the blob. This is because while in the metadata (the file allocation table of the blob) the block is free, but in the blob it is not. Microsoft Azure Storage is a sparse file system, which means the data is not charged; the allocated data in the blob means that over time the blob will expand. This is because the guest operating system believes there is no more free space.

With TRIM support, the guest operating system instructs the storage stack that a block of data should be deleted. Azure Storage will not allocate that block of data and you are not charged for it.

TRIM support is available on Windows Server 2012 R2 virtual machines for both the OS and data disks. For Windows Server 2008 R2 virtual machines, TRIM support is only available for the OS disk. For Linux servers, TRIM support is not available yet.

Basically, it comes down to TRIM enabling you to only pay for the amount of disk space you see being consumed in the virtual machine.

Monitoring Microsoft Azure

Monitoring your infrastructure running on Microsoft Azure is just as important as monitoring your on-premises infrastructure. In this section, we will get a high-level overview of available ways to get an insight in health, and performance and capacity of infrastructure components in Azure.

Microsoft Health Dashboard

We want to know the status of Microsoft Azure services like Storage, Network, Active Directory, and Compute at the highest possible level.

Microsoft provides the so-called *Service Dashboard* or *Health Dashboard*. This is a web-based dashboard providing the actual health status of all Azure services. For each service, you can further zoom in to Azure datacenters. The dashboard shows four statuses: **Normal Service Availability**, **Performance Degradation**, **Service Interruption**, and **Information**.

The dashboard URL is `http://www.windowsazure.com/en-us/support/service-dashboard/`.

The status of each service and Azure region can be monitored using a RSS feed. If you add the RSS feed to an application supporting RSS feeds, you will be able to have an automated push of status information.

Besides proving up-to-date status info, it is also possible to see historical data. This makes it very easy to search and see whether a particular Azure service in a particular period was affected. Microsoft informs customers about the progress of bringing the state of a service back to normal. However, the cause of the problem is not stated in the service dashboard.

Issues that had a serious impact on availability or performance for multiple customers are often documented in a Post Mortem blog. These blogs are published at MSDN.com and often titled *Summary of Microsoft Azure Service Disruption*. They provide a detailed description of what went wrong, why it went wrong, and what Microsoft has done to prevent similar issues in the future. These post mortems are very interesting to read as they often provide a unique insight into the inner workings of Microsoft Azure.

The Azure Health Dashboard will not warn you when a virtual machine fails, when an application fails, or any other failure in the infrastructure you are responsible for. We have several options available to have a more detailed insight.

First, the Azure Management Portal is able to provide information about service types and their performance, capacity, and health. Rules can be created which send an e-mail alert when a user-defined metric crosses a threshold value.

For the virtual machine service metrics, CPU percentage, disk read bytes/s, disk write/s, network in and network out can be monitored.

The storage service offers many alerts. Examples are alerts on failed authentication, inbound and outbound data transfers, and capacity and availability.

Rules that are used to monitor services are created in the Azure Management Portal by selecting **Management Services** in the left pane. Then, select **Alert** in the top menu. Next, click on **Add rule** in the bottom menu.

Another option for monitoring PaaS-related applications is using third-party monitoring tools. Many of them are offered as a SaaS service themselves. The setup is very easy. I used AzureWatch myself for a while. AzureWatch allows you to monitor cloud services and virtual machines, Azure Websites, SQL Azure databases, Azure storage accounts, and web HTTP/HTTPS URLs (endpoints).

AzureWatch is especially useful to scale down your instances when demand is low and scale up when demand increases. Automated scale up and scale down can also be done using Azure features.

In November 2014 Microsoft made available the Preview of Azure Operational Insights. Microsoft Azure Operational Insights is a Software as a Service offering which allows customers to monitor both Azure and on-premises components. A similar Microsoft service called System Center Advisor has been integrated in Operational Insights.

Monitoring using System Center Operations Manager

Microsoft Azure does not provide an API like Amazon CloudWatch does. Such an API allows third-party software or your in-house written scripts to monitor availability and performance of Azure services from a remote.

Remote monitoring of Azure virtual machines can, for example, be done using PowerShell. PowerShell remoting needs to be enabled in a virtual machine running Windows Server. Port 5986 must be open in the firewall of the guest. If you're not using a site-to-site VPN, you will also need to create an endpoint allowing traffic to flow to port 5986 from the Internet.

So, we have to use the tooling which is used in on-premises infrastructures.

System Center Operations Manager (SCOM), part of Microsoft System Center, allows monitoring of availability and performance of many components in an infrastructure. It is by far the most comprehensive monitoring tool for Microsoft solutions. SCOM is able to monitor non-Microsoft software and devices as well, for example, routers, Linux servers, or VMware vCenter. SCOM uses so-called management packs to get knowledge about the items it monitors.

One of the **management packs** (MP) available is the **System Center Monitoring Pack** for Microsoft Azure Application. This MP monitors applications that are deployed in the Azure platform as a service offering.

When you have deployed your own virtual machines in Azure, you can use any available MP to monitor availability and performance, just like doing the same thing on-premises. You will need a site-to-site VPN to prevent having to open all kinds of ports while at the same time weakening security.

Monitoring via open source tools

Other monitoring tools such as OpsView, Nagios, and Zabbix can be used for the purpose of monitoring as well. Microsoft Open Tech released a couple of plugins for both Nagios and Zabbix. These plugins are for:

- Microsoft Azure Storage (ingress, egress, requests, success ratio, availability, latency, and more)
- Microsoft Azure SQL databases( )(ingress, egress, requests, success ratio, availability, latency, and so on)
- Microsoft Azure Active Directory to monitor changes in user and group information (userdelta and groupdelta)
- Microsoft Azure **Platform as a Service** (**PaaS**) worker roles

Shutting down virtual machines

As you know, Microsoft charges compute per minute usage. If a virtual machine is not running, you are not charged for compute costs. However, to benefit from that you must shut down using the right method.

Virtual machines running in Microsoft Azure can be shut down using two methods:

- From inside the guest operating system
- From the Azure Management console

When a virtual machine is shut down from the guest operating system, it will keep its IP address. However, Microsoft will still charge you for compute costs even when the virtual machine is not running. This is because the virtual machine still has reservations open of compute resources, although it is not running. This can be compared to leaving your hotel room earlier but not checking out.

To prevent being charged for compute costs, a virtual machine needs to be shut down using the Azure Management console. What will happen is that the virtual machine status is shown as **Stopped deallocated**. The disadvantage of this method is that you might lose the IP address assigned to the virtual machine. This happens when there are no running virtual machines in a single cloud service.

Monitoring Azure and on-premises infrastructures

The software runs in the Azure North America datacenter.

It has four main features:

- Log Management
- Capacity Planning
- Change Tracking
- Update Assessment

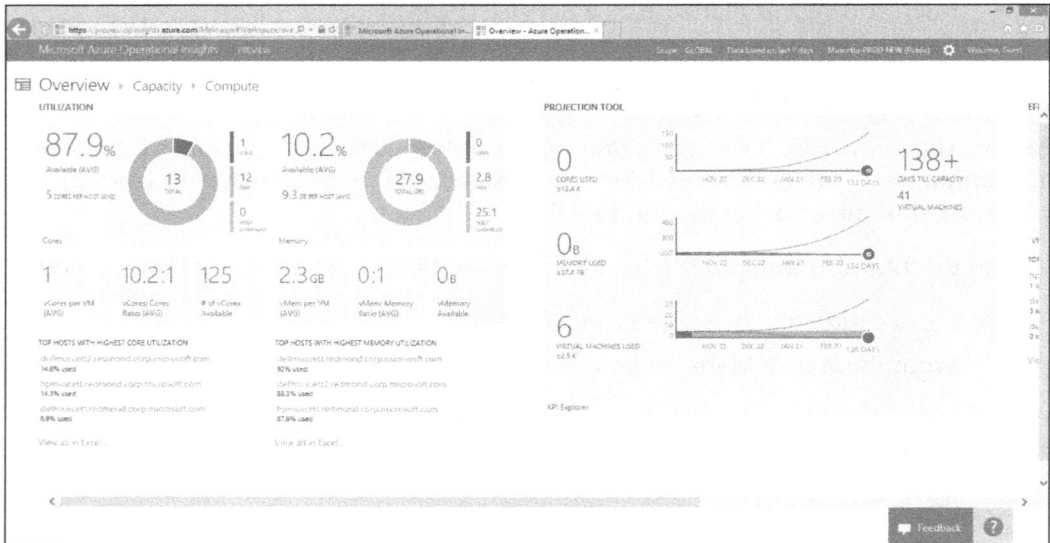

Log Management analyzes logfiles for errors. It will collect events from eventlogs like the System log of a Windows server. Administrators can run all kinds of queries to identify potential issues in their infrastructure.

Capacity planning provides insight into the capacity of the datacenter. It enables you to perform what-if scenarios. It will predict when a datacenter will have unsufficient resources.

Change Tracking keeps an eye on changes on systems.

Update Assessment will scan the server for missing updates and provide reporting.

Operational Insights uses agents that are deployed on servers and virtual machines. The agents use so-called Intelligence Packs to collect information. At the moment (January 2015) there are 8 Intelligence Packs available.

The service is offered in three tiers: Free, Standard, and Premium. The free tier has a limit on the amount of data collected daily and date will be deleted after 7 days. The Standard and Premium tiers do not have a limit on the amount of data collected daily and have greater data retention periods.

Mobile management of Microsoft Azure

When you are not sitting at your desk, it is possible to manage Microsoft Azure services using mobile devices. A short overview of useful apps is as follows:

- As the Azure Management Portal is written in HTML5, it will work perfectly on any mobile device installed with a HTML5-compatible browser. As long as the screen of the device is big enough, management will work perfectly. I used an Apple iPad and had no issues at all.

- Microsoft offers a free Remote Desktop app available for iOS, Android, and Windows Phone. This app allows connections to Windows Server running on Azure.

- Quite a few SSH apps are available to manage Linux machine from mobile devices.

- CloudTools for Microsoft Azure is an iOS app that allows you to manage Azure services. It shows the health status of services, deployments, services, and much more. It is targeted at the PaaS service. The cost for this app is $4.99.

Tips and tricks

This section has some useful tips to make the management of Microsoft Azure a bit easier.

How to reset the IP configuration of a virtual machine

Virtual machines running on Microsoft Azure do not have a possibility for console access. Console access can become handy when the guest operating system does not have network connectivity. Without network connectivity, an Azure virtual machine cannot be accessed over RDP so cannot be managed either.

Loss of network connectivity can occur when an administrator makes a mistake in the networking configuration. Someone might have filled in the wrong IP address, for example.

So how do we regain access to this virtual machine if there is no network connectivity? There are two options. The most efficient one is to adjust the size of the virtual machine.

The procedure is as follows:

1. Stop the virtual machine using the Azure Management Portal.
2. Select the configure menu item.
3. Change the virtual machine size and click on **Save**.
4. Restart the virtual machine.
5. Connect using RDP or SSH.

The other option is to download the VHD file that contains the guest operating system. Set the IP address to dynamic (DHCP) and upload the VHD file again. Recreate the virtual machine using the VHD and start the virtual machine. This is obviously more complex and time consuming.

However, this trick will not be able to restore RDP connectivity in all situations.

Checking the usage of Azure resources

Azure has soft quotas on a number of resources:

- Cores
- Cloud services
- Storage accounts

To check the number of cores in use, the number of cloud services and the number of storage accounts in use, go the **Settings** in **Azure Management Portal**. Then, select the **Usage** menu item.

The following screenshot shows an example of **Usage**. If the maximum of 20 cores has been reached, Microsoft support can be contacted to upgrade the number of cores. There is no cost associated with this upgrade.

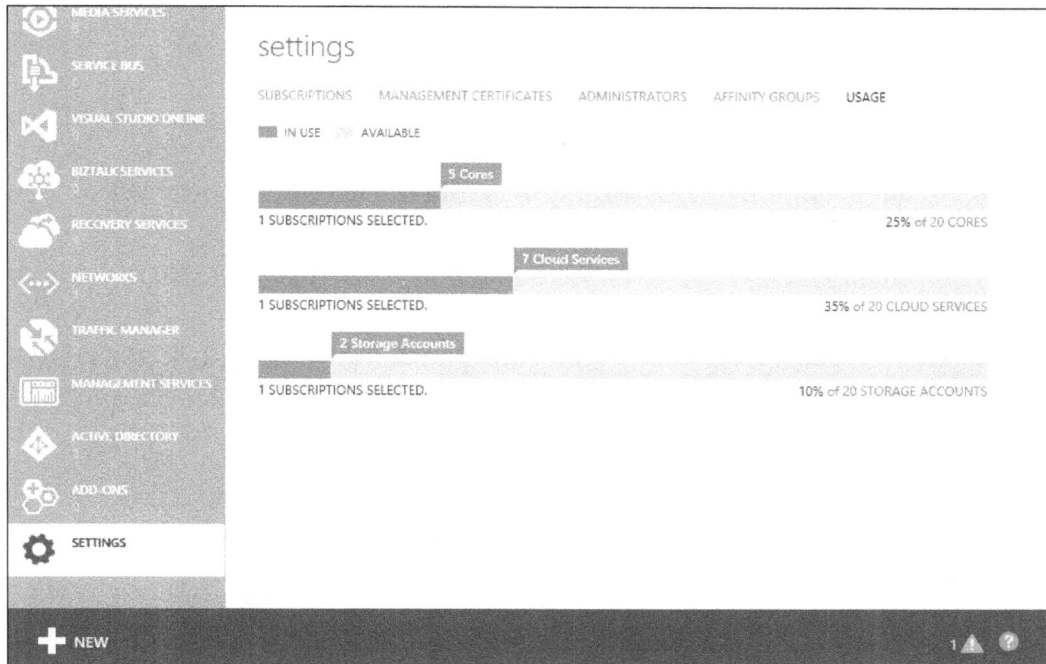

Automation

Automation is one of the most important features of cloud computing. Provisioning speed and agility can be reached by running scripts instead of doing things manually.

Several methods are available to automate certain tasks in Microsoft Azure. We will discuss all methods in later sections of the chapter:

- Microsoft Azure Automation
- REST API calling the service management API
- Windows PowerShell
- System Center Orchestrator
- Microsoft Azure Command-line Interface

Performing manual administrative tasks is done in **Azure Management Portal**. However, for certain repetitive tasks, you want to use automation. I advise you to start using PowerShell first. Most common tasks can be performed using this. For some other tasks, REST can be used.

Managing Azure using PowerShell

Knowledge of how to use PowerShell will save you a lot of time. PowerShell is being pushed by Microsoft as the tool for configuration and deployment of workloads in Azure. In some solutions, there is no graphical user interface feature available to perform a task and only a PowerShell script can do the job.

Some of us might be a bit too lazy to study PowerShell and believe it is hard to learn. I will try to prove it is actually very easy to learn.

To be able to use PowerShell for management of Microsoft Azure, we need to install the Microsoft Azure PowerShell module first. Besides the Microsoft PowerShell commandlets, there are also third-party commandlets (cmdlets) available. The Cerebrata Azure Management cmdlets are very useful.

Installation of the PowerShell module

Use the Microsoft Web Platform installer to install the PowerShell module. It can be found at `http://go.microsoft.com/fwlink/p/?linkid=320376&clcid=0x409`.

Install the web platform and accept the defaults. Installing the module also installs a customized console for Azure PowerShell. You can run the cmdlets from either the standard Windows PowerShell console or the Azure PowerShell console.

After the installation of PowerShell for Azure has completed, we are ready for authentication to our Azure subscription.

This can be done in two ways:

- Run PowerShell and authenticate using an organizational account / Microsoft account and the associated password
- Use a certificate

Running PowerShell and authenticating there can make it easier to manage access to a subscription, but may disrupt automation since it only retains the credentials for 12 hours so is not suitable for long-running tasks. We are going to use the certificate. To do so, perform the following steps:

1. Start the PowerShell for Azure console using **Run As Administrator**. How to do this depends on your system. For Windows 8 or Windows Server 2012 or later, type `power` on the **Start** screen. This command will search for all programs whose name starts with "power". For other systems, go to **Programs | Microsoft Azure | Microsoft Azure PowerShell**.

2. Type the command: `Get-AzurePublishSettingsFile`.

3. This will open a browser window which connects to Azure Management Portal. Type in the credentials of your subscription.

4. Next, you will be asked to select a folder for a file named `<subscription>-downloaddate-credentials.publishsettings`. Save this file and remember the location.

5. In PowerShell, type `Import-AzurePublishSettingsFile <path to the.publishsettings file>`.

6. You might have to change the execution policy. By default, PowerShell will restrict running scripts. You can change the policy.

7. In PowerShell, type `Set-ExecutionPolicy –ExecutionPolicy unrestricted`. This will run any script. If you want a restriction for running scripts, see the other options.

We are now ready to use PowerShell commands for the management of Azure.

> While using the certificate method makes it easier to use automation for long-running tasks, this method makes it harder to manage access to a shared subscription, such as when more than one person is authorized to access the account.

Managing Azure using command-line tools

The command-line tools are a very easy way to start using automation to manage Azure. Unlike PowerShell, which is very powerful but has a steep learning curve, the command line tools are quite easy to use. In this chapter, we will learn how to use the tools. Also, the command-line tools are available not only for Windows, but also for Mac and Linux. So, the command-line tools are suitable to get a consistent tool for multiple platforms.

First, we need to download the free Microsoft command-line tool. The software can be downloaded from `http://www.windowsazure.com/en-us/develop/mobile/tutorials/command-line-administration/`.

We select the Windows installer. Install the software and choice the defaults. After the installation has finished, start a Command Prompt.

Type in `Azure`. If the response is **Azure is not recognized as an internal or external command**, make sure `C:\Program Files (x86)\Microsoft SDKs\Microsoft Azure\CLI\wbin` is part of the path setting of the Command Prompt.

The first step in enabling command line management is to import the publish settings or subscription settings. These contain secure credentials and additional information about subscriptions.

At the command prompt type in `azure account download`.

Save the `.publishsettings` file to your workstation and remember the location. Make sure there is no space in the filename.

Then import the `.publishsettings` file using the following command. Replace the path to the settings file with the location of the file storage in the previous step.

```
azure account import <path-to-settings-file>
```

After importing your publish settings, you should delete the `.publishsettings` file for security reasons.

The `azure vm` command will show the possible commands. Many actions on virtual machines are possible.

The command-line syntax has three components: topic, verb, and options.

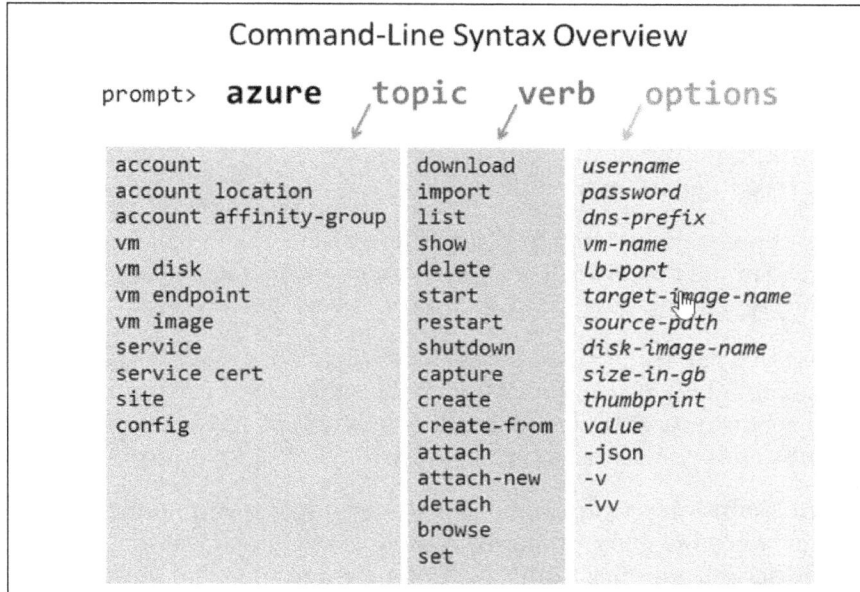

```
            Command-Line Syntax Overview

  prompt>  azure    topic    verb    options

    account               download      username
    account location      import        password
    account affinity-group list         dns-prefix
    vm                    show          vm-name
    vm disk               delete        lb-port
    vm endpoint           start         target-image-name
    vm image              restart       source-path
    service               shutdown      disk-image-name
    service cert          capture       size-in-gb
    site                  create        thumbprint
    config                create-from   value
                          attach        -json
                          attach-new    -v
                          detach        -vv
                          browse
                          set
```

Microsoft Azure Automation

Microsoft Azure Automation uses PowerShell workflows that provide the ability to automate administrative processes to manage and deploy cloud servers or any other function that a Windows PowerShell script can perform. It is based on Windows PowerShell 4.0.

PowerShell scripts are called runbooks. While Azure tasks can be performed using PowerShell scripts initiated from on-premises clients, Azure Automation offers a workflow execution engine. Runbooks can be scheduled and are executed in Azure. Two versions of runbooks exist. The draft version is used for editing and the published version is used for execution.

Customers do not have to rely on their on-premises hardware and Internet connection to be able to execute scripts. Azure Automation offers a highly scalable and available script execution engine.

To import PowerShell cmdlets into Azure Automation's so-called Integration Modules are used. This is a package that contains a Windows PowerShell Module.

The pricing of Azure Automation is based on:

- Runtime of the job
- Number of runbooks
- Size of the integration module

Azure Automation has the ability to run scripts inside Azure virtual machines without the use of the PowerShell endpoint or PowerShell Remoting. Company policies might prevent opening an endpoint for PowerShell access.

The VM Agent that can be installed at the deployment of a new virtual machine provides a way to interact with the VM. It enables the Azure Fabric Controller to perform tasks inside a virtual machine. One method of access the VM Agent provides is the ability to use the Azure VM Custom Script Extension.

Custom Script Extension scripts can be used for example to automatically configure a virtual machine once the guest operating system is running. Custom Script Extension will download scripts and files from Azure storage and then run these inside the VM using PowerShell.

A good explanation of the use of Custom Script Extension can be found here:

```
http://fabriccontroller.net/blog/posts/customizing-your-microsoft-
azure-virtual-machines-with-the-new-customscript-extension/
```

Azure Automation was in Preview and free at the time of writing this book.

Managing Azure using REST API

Another way to automate is using REST API. This is a standard method of enabling automation using a standard set of commands over HTTPS. REST API is not exclusively available in Microsoft Azure. Many cloud platforms such as Amazon and VMware vCloud Air offer REST API. It is also available in storage solutions (Nutanix) or backup (Veeam Backup & Replication).

REST API does not use an user account and password for authentication. To authenticate using REST, you will need a X509 certificate. These certificates can be self-signed, since they are used only for private communication between an application using the Service Management API and Azure Management Service. They can be or through using the makecert utility. Each subscription can have a maximum of 400 certificates.

While this book is not on automation, it is important to understand the basics of using REST API.

Microsoft Azure has several REST APIs available. The most frequently used one is the one connected to the Service Management API. There is also a Storage Services API. If you search for Microsoft Azure Storage Metrics, you will find a lot of information on how to query storage related data.

The purpose of the service management API is to allow third parties to programmatically access Microsoft Azure. The API is used by software vendors for tooling such as monitoring Azure or deploying services.

The API allows us to perform almost all tasks available in the Management Portal but now using scripts. You can create, stop, start, and delete virtual machines.

It supports the entire Azure Service lifecycle of deployment, configuration, staging, suspension, and deletion of Azure Services.

The API is available in two versions. Each version has a version number that looks like this: YYYY-MM-DD.

Each version of the API offers new commands and depreciated commands. So when calling the API, you must send the API version number using `x-ms-version`.

Authentication is done using a X509 v3 certificate. Each subscription can have a maximum of 400 certificates. You can either use IIS, the makecert tool, or the Visual Studio publish wizard to create self-signed certificates.

This Microsoft site has all the information you need to learn more about the Service Management REST API: `http://msdn.microsoft.com/en-us/library/windowsazure/ee460799.aspx`.

Exploring the service management API

To start exploring the Service Management API, we need to perform a couple of tasks:

1. Create a self-signed certificate.
2. Upload the certificate to Azure.
3. Explore the API.

To explore the API, a REST client is very handy. Several clients are available. Some good ones are RESTClient, which is a plugin for Firefox, and Fiddler for Chrome.

Introducing System Center Orchestrator

System Center Orchestrator is a software component of the System Center suite that allows us to automate tasks, for example, deploying an application on a server or provisioning a virtual machine on Microsoft Azure.

Instead of writing a PowerShell script or directly addressing the Service Management API, Orchestrator allows a relatively simple drag and drop of out-of-the-box tasks.

Orchestrator is an orchestration engine. Its knowledge of functions is received by importing so-called Integration Packs. Many Integration Packs are available. The Microsoft Azure Integration Pack contains a lot of activities that can be used to automate tasks. Available activities include creation, modification, and deletion of virtual machines as well as management of virtual machine images.

It is important to understand that the Azure Integration Pack uses a specific version of the service management API. So, when a new API is released, you will not be able to benefit from new functions in that release until Microsoft releases a new integration pack.

The procedure to use the Azure Integration Pack is as follows:

1. Download the Azure Integration Pack.
2. Register and deploy. Register it with the Orchestrator Management Server and then deploy it to runbook servers and Runbook Designers.
3. Configure the Azure connection.

As with all connections to the API, you will need a certificate. A connection establishes a reusable link between Orchestrator and Microsoft Azure. You can specify as many connections as you require to create links to multiple Microsoft Azure subscriptions.

Licensing and license mobility

Correct licensing of applications and operating systems is not an easy task. Many vendors have special rules when transferring licenses to a multi-tenant cloud infrastructure. Make sure you understand the licensing rules of the vendor. If uncertain, discuss this with your vendor. It may prevent some nasty fines from the vendor for not respecting the licensing end user agreement.

Basically, two scenarios are possible for licensing:

- You use licenses offered by the cloud vendor. This is the easy option. You pay the service provider a monthly fee for using the license and you are done. However, the availability of licenses is restricted. Windows Server will always be an option, along with SQL Server and SharePoint. Your service provider will not offer all the application licenses you are currently using.
- Use your own licenses in Microsoft Azure. We will discuss this in depth.

When using your owned licenses in a public cloud, there are a couple of possible restriction you should be aware of:

- License mobility of licenses in a shared hardware environment
- Licenses tied to physical sockets

The big difference in licensing depends on whether you are running your software on non-shared hardware or on shared hardware.

If your organization is running their licensed software on a non-shared hardware environment and your organization is the only user of that hardware, the same licensing rules applies as if the software is running on-premises.

If your software is running in a shared server environment, some vendors have restrictions for moving licenses from on-premises to a public cloud.

License mobility for Microsoft software

License mobility enables the owner of a software license to run that software either on-premises or on a hosted environment. Each vendor has its own license rules, so I will concentrate on the license mobility of Microsoft software.

Some Microsoft software is licensed by the Microsoft *License Mobility through Software Assurance*. This allows you to run selected software in a shared hardware environment offered by a service provider.

Windows server is not part of this License Mobility through SA, which means you cannot transfer Windows Server licenses from on-premises workloads to cloud workloads. For the licensing of Windows Server in the cloud, you will have to use the cloud provider Services Provider License Agreement licenses.

The following three requirements must be met by organizations wanting to move Microsoft licenses to the cloud:

- You will need to have a Volume Licensing program with SA to be able to move licenses to a cloud platform
- The service provider you are using must be an Authorized License Mobility Partner
- Fill in and submit a License Mobility Validation form

Products whose license is covered by the License Mobility through Software Assurance are listed in the Product Use Rights document, for example, Microsoft Exchange Server, Microsoft SharePoint Server, Microsoft Lync Server, and Microsoft Dynamics CRM business software.

In addition, the following products are also eligible for License Mobility through SA:

- SQL Server Standard: Per Processor and Server/CAL (processor and server licenses only) with Software Assurance
- System Center: All Server Management Licenses (MLs), including SMSE and SMSD with Software Assurance, System Center 2012 Standard, and Datacenter with Software Assurance

Microsoft restricts customers to deploy software in an environment in where hardware is shared by multiple organizations. To overcome this issue, some cloud providers offer a dedicated cloud service. Here, the customer is able to provision their own virtual machines on dedicated servers. So, the compute capacity is not shared with other tenants while physical network and storage is.

Licenses tied to physical sockets

Some vendors count the maximum number of servers an application can run on by the number of licenses for CPU sockets. In a cloud environment, this makes it impossible to use that software. In Microsoft Azure, there is no way customers can pin applications to specific physical host servers. However, vendors are changing their licensing. For example, Oracle now allows you to run Oracle software on Microsoft Azure.

Billing and cost management

Azure is very useful for its scale. Customers can create an unlimited number of servers and consume unlimited amounts of storage. However, this can be costly if there is no management of the consumption.

In server virtualization, *server sprawl* is used for a symptom where many virtual machines are running, while nobody really knows what the purpose is of some of those servers. It is so easy to create a virtual machine while the perception is that there are no associated costs.

Azure has two ways of charging:

- Pay upfront using an Enterprise Agreement. The customer has a commitment with Microsoft to pay in advance for a certain amount of resources.
- Pay by credit card or invoice. This is the pay-as-you-go model.

Microsoft makes an invoice available once per month. This is a PDF file that provides an overview of the costs per Azure service (virtual machines, data management, identity, recovery services, and so on).

The only way to get a more detailed insight into costs is by downloading a comma-separated variable file CSV file from Azure. The CSV file provides an overview of costs for all the services you consumed. The CSV file shows which services are consumed and for how long for each day.

Currently, cost management on Microsoft Azure is quite limited. Azure lacks an **application programming interface** (**API**) like Amazon provides that can be used to query actual costs by third-party software. However, Microsoft Azure Pack, which is used in private clouds as well as in clouds managed by service providers, does provide such an API.

To get insight into costs and produce reports, *Cloud Cruiser* can be used. This is a third-party tool that is able to display the costs made by customers (showback) or charge customers for consumption of cloud resources (chargeback) in real time.

Part of Microsoft Azure Pack is a free edition of Cloud Cruiser. This edition is limited in the number of objects it can handle. The commercially available version does not have such a limit.

Understanding the CSV

The CSV which contains detailed consumption information is a bit difficult to understand. Consumption is shown per day. You might notice a virtual machine that has been running the whole day but has been charged for 16 hours; or a single virtual machine running for 24 hours was billed for 48 hours that particular day.

The explanation for this billing is that compute hours for all instances are converted into small A1 instance hours. For example, one clock hour of a medium (A2) cloud services instance will be presented on your bill as two small (A1) cloud services instance hours.

The following figure shows the conversion:

CLOUD SERVICES INSTANCE	CLOCK HOURS	SMALL INSTANCE HOURS
Extra Small (A0)	1	1/4 hour
Small (A1)	1	1 hour
Medium (A2)	1	2 hours
Large (A3)	1	4 hours
Extra Large (A4)	1	8 hours

Summary

In this chapter, we took another step towards learning about Microsoft Azure infrastructure services. To allow user accounts in on-premises AD access to Azure, you learned how to set( )up directory synchronization. You now understand how to handle VHD files and know the restrictions on moving licenses to the cloud.

Also, you learned about monitoring Microsoft Azure services such as storage and virtual machines, and their billing and cost management.

You also learned how to configure Azure. In *Chapter 8, Migrating to Microsoft Azure*, you will learn about the available options, including the tools used for this move.

7
High Availability, Protection, and Recovery using Microsoft Azure

Microsoft Azure can be used to protect your on-premise assets such as virtual machines, applications, and data. In this chapter, you will learn how to use Microsoft Azure to store backup data, replicate data, and even for orchestration of a failover and failback of a complete data center.

You will also learn how applications and the data running on Azure are protected by the Azure infrastructure and what we can do to get maximum uptime for our applications.

We will focus on the following topics:

- Microsoft Failover clustering
- Microsoft Azure Backup Vault for storage of backup data
- Azure Site Recovery for failover and failback of virtual machines
- SQL Server Replication to protect SQL databases
- Microsoft StorSimple
- Azure snapshots to protect Azure virtual machines

High availability in Microsoft Azure

One of the most important limitations of Microsoft Azure is the lack of an SLA for single-instance virtual machines. If a virtual machine is not part of an availability set, that instance is not covered by any kind of SLA. The reason for this is that when Microsoft needs to perform maintenance on Azure hosts, in many cases, a reboot is required. Reboot means the virtual machines on that host will be unavailable for a while. So, in order to accomplish High Availability for your application, you should have at least two instances of the application running at any point in time. As mentioned in previous chapters Microsoft is working on some sort of hot patching which enables virtual machines to remain active on hosts being patched. Details are not available at the moment of writing.

High Availability is a crucial feature that must be an integral part of an architectural design, rather than something that can be "bolted on" to an application afterwards. Designing for High Availability involves leveraging both the development platform as well as available infrastructure in order to ensure an application's responsiveness and overall reliability. The Microsoft Azure Cloud platform offers software developers PaaS extensibility features and network administrators IaaS computing resources that enable availability to be built into an application's design from the beginning. The good news is that organizations with mission-critical applications can now leverage core features within the Microsoft Azure platform in order to deploy highly available, scalable, and fault-tolerant cloud services that have been shown to be more cost-effective than traditional approaches that leverage on-premises systems.

Microsoft Failover Clustering support

Windows Server Failover Clustering (WSFC) is not supported on Azure. However, Microsoft does support SQL Server AlwaysOn Availability Groups. For AlwaysOn Availability Groups, there is currently no support for availability group listeners in Azure. Also, you must work around a DHCP limitation in Azure when creating WSFC clusters in Azure. After you create a WSFC cluster using two Azure virtual machines, the cluster name cannot start because it cannot acquire a unique virtual IP address from the DHCP service. Instead, the IP address assigned to the cluster name is a duplicate address of one of the nodes. This has a cascading effect that ultimately causes the cluster quorum to fail, because the nodes cannot properly connect to one another.

So if your application uses Failover Clustering, it is likely that you will not move it over to Azure. It might run, but Microsoft will not assist you when you encounter issues.

Load balancing

Besides clustering, we can also create highly available nodes using load balancing. Load balancing is useful for stateless servers. These are servers that are identical to each other and do not have a unique configuration or data.

When two or more virtual machines deliver the same application logic, you will need a mechanism that is able to redirect network traffic to those virtual machines. The Windows **Network Load Balancing** (**NLB**) feature in Windows Server is not supported on Microsoft Azure. An Azure load balancer does exactly this. It analyzes incoming network traffic of Azure, determines the type of traffic, and reroutes it to a service.

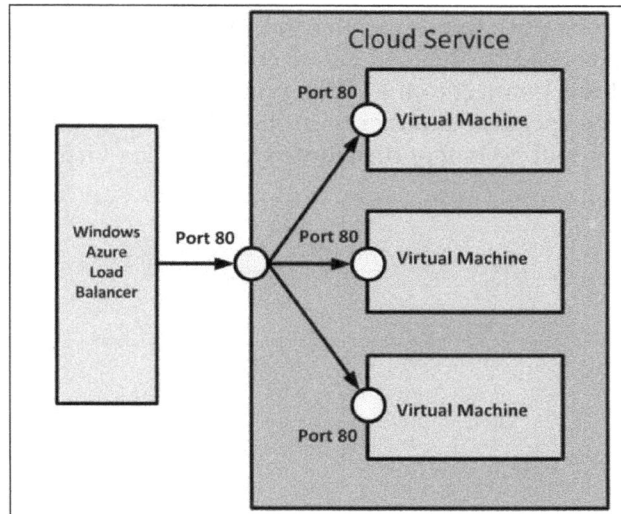

The Azure load balancer is running provided as a cloud service. In fact, this cloud service is running on virtual appliances managed by Microsoft. These are completely software-defined. The moment an administrator adds an endpoint, a set of load balancers is instructed to pass incoming network traffic on a certain port to a port on a virtual machine. If a load balancer fails, another one will take over.

Azure load balancing is performed at layer 4 of the OSI mode. This means the load balancer is not aware of the application content of the network packages. It just distributes packets based on network ports.

To load balance over multiple virtual machines, you can create a load-balanced set by performing the following steps:

1. In **Azure Management Portal**, select the virtual machine whose service should be load balanced.

2. Select **Endpoints** in the upper menu.

3. Click on **Add**.

4. Select **Add a stand-alone endpoint** and click on the right arrow.

5. Select a name or a protocol and set the public and private port.

6. Enable **create a load-balanced set** and click on the right arrow.

7. Next, fill in a name for the load-balanced set.

8. Fill in the probe port, the probe interval, and the number of probes. This information is used by the load balancer to check whether the service is available. It will connect to the probe port number; do that according to the interval. If the specified number of probes all result in unable to connect, the load balancer will no longer distribute traffic to this virtual machine.

ADD ENDPOINT

Configure the load-balanced set

Endpoints that are load-balanced across multiple virtual machines are added to a load-balanced set.

LOAD-BALANCED SET NAME

webserver   ×

PROBE PROTOCOL

TCP

PROBE PORT

80

PROBE INTERVAL

15   SECONDS

NUMBER OF PROBES

2

---

9. Click on the check mark.

The load balancing mechanism available is based on a hash. Microsoft Azure Load Balancer uses a five tuple (source IP, source port, destination IP, destination port, and protocol type) to calculate the hash that is used to map traffic to the available servers.

A second load balancing mode was introduced in October 2014. It is called Source IP Affinity (also known as session affinity or client IP affinity). On using Source IP affinity, connections initiated from the same client computer go to the same DIP endpoint.

These load balancers provide high availability inside a single data center. If a virtual machine part of a cluster of instances fails, the load balancer will notice this and remove that virtual machine IP address from a table.

However, load balancers will not protect for failure of a complete data center. The domains that are used to direct clients to an application will route to a particular virtual IP that is bound to an Azure data center.

To access application even if an Azure region has failed, you can use Azure Traffic Manager. This service can be used for several purposes:

- To failover to a different Azure region if a disaster occurs
- To provide the best user experience by directing network traffic to Azure region closest to the location of the user
- To reroute traffic to another Azure region whenever there's any planned maintenance

The main task of Traffic Manager is to map a DNS query to an IP address that is the access point of a service.

This job can be compared for example with a job of someone working with the X-ray machine at an airport. I'm guessing that you have all seen those multiple rows of X-ray machines. Each queue at an X-ray machine is different at any moment. An officer standing at the entry of the area distributes people over the available X-rays machine such that all queues remain equal in length.

Traffic Manager provides you with a choice of load-balancing methods, including performance, failover, and round-robin. Performance load balancing measures the latency between the client and the cloud service endpoint. Traffic Manager is not aware of the actual load on virtual machines servicing applications.

As Traffic Manager resolved endpoints of Azure cloud services only, it cannot be used for load balancing between an Azure region and a non-Azure region (for example, Amazon EC2) or between on-premises and Azure services.

It will perform health checks on a regular basis. This is done by querying the endpoints of the services. If the endpoint does not respond, Traffic Manager will stop distributing network traffic to that endpoint for as long as the state of the endpoint is unavailable.

Traffic Manager is available in all Azure regions. Microsoft charges for using this service based on the number of DNS queries that are received by Traffic Manager. As the service is attached to an Azure subscription, you will be required to contact Azure support to transfer Traffic Manager to a different subscription.

The following table shows the difference between Azure's built-in load balancer and Traffic Manager:

	Load balancer	Traffic Manager
Distribution targets	Must reside in same region	Can be across regions
Load balancing	5 tuple Source IP Affinity	Performance, failover, and round-robin
Level	OSI layer 4 TCP/UDP ports	OSI Layer 4 DNS queries

Third-party load balancers

In certain configurations, the default Azure load balancer might not be sufficient. There are several vendors supporting or starting to support Azure. One of them is Kemp Technologies.

Kemp Technologies offers a free load balancer for Microsoft Azure. The **Virtual LoadMaster (VLM)** provides layer 7 application delivery. The virtual appliance has some limitations compared to the commercially available unit. The maximum bandwidth is limited to 100 Mbps and High Availability is not offered. This means the Kemp LoadMaster for Azure free edition is a single point of failure. Also, the number of SSL transactions per second is limited.

One of the use cases in which a third-party load balancer is required is when we use Microsoft Remote Desktop Gateway. As you might know, Citrix has been supporting the use of Citrix XenApp and Citrix XenDesktop running on Azure since 2013. This means service providers can offer cloud-based desktops and applications using these Citrix solutions.

To make this a working configuration, session affinity is required. Session affinity makes sure that network traffic is always routed over the same server.

Windows Server 2012 Remote Desktop Gateway uses two HTTP channels, one for input and one for output, which must be routed over the same Remote Desktop Gateway. The Azure load balancer is only able to do round-robin load balancing, which does not guarantee both channels using the same server.

However, hardware and software load balancers that support IP affinity, cookie-based affinity, or SSL ID-based affinity (and thus ensure that both HTTP connections are routed to the same server) can be used with Remote Desktop Gateway.

Another use case is load balancing of **Active Directory Federation Services** (**ADFS**). Microsoft Azure can be used as a backup for on-premises **Active Directory** (**AD**). Suppose your organization is using Office 365. To provide single sign-on, a federation has been set up between Office 365 directory and your on-premises AD. If your on-premises ADFS fails, external users would not be able to authenticate. By using Microsoft Azure for ADFS, you can provide high availability for authentication.

Kemp LoadMaster for Azure can be used to load balance network traffic to ADFS and is able to do proper load balancing. To install Kemp LoadMaster, perform the following steps:

1. Download the **Publish Profile** settings file from `https://windows.azure.com/download/publishprofile.aspx`.

2. Use PowerShell for Azure with the `Import-AzurePublishSettingsFile` command.

3. Upload the KEMP supplied VHD file to your Microsoft Azure storage account.

4. Publish the VHD as an image.

5. The VHD will be available as an image. The image can be used to create virtual machines.

The complete steps are described in the documentation provided by Kemp.

Geo-replication of data

Microsoft Azure has geo-replication of Azure Storage enabled by default. This means all of your data is not only stored at three different locations in the primary region, but also replicated and stored at three different locations at the paired region.

However, this data cannot be accessed by the customer. Microsoft has to declare a data center or storage stamp as lost before Microsoft will failover to the secondary location.

In the rare circumstance where a failed storage stamp cannot be recovered, you will experience many hours of downtime. So, you have to make sure you have your own disaster recovery procedures in place.

Zone Redundant Storage

Microsoft offers a third option you can use to store data. **Zone Redundant Storage (ZRS)** is a mix of two options for data redundancy and allows data to be replicated to a secondary data center / facility located in the same region or to a paired region. Instead of storing six copies of data like geo-replicated storage does, only three copies of data are stored. So, ZRS is a mix of local redundant storage and geo-replicated storage. The cost for ZRS is about 66 percent of the cost for GRS.

Snapshots of the Microsoft Azure disk

Server virtualization solutions such as Hyper-V and VMware vSphere offer the ability to save the state of a running virtual machine. This can be useful when you're making changes to the virtual machine but want to have the ability to reverse those changes if something goes wrong.

This feature is called a snapshot. Basically, a virtual disk is saved by marking it as read only. All writes to the disk after a snapshot has been initiated are stored on a temporary virtual disk. When a snapshot is deleted, those changes are committed from the delta disk to the initial disk.

While the Microsoft Azure Management Portal does not have a feature to create snapshots, there is an ability to make point-in-time copies of virtual disks attached to virtual machines.

Microsoft Azure Storage has the ability of versioning. Under the hood, this works differently than snapshots in Hyper-V. It creates a snapshot blob of the *base blob*. Snapshots are by no ways a replacement for a backup, but it is nice to know you can save the state as well as quickly reverse if required.

Introduction to geo-replication

By default, Microsoft replicates all data stored on Microsoft Azure Storage to the secondary location located in the paired region. Customers are able to enable or disable the replication. When enabled, customers are charged.

When Geo Redundant Storage has been enabled on a storage account, all data is asynchronous replicated. At the secondary location, data is stored on three different storage nodes. So even when two nodes fail, the data is still accessible.

However, before the read access Geo-Redundant feature was available, customers had no way to actually access replicated data. The replicated data could only be used by Microsoft when the primary storage could not be recovered again.

Microsoft will try everything to restore data in the primary location and avoid a so-called geo-failover process. A geo-failover process means that a storage account's secondary location (the replicated data) will be configured as the new primary location. The problem is that a geo-failover process cannot be done per storage account, but needs to be done at the storage stamp level. As you learned in *Chapter 3, Understanding the Microsoft Azure Architecture*, a storage stamp has multiple racks of storage nodes. You can imagine how much data and how many customers are involved when a storage stamp needs to failover. Failover will have an effect on the availability of applications. Also, because of the asynchronous replication, some data will be lost when a failover is performed.

Microsoft is working on an API that allows customers to failover a storage account themselves. When geo-redundant replication is enabled, you will only benefit from it when Microsoft has a major issue. Geo-redundant storage is neither a replacement for a backup nor for a disaster recovery solution.

Microsoft states that the **Recover Point Objective** (RPO) for Geo Redundant Storage will be about 15 minutes. That means if a failover is required, customers can lose about 15 minutes of data. Microsoft does not provide a SLA on how long geo-replication will take.

Microsoft does not give an indication for the **Recovery Time Objective** (RTO). The RTO indicates the time required by Microsoft to make data available again after a major failure that requires a failover. Microsoft once had to deal with a failure of storage stamps. They did not do a failover but it took many hours to restore the storage service to a normal level.

In 2013, Microsoft introduced a new feature called **Read Access Geo Redundant Storage (RA-GRS)**. This feature allows customers to perform reads on the replicated data. This increases the read availability from 99.9 percent when GRS is used to above 99.99 percent when RA-GRS is enabled.

Microsoft charges more when RA-GRS is enabled. RA-GRS is an interesting addition for applications that are primarily meant for read-only purposes. When the primary location is not available and Microsoft has not done a failover, writes are not possible.

The availability of the Azure Virtual Machine service is not increased by enabling RA-GRS. While the VHD data is replicated and can be read, the virtual machine itself is not replicated. Perhaps this will be a feature for the future.

Disaster recovery using Azure Site Recovery

Disaster recovery has always been on the top priorities for organizations. IT has become a very important, if not mission-critical factor for doing business. A failure of IT could result in loss of money, customers, orders, and brand value.

There are many situations that can disrupt IT such as:

- Hurricanes
- Floods
- Earthquakes
- Disasters such as a failure of a nuclear power plant
- Fire
- Human error
- Outbreak of a virus
- Hardware or software failure

While these threads are clear and the risk of being hit by such a thread can be calculated, many organizations do not have a proper protection against those threads.

In three different situations, disaster recovery solutions can help an organization to continue doing business:

- Avoiding a possible failure of IT infrastructure by moving servers to a different location.
- Avoiding a disaster situation, such as hurricanes or floods, since such situations are generally well known in advance due to weather forecasting capabilities.

- Recovering as quickly as possible when a disaster has hit the data center. Disaster recovery is done when a disaster unexpectedly hit the data center, such as a fire, hardware error, or human error.

Some reasons for not having a proper disaster recovery plan are complexity, lack of time, and ignorance; however, in most cases, a lack of budget and the belief that disaster recovery is expensive are the main reasons. Almost all organizations that have been hit by a major disaster causing unacceptable periods of downtime started to implement a disaster recovery plan, including technology immediately after they recovered. However, in many cases, this insight came too late. According to Gartner, 43 percent of companies experiencing disasters never reopen and 29 percent close within 2 years.

Server virtualization has made disaster recovery a lot easier and cost effective. Verifying that your DR procedure actually works as designed and matches RTO and RPO is much easier using virtual machines.

Since Windows Server 2012, Hyper-V has a feature for asynchronous replication of virtual machine virtual disks to another location. This feature, Hyper-V Replica, is very easy to enable and configure. It does not cost extra. Hyper-V Replica is storage agnostic, which means the storage type at the primary site can be different than the storage type used in the secondary site. So, Hyper-V Replica perfectly works when your virtual machines are hosted on, for example, EMC storage while in the secondary a HP solution is used.

While replication is a must for DR, another very useful feature in DR is automation. As an administrator, you really appreciate the option to click on a button after deciding to perform a failover and sit back and relax. Recovery is mostly a stressful job when your primary location is flooded or burned and lots of things can go wrong if recovery is done manually.

This is why Microsoft designed Azure Site Recovery. Azure Site Recovery is able to assist in disaster recovery in several scenarios:

- A customer has two data centers both running Hyper-V managed by System Center Virtual Machine Manager. Hyper-V Replica is used to replicate data at the virtual machine level.

- A customer has two data centers both running Hyper-V managed by System Center Virtual Machine Manager. NetApp storage is used to replicate between two sites at the storage level.

- A customer has a single data center running Hyper-V managed by System Center Virtual Machine Manager.

- A customer has two data centers both running VMware vSphere. In this case InMage Scout software is used to replicate between two datacenters. Azure is not used for orchestration.

- A customer has a single data centers not managed by System Center Virtual Machine Manager.

In the second scenario, Microsoft Azure is used as a secondary data center if a disaster makes the primary data center unavailable.

Microsoft announced also to support a scenario where vSphere is used on-premises and Azure Site Recovery can be used to replicate data to Azure. To enable this InMage software will be used. Details were not available at the time this book was written.

In the first two described scenarios Site Recovery is used to orchestrate the failover and failback to the secondary location. The management is done using Azure Management Portal. This is available using any browser supporting HTML5. So a failover can be initiated even from a tablet or smartphone.

Using Azure as a secondary data center for disaster recovery

Azure Site Recovery went into preview in June 2014. For organizations using Hyper-V, there is no direct need to have a secondary data center as Azure can be used as a target for Hyper-V Replica.

Some of the characteristics of the service are as follows:

- Allows nondisruptive disaster recovery failover testing

- Automated reconfigure of network configuration of guests

- Storage agnostic supports any type of on-premises storage supported by Hyper-V

- Support for VSS to enable application consistency

- Protects more than 1,000 virtual machines (Microsoft tested with 2,000 virtual machines and this went well)

To be able to use Site Recovery, customers do not have to use System Center Virtual Machine Manager. Site Recovery can be used without this installed. System Center Virtual Machine Manager. Site Recovery will use information such as? virtual networks provided by SCVMM to map networks available in Microsoft Azure.

Site Recovery does not support the ability to send a copy of the virtual hard disks on removable media to an Azure data center to prevent the initial replication using WAN (seeding). Customers will need to transfer all the replication data over the network. ExpressRoute will help to get a much better throughput compared to a site-to-site VPN over the Internet.

Failover to Azure can be as simple as clicking on a single button. Site Recovery will then create new virtual machines in Azure and start the virtual machines in the order defined in the recovery plan. A recovery plan is a workflow that defines the startup sequence of virtual machines. It is possible to stop the recovery plan to allow a manual check, for example. If all is okay, the recovery plan will continue doing its job. Multiple recovery plans can be created.

Microsoft **Volume Shadow Copy Services (VSS)** is supported. This allows application consistency. Replication of data can be configured at intervals of 15 seconds, 5 minutes, or 15 minutes. Replication is performed asynchronously.

For recovery, 24 recovery points are available. These are like snapshots or point-in-time copies. If the most recent replica cannot be used (for example, because of damaged data), another replica can be used for restore. You can configure extended replication. In extended replication, your Replica server forwards changes that occur on the primary virtual machines to a third server (the extended Replica server). After a planned or unplanned failover from the primary server to the Replica server, the extended Replica server provides further business continuity protection. As with ordinary replication, you configure extended replication by using Hyper-V Manager, Windows PowerShell (using the -Extended option), or WMI.

At the moment, only VHD virtual disk format is supported. Generation 2 virtual machines that can be created on Hyper-V are not supported by Site Recovery. Generation 2 virtual machines have a simplified virtual hardware model and support **Unified Extensible Firmware Interface (UEFI)** firmware instead of BIOS-based firmware. Also, boot from PXE, SCSI hard disk, SCSCI DVD, and Secure Boot are supported in Generation 2 virtual machines.

However on March 19 Microsoft responded to numerous customer requests on support of Site Recovery for Generation 2 virtual machines. Site Recovery will soon support Gen 2 VM's. On failover, the VM will be converted to a Gen 1 VM. On failback, the VM will be converted to Gen 2. This conversion is done till the Azure platform natively supports Gen 2 VM's.

Customers using Site Recovery are charged only for consumption of storage as long as they do not perform a failover or failover test.

Failback is also supported. After running for a while in Microsoft Azure customers are likely to move their virtual machines back to the on-premises, primary data center. Site Recovery will replicate back only the changed data.

Mind that customer data is not stored in Microsoft Azure when Hyper-V Recovery Manager is used. Azure is used to coordinate the failover and recovery. To be able to do this, it stores information on network mappings, runbooks, and names of virtual machines and virtual networks. All data sent to Azure is encrypted.

By using Azure Site Recovery, we can perform service orchestration in terms of replication, planned failover, unplanned failover, and test failover. The entire engine is powered by Azure Site Recovery Manager.

Let's have a closer look on the main features of Azure Site Recovery. It enables three main scenarios:

- Test Failover or DR Drills: Enable support for application testing by creating test virtual machines and networks as specified by the user. Without impacting production workloads or their protection, HRM can quickly enable periodic workload testing.

- Planned Failovers (PFO): For compliance or in the event of a planned outage, customers can use planned failovers, virtual machines are shutdown, final changes are replicated to ensure zero data loss, and then virtual machines are brought up in order on the recovery site as specified by the RP. More importantly, failback is a single-click gesture that executes a planned failover in the reverse direction.

- Unplanned Failovers (UFO): In the event of unplanned outage or a natural disaster, HRM opportunistically attempts to shut down the primary machines if some of the virtual machines are still running when the disaster strikes. It then automates their recovery on the secondary site as specified by the RP.

If your secondary site uses a different IP subnet, Site Recovery is able to change the IP configuration of your virtual machines during the failover.

Part of the Site Recovery installation is the installation of a VMM provider. This component communicates with Microsoft Azure. Site Recovery can be used even if you have a single VMM to manage both primary and secondary sites.

Site Recovery does not rely on availability of any component in the primary site when performing a failover. So it doesn't matter if the complete site including link to Azure has been destroyed, as Site Recovery will be able to perform the coordinated failover.

Azure Site Recovery to customer owned sites is billed per protected virtual machine per month. The costs are approximately €12 per month. Microsoft bills for the average consumption of virtual machines per month. So if you are protecting 20 virtual machines in the first half and 0 in the second half, you will be charged for 10 virtual machines for that month.

When Azure is used as a target, Microsoft will only charge for consumption of storage during replication. The costs for this scenario are €40.22/month per instance protected.

As soon as you perform a test failover or actual failover Microsoft will charge for the virtual machine CPU and memory consumption.

Requirements

To be able to use Azure Site Recovery, the following items are required:

- System Center 2012 SP1 with latest cumulative update or System Center 2012 R2. Mind for small businesses Microsoft also offers Site Recovery without the need for System Center.
- A certificate.
- A Microsoft Azure subscription with the Site Recovery feature enabled.
- At least one on-premises data center with at least one instance of SCVMM 2012.

Configuring Azure Site Recovery

Enabling Azure Site Recovery involves the following steps:

1. Enable the Site Recovery vault.
2. Create and upload a certificate.
3. Download and install the Recovery Manager provider.
4. Choose which clouds should be protected.
5. Map networks.
6. Enable the virtual machines that should be protected.

A step-by-step instruction guide on how to configure Azure Site Recovery will take too many pages. You will find an excellent how-to at http://msdn.microsoft.com/en-us/library/dn788903.aspx.

In the previous chapter we discussed how to recover to Azure. One of the requirements for this scenario is Virtual Machine Manager. Not every organization needs Virtual Machine Manager. Many organizations use Hyper-V managed by native Microsoft tools or by third party such as like 5Nine Manager for Hyper-V.

In December 2014 Microsoft announced **Disaster recovery for branch offices and SMB through Azure Site Recovery**. This allows organizations that do not use Virtual Machine Manager to use Azure as a replication target.

The procedure to protect virtual machines running on Hyper-V is described in this Microsoft blogpost: http://azure.microsoft.com/en-us/documentation/articles/hyper-v-recovery-manager-hypervsite/.

Installing a replica Active Directory controller in Azure

Microsoft Azure can be used as a secondary location to keep a copy of Active Directory. If a disaster hits the primary site that makes Active Directory partly or totally unavailable, you have at least Active Directory still operational in a secondary location.

Think about how much time this saves compared to having to fully restore one of your most crucial assets. You can have an Active Directory server in Microsoft Azure as a replica. In this section, I will describe the steps you need to take to create such a replica.

The requirements include a VPN connection between your on-premises infrastructure and the Microsoft Azure network. For security reasons, it is not advised to have Active Directory replication over the public interface of Microsoft Azure using endpoints.

This webpage provides step-by-step instructions on how to configure AD replication to Azure: http://blogs.technet.com/b/keithmayer/archive/2013/01/20/step-by-step-extending-on-premises-active-directory-to-the-cloud-with-windows-azure-31-days-of-servers-in-the-cloud-part-20-of-31.aspx.

Using Microsoft Azure as a backup target

Storage in Microsoft Azure has many advantages. Capacity is almost unlimited, so there is no need for so-called forklift upgrades when using on-site storage. Provisioning of new storage capacity is done with few mouse clicks. You won't be able to do that when extending on-premises storage, as this involves placing cabinets in racks, supplying power, networking, and IO.

Microsoft Azure provides two options to use storage as a backup target:

- Using regular Azure Storage
- Using Azure Backup

Azure Storage is the regular blob storage that is used by many applications, virtual machine hard disks, and so on.

Azure Backup is especially targeted for storage of backup data. Microsoft charges the two quite differently. Azure Backup is almost eight times more expensive than Azure Storage. For Azure Backup, Microsoft does not charge for bandwidth, transactions, or computation. Data stored in Azure Backup is compressed.

Azure Storage can be used by many backup applications as a backup target. Some examples are Veeam Backup & Replication Cloud Edition.

Veeam Backup & Replication Cloud Edition features a virtual Disk. When enabled, administrators are able to mount any Azure Storage account as a drive letter in Windows Explorer.

Microsoft has a service that uses these capabilities of cloud storage. Azure Backup is a simple way to protect and recover files. The service can be accessed using an agent that supports Windows Server and Data Protection Manager.

Note that this is not yet an enterprise-ready solution. It lacks features such as a one-step bare metal recovery. Still, Azure Backup is very useful in branch offices, small and medium business, and other same-size environments.

When using the Microsoft supplied Windows Server Backup or DPM agent, all data is encrypted using a passphrase you select. The bandwidth usage can be throttled depending on the time of the day.

Some characteristics of the agent are:

- It supports bandwidth throttling
- It supports file servers, SQL Server, SharePoint, and Exchange
- It supports incremental backups that reduce bandwidth consumption
- It supports recovery to other than original server
- It supports data encrypting executed on-premises
- The ability to recover individual files

Microsoft Azure Backup has a limitation of maximum 1.65 TB (after installation of update KB2989574) of data per volume that can be backed up in one backup operation. The standalone server and DPM solutions have different retention maximums. In the standalone server scenario, backups can be retained in the vault for up to 30 days. This is configurable in the Windows Azure Backup agent's scheduling wizard.

Azure Backup lets you set multiple retention policies on backup data. Backup data can be stored for multiple years by maintaining more backup copies near term, and less backup copies as the backup data becomes aged. The number of backup copies that can be stored at Azure is 366.

Azure Backup integrates with the Azure Import service to send the initial backup data to Azure datacenter. This capability will enable the customers to ship the initial backup data through disk to the nearest Azure datacenter.

Many backup applications such as Veeam Backup & Replication, CA ARCserve, and Microsoft Data Protection Manager provide the ability to use Microsoft Azure as a storage target. Also, backup data directly from Windows Server can be stored in Microsoft Azure.

While capacity is unlimited, there are some caveats:

- In a scenario in which you like to backup local servers to Microsoft Azure, you should keep in mind the time required to restore that data. It can take a considerate amount of time to restore the data especially over slow WAN connections.

- While costs of cloud-based storage are dropping, in many scenarios it is more expensive than on-premises storage. Cloud-based storage is charged per month. Customers are not only charged on consumed storage capacity, but also for IO transactions and data that leaves the data center. This, however, is relatively very small percentage of the total costs.

- The costs per GB of Azure Backup are relatively high in comparison to the Azure Storage offering.. At the time of writing this, costs are seven times higher than regular Azure Storage.

To use Azure Vault, it is not required to have a site-to-site VPN connection.

In this section, you are going to learn how to use Microsoft Azure for a backup target. We will do that in the following steps:

1. Enable the Backup Vault.

2. Create a certificate.

3. Download and install the backup agent.

4. Create a backup schedule.

Step 1 – enabling Azure Vault

The first step is to enable the Azure Vault. The Vault is a storage location dedicated to the storage of backup data. Data stored in Azure Vault cannot be access using storage accounts connected to your Azure subscription. The steps to enable an Azure Vault are as follows:

1. In Azure Management Portal, select the **New** button in the left corner.

2. Navigate to **Data Services | Recovery Services | Backup Vault | Quick create**.

3. Fill in a name for the vault and select the region in which you like to storage data in that vault.

> It is wise to select a different region for the backup Vault than the region of the servers you want to backup. This is true for the backup of on-premises servers as well as for Azure virtual machines. Suppose the east coast of the US is hit by a hurricane and your data center, power, or network connections are affected. There is a change the Azure data center is affected as well if located in the same region.

4. Click on **Create Vault**.

> It can take a while for the backup vault to be created. To check the status, you can monitor the notifications at the bottom of the portal. After the backup vault has been created, a message will tell you that the vault has been successfully created and it will be listed in the resources for Recovery Services as **Online**.

The next step is to create certificates. For each server you like to store backups of in the Azure Vault, you need to create a certificate.

Step 2 – creating a certificate

To connect to Vault, we need a certificate. We have two options here:

- Use any valid **Secure Sockets Layer** (**SSL**) certificate that is issued by a **certification authority** (**CA**) that is trusted by Microsoft (and whose root certificates are distributed through the Microsoft Root Certificate Program).

- Create your own certificate. This is created using the makecert tool. How to get this tool is described in *Chapter 4, Building an Infrastructure on Microsoft Azure*, of this book, in which we set up a client-to-site VPN connection.

Makecert is included in the Windows SDK for Windows 7 and Windows SDK for Windows 8. These can be downloaded for free. During the setup of the SDK, select **Windows software Development kit**. Deselect all other installation features.

After the installation is complete, makecert.exe can be located in the C:\Program Files (x86)\Windows Kits\8.0\bin\x64 folder.

Azure Vault has some requirements regarding attributes of the certificate:

- They must have key length of at least 2048 bits key

- Enhanced key usage should be Client Authentication

- The validity period should not exceed 3 years (the certificate should be an x.509 v3 certificate)

The certificate we created earlier to connect App Controller to Microsoft Azure cannot be used for this purpose. This is since that certificate uses Server Authentication as Enhanced Key Usage.

To create a certificate using the makecert tool, start a command prompt with the **run as administrator** option. If you start the Command Prompt without administrative privilege, the creation will fail. Do this when signed in to the Window Server you want to back up.

Type in the following command:

```
makecert.exe -r -pe -n CN=AzureBackup -ss my -sr localmachine -eku
1.3.6.1.5.5.7.3.2 -e 01/19/2015 -len 2048 AzureBackup.cer
```

The used parameter CN in the previous command is the name you like to give the certificate. Make sure the date entered in the -e parameter is not more than 3 years from the current date.

After the certificate has been created, upload it to Azure by performing the following steps:

1. In **Azure Management Portal**, click on **Recovery Services**.

2. Click on the vault you created in the previous step.

3. Click on the **Manage Certificate** button in the lower menu bar.

4. Navigate to the folder containing the .cer certificate, select it, and click on the check mark.

5. If the certificate is fine, there will be no errors shown. The certificate can be checked by selecting the backup vault and then click on **Dashboard**. Details on the certificate are shown on the right-hand side of the screen.

Step 3 – downloading and installing the Azure Backup agent

Microsoft provides free clients for the following operating systems and applications:

- Microsoft Data Protection Manager 2012 SP1 and later
- Windows Server 2012
- Windows Server 2012 Essentials
- Windows Server 2012 R2
- Windows 7 Service Pack 1, Windows 8 and Windows 8.1
- Windows Server 2008 R2 with Service Pack 1 (SP1)
- Windows Server 2008 with Service Pack 2 (SP2)

In the portal, select the backup vault. Next, select the **Dashboard** menu item. On the right, you will see a link to download the backup agent.

After the download has finished, start the setup. Accept or change the defaults of your choice. The required components will be installed automatically.

After a successful installation, a shortcut to **Windows Server Backup** is located in the **Administrative Tools** folder.

We are now going to configure Azure Backup to it is able to access the previously created Azure Vault. We also make sure our data is encrypted by using an encryption key.

1. Start **Windows Server Backup** and select **Backup** in the left pane.

2. Click on **Register server** in the right pane.

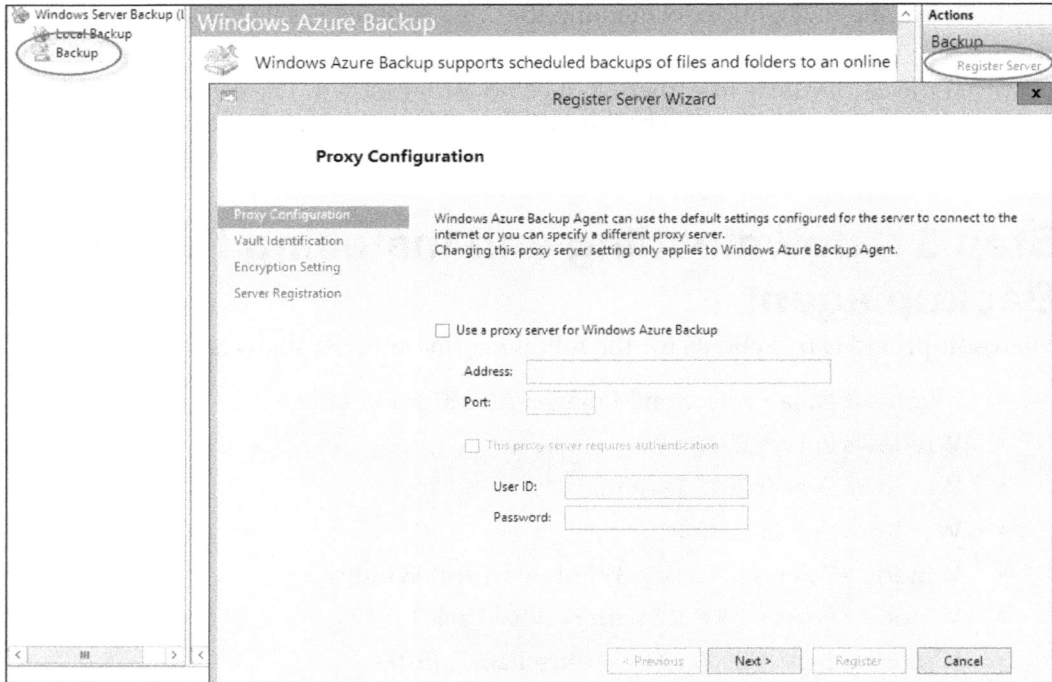

3. Fill in a proxy server if appropriate. Click on **Next**.

4. At the vault identification, click on the **Browse** button and select the `.cer` certificate we uploaded to Azure in the previous steps. When the correct certificate has been selected, you are presented with a location of the Azure Vault. Select it and click on **Next**.

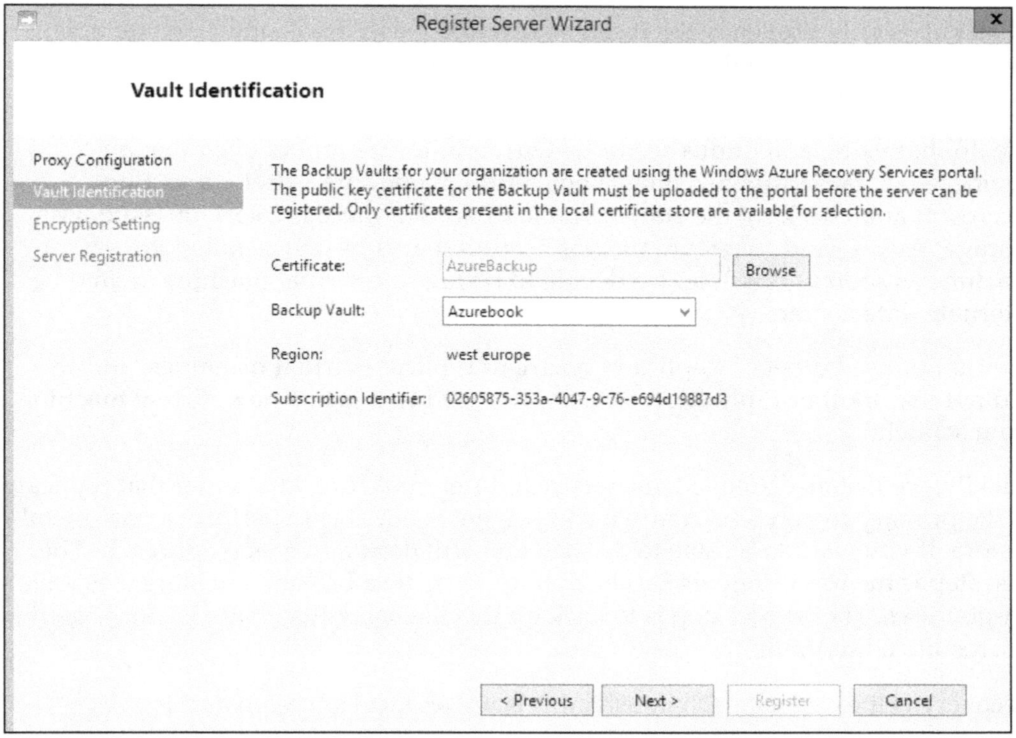

5. Next, fill in a passphrase to encrypt the backup data. Select a file to store the passphrase. Make sure to store the passphrase file in a secure location such as a USB key stored in a safe. If the passphrase is lost, nobody will be able to recover the data stored in Azure.

6. Click on **Register**.

Step 4 – creating a backup schedule

The next step is to schedule a backup. This is a straightforward process. First, you select files and folders to include in the backup. The next step is to configure a schedule. A maximum of three backups can be made at on the same day. On the next screen of the wizard, you can specify the number of days for which backup should be retained. That is it. You now can Microsoft Azure to store backup data.

Restoring data is very simple. Just click on the **Recover data** button and you are guided by a wizard through the restoration process.

Recovery of virtual machines

A backup is only proven when it can be restored. So in this chapter, we are not focusing on how to install the agent and make backups. In this section, we are going to learn to perform a restore.

We do that using a fictitious scenario. Our monitoring tool noticed that a business-critical virtual machine is not running anymore. After contacting Microsoft and checking the status, you learned that there is a serious issue with storage. As we need to restore the application that runs on the failed virtual machine as soon as possible, we decide to restore the virtual machine in an alternate data center.

We cannot use Hyper-V Replica in Azure to replicate virtual machines, and we did not use another replication tool. So, we need to install a new virtual machine from scratch.

Luckily, we installed Active Directory in a different Azure data center that replicates to the primary region. The Azure Backup agent is not able to perform a bare metal restore. If you want to be able to do that, you will need a two-step approach. The first step is the use Windows Server Backup to create a backup and store it as a file on-premises. The second step is to back up this file using the Azure Backup agent to Microsoft Azure Vault.

Recovery is the opposite. Obviously, this is not an ideal situation as it is time-consuming and error-prone.

Using Microsoft StorSimple

Traditional SAN storage is often expensive. Each time when the maximum capacity has been reached, another large investment has to be made to acquire more storage. It does not scale very much because of those large capital investments.

In many cases, however, the data stored on a SAN is hardly accessed. So, why not move this data to the cloud? That is exactly what Microsoft StorSimple does; archiving hardly used data to Microsoft Azure while keeping the data accessible for applications and users.

Microsoft StorSimple is a hardware appliance that offers primary storage, archive, backup, and disaster recovery in one solution. Microsoft Azure Storage is used as a cheap and scalable storage tier to store archive, backup, and disaster recovery data. Other supported cloud platforms are, for example, Atmos, OpenStack, HP, and Amazon Web Services to name a few. However, StorSimple will only support Microsoft Azure as a storage target when the next firmware version has been released.

StorSimple is a so-called **cloud integration storage (CiS)** solution. It can archive unstructured data. That are common files like those created by Office, Photo editing software, and so on. StorSimple cannot be used to archive database files, virtual hard disks of operational virtual machines, or files such as Outlook .pst files.

Significant cost-saving over traditional storage and backup is accomplished by using Microsoft Azure Storage as its lowest storage tier storing archives and backup data. The solution replaces tape handling hardware offsite backup as backup data is stored in Azure as well.

Of all data created over time, on average 85 percent or more is regarded as cold. This means it is hardly ever accessed. The hardware appliance contains three tiers of local storage plus it uses cloud storage as the lowest tier.

The available tiers are as follows:

- SSD: Linear (raw tier 1)
- SSD: Deduplicated (tier 2), and concurrent inline block-level dedupe
- SAS: Deduplicated and compressed (tier 3)
- Cloud: Deduplicated, compressed, and encrypted (tier 4)

The life cycle of data starts when it is written in NVRAM. This is RAM that is battery-backed. Then, the data is written to SSD. Data is not compressed or deduped while stored in tier 1.

When data is not accessed for a while, blocks are deduplicated but still stored on SSD. The dedupe rate depends on the type of data. Storage capacity can be increased 2 to 5 times because of the deduplication.

When blocks are getting cooler they are compressed and moved to the SAS tier. Note that blocks are automatically tiered but not complete files. So, the most frequently accessed blocks of files remain stored on the fastest SSD tier, ensuring good performance.

The final stage of the data life cycle is the cloud tier. Data is encrypted and moved to Azure (or any other cloud storage).

The metadata that is used to track the location of each block is always stored locally on the StorSimple device.

Weighted Storage Layout is the technology that determines when a block of data is moved to another tier. It analyzes frequency of use, age of data, reference counts, and preferences set by administrators to decide for data move.

The last tier of storage is cloud as a tier. StorSimple is able to move data that is not accessed frequently to Microsoft Azure Storage. Note that it does not use Azure Backup Vault that has much higher costs per GB than Microsoft Azure Storage.

To make sure data stored in Azure is safe, AES-256 military-grade encryption is used for all data leaving the appliance. Only the customer has access to the encryption key. The data is presented to physical servers and virtualization hosts over the iSCSI protocol. Both Hyper-V and VMware vSphere are supported.

Many components of the appliance are redundant: power supply, storage controller, and network interface. The disk configuration is RAID-10 with a hot spare hard disk. Software upgrades are nondisruptive.

StorSimple is available in four models ranging in a storage capacity from 2 TB to 40 TB. A typical use case for StorSimple is for storage of file server data. The data stored on a file server is typically accessed frequently within weeks after creation. Then, the data is hardly accessed and is a candidate to be archived.

Another typical use case is for projects. Projects run for a limited time. After the project has finished, that data needs to be available for archiving. Storing that kind of data on cheap storage will reduce the TCO for storage a lot.

StorSimple has two types of snapshots. A snapshot is a point in time picture of the data in a volume at a given time. Local snapshots are like traditional backup. The main purpose is to recover accidentally deleted files. Each snapshot only stores changed data compared to the previous snapshot. The local snapshot is deduplicated and compressed. This has no performance impact, since it *doesn't* have to go out and read through all metadata to work out what blocks or files have changed, like a traditional backup. Reading through file information is one of the worst enemies of backing up unstructured data; if you have millions of files (which is common) it can take hours just to read through the data to work out what files have changed *before you back up a single file*. So, StorSimple can efficiently give you local points in time for quick restores that are near instant to backup and restore from.

Cloud snapshots allow us to create a snapshot of a StorSimple volume and replicate that snapshot to Azure for archiving and disaster recovery purposes. The first cloud snapshot contains the whole dataset. Later snapshots only contains the block changes. These cloud snapshots are policy-based and can be kept for hours, days, weeks, months, or years as required.

StorSimple supports a maximum of 64 storage accounts per system.

Restoring individual files

Restoring accidentally deleted files is very simple. An administrator connects to a local or cloud snapshot, clones it, and then mounts it as a drive letter or mount point. Files can then be copied from the clone back to the original volume.

Disaster recovery using Microsoft StorSimple

A unique feature of the StorSimple appliance is the ability to quickly recover from a volume failure or complete loss of a data center. StorSimple creates VSS snapshots of volumes and stores these in Azure Storage or any other supported cloud. If your primary data center has failed, the recovery of data can be performed easily and quickly.

A high level overview of the steps to recover when a data center is lost is as follows:

1. Install a replacement StorSimple device in the recovery location.

2. Connect it to the Microsoft Azure Storage account.

3. Fill in the encryption key.

4. Publish the volumes to the servers by mounting the cloud snapshots.

5. While the data is still physically located in Azure storage, applications will be able to access the data. If data is accessed, it is transferred from Azure to the StorSimple appliance.

While in a traditional disaster recovery all data is restored in one go, StorSimple restores only the requested data (hot data). Data that is not requested (cold data) is automatically restored at a later time. This so-called thin restore downloads the metadata map that describes the state of the system and provides an image of the volume's contents at the time a snapshot is taken. This map is typically 0.1 percent the size of the stored data.

As soon as the metadata map has been downloaded, systems are able to access data. For applications and users, it shows all data to be local.

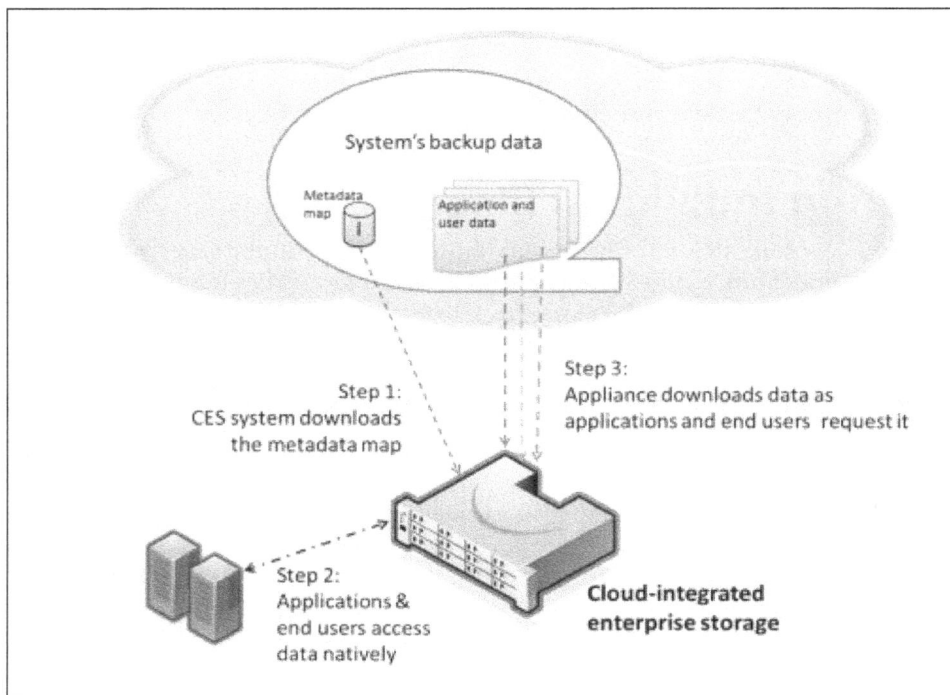

Microsoft has temporary offers of which StorSimple appliances are free if customers purchase $50,000 or $100,000 of Azure storage per year. Free 1 year Gold support is included in this offer.

Backing up and restoring Azure virtual machines

If you are using Microsoft Azure to host legacy applications vague, you are likely to want a backup of virtual machines.

Backup data should never be stored in the same physical location as the live data. So, we must make sure backup data is stored in another location than the Azure region that hosts our virtual machines.

As Microsoft Azure data centers do not provide backup to tape and no physical access to collect tapes, the only option to get data offsite is by using disk to disk copy.

We have three options to do that:

- Store backup data in our on-premises data center
- Store backup data in another Azure region
- Store backup data in a non-Microsoft Azure cloud

Storing backup data in an on-premises data center will mean all the backup data is transferred over a site to site VPN. This can take quite some time for the transfer to finish. Apart from data, Microsoft will charge for data leaving Azure.

Another aspect to consider is the time it will take to restore data. In case of a restore, data has to be transferred back from on-premises to the Azure data center.

Storing data in another Azure data center is another option. Note that Microsoft will charge for egress data leaving an Azure data center with destination on-premises or another Azure data center. Bandwidth available for inter-Azure data center traffic is about 10 GB per hour.

Using PowerShell, we have an option to copy blobs from one Azure data center to another. The disadvantage of a blob copy is that the virtual machine accessing that blob should be shutdown. So, in most cases, we cannot use this method. You might think, "So what about geo-replication?". Microsoft makes sure that data is replicated to another data center.

Geo-replicated data is a type of insurance for Microsoft. If Microsoft is not able to recover data due to unavailability in a storage stamp or complete data center, they can decide to make the replicated data primary. Note that as a customer, you have no control over accessing that data.

Microsoft offers read access geo-replication that is in a preview at the time of writing this book. This enables customers to read from the geo-replicated storage. This is ideal for a backup solution.

At the time of writing this, there are no third-party tools that are able to read data from geo-replicated storage. Each blob in the primary location is addressed by using a URL. To read the replicated data a different URL is required.

I do expect that backup vendors will support RA-GRS. This enables customers to restore their data themselves.

Summary

In this chapter, you learned about ways to protect virtual machines running both on-premises and in Microsoft Azure. Microsoft is frequently adding new features that help to protect applications. Azure Site Recovery is a very interesting service to protect Hyper-V virtual machines without huge investments in data center facilities, hardware, and software.

In the next chapter we are going to learn how physical and virtual servers can be migrated to Azure using various types of tools. Microsoft offers some sophisticated tools that allows us to migrate servers to Azure with very limited downtime.

8
Migrating to Microsoft Azure

In the previous chapters, you learned about Azure and how you can extend your on-premises infrastructure to Microsoft Azure. Use case scenarios for linking Azure to on-premise infrastructures are, for example, using a replica of Active Directory or SQL Server in Azure. You also learned how to use Azure to back up data and for disaster recovery orchestration.

In this chapter, we will discuss how to migrate servers, including the applications running on them, to Microsoft Azure as easily as possible.

When you begin planning your migration, you need to consider several key factors, such as cost, business and technical requirements, timeline, and any testing that will be required in the migration process. This chapter focuses mainly on the technical aspects.

In this chapter, we will describe a couple of scenarios for the migration of applications to Microsoft Azure:

- Migrating a Hyper-V virtual machine to Microsoft Azure
- Migrating a VMware vSphere virtual machine to Microsoft Azure
- Migrating an Amazon EC2 virtual machine to Microsoft Azure
- Migrating a physical server to Microsoft Azure

Before moving your servers to Microsoft Azure, you should check a couple of things.

Premigration checks

Let's check the following items and make sure they are available before moving applications to Azure or any other cloud:

- Make sure Microsoft Azure supports the guest operating system. You can check this at `http://msdn.microsoft.com/en-us/library/azure/ee924680.aspx`.

- Check whether the disk volume size of the on-premises server is supported by Microsoft Azure.

- Make sure the application software does not require a dongle for licensing.

- Make sure the software vendor allows moving a license to the cloud or a shared server environment. Some vendors state the license is tied to the instance it was originally installed on. Moving the license to a multitenant infrastructure is not always allowed.

- If you are using an OEM license of Windows Server, you will first need to adjust the license to a volume license. After an OEM license has moved to a server with different hardware than the one it was installed on, it will not boot anymore. This is because an OEM license is glued to the hardware it was installed on.

- Does the SLA of Microsoft meet your expectations of availability? Remember, Microsoft does not provide an SLA for a single virtual machine. The VM needs to be part of an availability set to be able to get a SLA for it.

- Make sure the license is allowed by the software vendor to be moved to the cloud.

The right for movement of licenses to platforms other than the one a license was originally installed on is called license mobility by Microsoft.

License mobility

When a software license has been acquired and installed on a server (either physical or virtual), it is assigned to that server. It is very common for software vendors to disallow licenses to move freely over servers.

One of the reasons for software vendors to disallow free movement of licenses is to prevent customers purchasing a single license that can be used for 24 hours. For example, in a scenario where a customer is using the *follow the sun* principle, software could follow shifts of people working in Asia, then to Europe, and then to the USA. Another reason is software vendors' fear of reduced income when a virtual server running in a multitenant infrastructure is shared by multiple organizations. Instead of selling a license to each organization, only one license would technically be enough.

It is a bit like if a car manufacturer does not allow his cars to be used by a lease company. The car manufacturer only allows selling to consumers directly.

It all comes down to making sure software vendors make the best possible revenue. When software is moved to Azure or any other cloud, we need to verify that this is allowed. Each vendor has its own policies, and understanding the policies is very difficult.

We will focus on policies for Microsoft software in this chapter. We will start looking at licenses with Microsoft Windows Server and desktop operating systems such as Windows 8. It is not allowed to move those licenses to Microsoft Azure. Using Windows client operating systems on Microsoft Azure is not allowed at all.

Windows Server needs to be licensed using the Microsoft **Service Provider License Agreement (SPLA)**. This means customers will need to lease a Windows Server license and pay Microsoft for that. The ability to move Microsoft applications to the cloud depends on the application.

First, a customer will need to have purchased Software Assurance on the product. **Software Assurance (SA)** is a commitment to Microsoft that provides customers with many benefits. One of the benefits of SA is the ability to reuse (move) licenses in the cloud.

Not all Microsoft products are eligible for this right, which Microsoft calls *License Mobility through Software Assurance*. Customer benefits of each Microsoft product are described in a document titled *Product Use Rights* (PUR). This document is updated almost each month. The most recent PUR is published at `http://www.microsoft.com/licensing/products/products.aspx`.

Examples of products that are eligible for License Mobility through SA are:

- Exchange Server 2007 and 2013
- Forefront Identity Manager 2010 R2
- Lync Server 2013
- Microsoft Dynamics CRM 2013 Server
- SharePoint Server 2013
- SQL Server 2014 Standard, Enterprise, and Business Intelligence

Before you move the license to Microsoft Azure, you have to fill in a form to notify Microsoft that you are moving licenses. License Mobility is only allowed to shared data centers that are an Authorized Mobility Partner.

Once we are sure that the license can be moved, it is time to plan for the migration. Let's see what our options are.

Migration options

A few techniques are available to migrate a virtual machine from on-premises to the cloud. In this section, we will discuss the techniques for a migration using Azure as a destination:

- **Offline conversion with considerable downtime**: A conversion is required when the virtual machine running on-premises is using a format that is not supported by the native cloud platform. For example, VMware virtual machines use .vmdk virtual disk files. We cannot place those on Microsoft Azure without first converting the virtual disks to .vhd format.

- **Move with no downtime involved**: A move is basically transfer of the virtual machine without adjustments to the cloud platform. This can currently be done offline for virtual machines using VHD virtual disks running on Hyper-V. At the moment, it is not possible to perform an online migration using Hyper-V Live Migration. It is probably only a matter of time until we can do Live Migrations to the cloud and back.

- **Replication with limited downtime**: Replication means data on a source server is replicated to a target server. The target server is running on a cloud platform and is kept in sync with the source server. In most scenarios, replication is used for disaster recovery purposes, but it can be used to move virtual machines as well. The advantage of using replication is that there is almost no downtime. In July 2014, Microsoft acquired InMage, which has a very interesting migration tool. The tool is now called *Migration Accelerator for Azure*. We will have a look at this tool later.

- **Nesting**: This is a new technique that is available on a few cloud platforms. Basically, nesting means that the virtual machine is not converted but is running on top of a Cloud Application Hypervisor. Ravello Systems offer such a solution for Amazon Web Services, Rackspace, HP Cloud, and Google Compute Engine. VMware virtual machines can run without modifications on those cloud platforms. For Azure, nesting is not possible at the moment. Integration with Azure remains on the Ravello road map.

Offline conversion

The most basic conversion approach available is an offline conversion. A Hyper-V or VMware virtual disk is converted to the virtual disk format supported by Azure. This conversion is done offline. Depending on the size of the virtual disk, this conversion can take many hours. So, you really need to determine for how long applications can be offline by asking the owner of the application. Microsoft offers the Microsoft Virtual Machine Converter software to perform offline conversions.

Since release 3.0, Microsoft Virtual Machine Converter can do two types of conversions:

- Convert virtual machines running on VMware vSphere to either Hyper-V or Azure
- Convert physical servers running Windows Server 2008 or later or Windows Vista or later to Hyper-V

Microsoft Virtual Machine Converter is a free tool. Before the release of Azure Migration Accelerator, this was the only option to convert servers to Azure. Migration Accelerator is a much more mature and feature-rich solution.

Migrating a Hyper-V virtual machine to Microsoft Azure

Hyper-V supports `.vhd` and `.vhdx` virtual disk files. As Microsoft Azure is running Hyper-V as well and also supports both virtual disk types, the migration is quite easy.

In this scenario, we assume the virtual machine can be switched off during the migration to Microsoft Azure. If you cannot afford much downtime, you can use the free Azure Migration Accelerator tool.

The steps involved in migration are:

1. Shut down the virtual machine.
2. Upload all of the `.vhd` files to Microsoft Azure using one of the methods described in the previous chapters.
3. Create one or more disks in the Management Portal using the uploaded `.vhd` files.
4. Create a new virtual machine in Microsoft Azure.
5. Start the virtual machine.
6. Remove the integration tool.

Moving a virtual machine from Azure to on-premises

While the cloud offers many advantages, it may be required to move virtual machines from Azure to on-premises. Currently, this is not possible using Live Migration. Microsoft Azure data centers do not offer such a feature, although technically speaking this should be possible.

Microsoft does offer Live Migration without source and target hosts sharing the same storage. Also, NVGRE allows you to move virtual machines between two networks that are not part of the same network.

We have a few options available to move virtual machines from Azure to on-premises:

- Use a third-party tool and perform a V2V conversion
- Download the .vhd files

Using a third-party tool has the advantage that downtime can be reduced. Most tools offer the ability to copy the virtual machine data to a target server while the source server remains online. The source server is required to be offline only to copy the changed data.

Using a V2V method is described in the next section, where you will learn how to use Double-Take.

Converting a VMware vSphere virtual machine to Microsoft Azure

Virtual machines running on VMware ESXi use the VMDK virtual disk file format. As Azure is based on Hyper-V, it does not support the VMDK format. This implies we need to convert to VHD format.

Several tools can be used to perform such a migration. We will have a look at **Microsoft Virtual Machine Converter** (**MVMC**) 3.0, which is a free tool.

MVMC is designed to convert VMware virtual machines running Linux or Microsoft Windows to Hyper-V or Microsoft Azure. It supports Hyper-V running on Windows Server 2012 R2, Windows Server 2012, and Windows Server 2008 R2 SP1.

It also supports the conversion of virtual machines from VMware vSphere 5.5, VMware vSphere 5.0, and VMware vSphere 4.1 hosts.

MVMC requires an ESX, ESXi, or vCenter Server to connect to. The procedure used by MVMC is as follows:

1. A snapshot of the VMware virtual machine is taken.
2. The virtual machine is shut down.
3. The VMDK file(s) are converted to VHD format. The VHD file is initially stored on the computer that has MVMC installed.
4. The VHD file is uploaded to Microsoft Azure.

A prerequisite is to have a management certificate uploaded to Azure. This certificate is used by MVMC for authentication to Azure.

The procedure to create and upload a certificate is as follows:

1. Make sure `makecert` is available on the server that is used for the conversion.
2. Create the certificate.
3. Export the certificate without the private key to a `.cer` file.
4. Upload the `.cer` file to Azure using the Management Portal.

To create a management certificate, execute the following command on the machine on which you are installing MVMC (start a command prompt as an administrator for that):

```
makecert -sky exchange -r -n "CN=<CertificateName>" -pe -a sha1 -len
2048 -ss My "<CertificateName>.cer"
```

The result is a `.cer` file located in the working folder you started makecert in. The certificate is also added to your personal certificate store. You can check this by using MMC and adding the certificated snap-in.

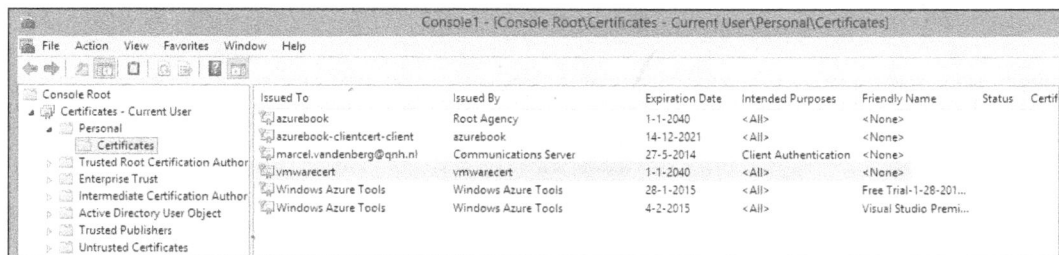

The next step is to add the certificate to the **Trusted Root Certificate Authorities** folder. To do so, select the `.cer` certificate in **Explorer** and double-click on it. Then, perform the following steps:

1. Select **Install Certificate**.
2. Select **Local Machine**.
3. Click on **Next**.
4. Select **Place all certificates in the following store**.
5. Click on **Browse**.
6. Select **Trusted Root Certification Authorities**.
7. Click on **Ok**.
8. Click on **Next**.
9. Click on **Finish**.

Next, upload the certificate to the Azure portal by performing the following steps:

1. Log in to Azure.
2. Select **Settings**.
3. Select **Management Certificates**.
4. Click on **Browse file**.
5. Select the `.cer` file you created earlier.
6. Click on the checkmark.

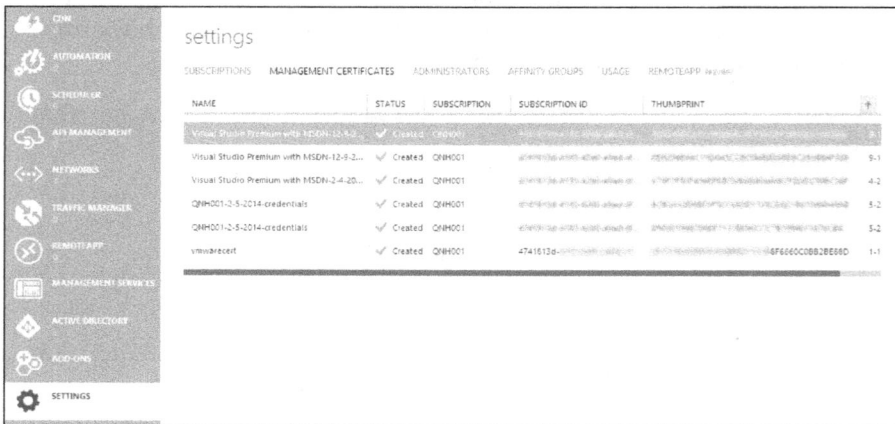

The actual conversion of a VMware virtual machine is quite simple. It is basically a next-next-finish operation.

Microsoft announced Azure Site Recovery will support VMware vSphere in the near future. By using Site Recovery you can easily migrate virtual machines to Azure. Microsoft Migration Accelerator will be used for this conversion and replication.

Migration using Migration Accelerator for Azure

Migration of virtual machines has so far involved some manual labor and downtime of the application. If downtime should be zero or close to zero, a great new tool is Microsoft Migration Accelerator for Azure. Migration Accelerator is able to synchronize source servers with a target in Azure. This is done over HTTPS while the source server is fully operational. To reduce network bandwidth, all data is compressed.

Migration Accelerator for Azure was introduced in September 2014 by Microsoft as a tool for migrations of virtual machines to Microsoft Azure. This tool is based on a tool called *Scout* made by a company called InMage, which Microsoft acquired in July 2014.

Migration Accelerator is an enterprise tool for almost zero downtime migrations of VMware, Hyper-V, Amazon Web Services, and physical servers to Azure. Both Windows and Linux are supported as the source operating system. However, during the preview of Migration Accelerator, support was limited to Windows Server 2008 R2, Windows Server 2012, and 2012 R2.

Migration Accelerator automates all aspects of migration including discovery of source workloads, remote agent installation, network adaptation, and endpoint configuration. With Migration Accelerator, you reduce cost and risk of your migration project.

Migration Accelerator creates a replica of a source server and keeps that replica in sync with the source server on-premises. This means that once both source and target servers are in sync; you can shut down the source server and then boot the target server to complete the migration.

Let's have a look into how Migration Accelerator works under the hood.

As Migration Accelerator was in a limited preview at the time of writing of this book, Microsoft provided limited information on this service. When you initially create the configuration server, make sure you assign a fixed IP address to this server. If the IP address changes, you will need to reinstall the Migration Accelerator software.

What the software does is creates a **virtual disk (VHD)** in Azure for each on-premises source target volume you want to move to Azure. This VHD is then attached to a dedicated server running in Azure. The advantage of not having a replica for each source server is reducing the computing costs in Azure.

To be able to use Migration Accelerator, it is not necessary to have a dedicated connection to Azure using ExpressRoute. It is perfectly possible to use a standard HTTPS Internet connection. However, it is to be noted that the bandwidth can be limited and data security can be an issue. The preferred way of migrating is using a site-to-site VPN or an ExpressRoute connection.

To get an understanding of how Microsoft Migration Accelerator works, we will first discuss the required components.

Components of Migration Accelerator

The following figure shows the components of Migration Accelerator:

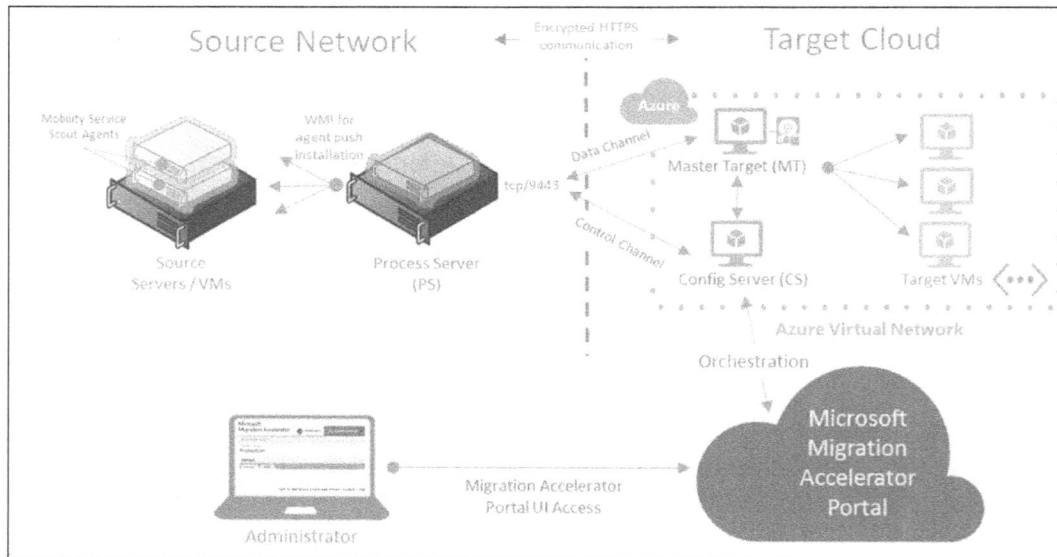

First, each on-premises source server requires a so called *Mobility Service agent* to be installed. This is an agent that can be deployed centrally on physical and virtual servers you would like to migrate to Azure. The agent is responsible for transferring data to the Process Server. To keep the source and target in sync, the agent captures all writes to the disk.

The **Process Server** (PS) is a virtual or physical server installed on-premises. It is responsible for receiving data changes from the source servers, performing compression, encryption, caching, and bandwidth management, before replicating to a secondary location for DR purposes. Data is not sent synchronously. This would have a negative effect on the performance of applications and the application would get a write acknowledge only after the write succeeded, both on the source and target server. The synchronization delay is kept at a minimum, which is about a few seconds.

Always make sure the Process Server is located at the same location as the source servers. This ensures that compute and IO overhead on the source server is kept at a minimum.

The **Master Target** (MT) server is a virtual machine running on Azure. This virtual machine has a virtual disk attached for each replicated on-premises volume. The MT server writes the data it receives from the PS.

If a source server requires a failover, the virtual disk is disconnected from the MT server and connected to a virtual machine on Azure. This means that during replication and synchronization, the actual target virtual machines are not running.

Make sure the size of the MT server is according to the documentation. Microsoft recommends an A4-size virtual machine. This has a maximum of 16 disks. As one disk is reserved for the retention point, an A4 virtual machine will allow the replication of 15 disks as the replication source.

The **Configuration Server** is a Microsoft Azure-based virtual machine that is responsible for communication between the MT server and the **Migration Accelerator** (MA) portal. It also controls the migration process.

The MA portal is a web portal that runs on Azure. You do not have to install this portal. It is provisioned for you when you decide to start using the MA. The portal can be accessed using a domain name such as `<url that is sent to you>.cloudapp.net`. The portal is the control center for your migrations. It will be able to discover source servers in your on-premises infrastructure. Also, the portal provides insight into the replication process.

Installing Migration Accelerator

Installation of the Migration Accelerator components is pretty straightforward. Make sure you have an affinity group, storage account, virtual network, and cloud service already configured before installing the Configuration Server and Master Target server.

First, install the Configuration Server and the Master Target server. Choose virtual machine size **A3** for the Configuration Server and **A4** for the Master Target server.

The Configuration Server communicates with the Process Server installed on-premises. To enable this communication, the Configuration Server requires a public IP address. Microsoft offers five public IP addresses for free for each standard Azure subscription. The soft limit is also five IP addresses, but this can be increased by requesting Microsoft support.

You first need to reserve a public IP address in Azure by using the PowerShell New-AzureReservedIP command. Then, use the reserved IP address for provisioning the virtual machine on which the Configuration Server will be installed.

The process of reserving a public IP is described at http://mythoughtsonit.com/2014/09/step-by-step-reserve-a-public-ip-address-in-azure/.

The Process Server requires Active Directory membership to be able to push the agent to each source virtual machine or physical server.

The following table shows the specification for the Process Server. The sizing depends on the data change rate. The cache disk is used to store replication data before it is copied to Azure.

If you have a daily change rate over 1 TB, it is advised to use additional Process Servers.

Data Change Rate	CPU	Memory	Boot Volume Capacity	Cache Disk Size	Total Disk Throughput Required	NIC Details
Up to 300 GB/day	4 cores	8 GB	40 GB	Minimum of 400 GB	15 – 20 MB/s	2 x 1 GigE with Static IP
Up to 700 GB/day	8 cores	16 GB	40 GB	Minimum of 790 GB	34.9 – 46.6 MB/s	2 x 1 GigE with Static IP
Up to 1 TB/day	8 cores	32 GB	40 GB	Minimum of 790 GB	51.2 – 68.27 MB/s	2 x 1 GigE with Static IP

Microsoft Azure supports operating system disks having a maximum size of 127 GB. Data disks can be up to 1 TB in size. If the source servers have disks larger than the supported size in Azure, you will need to shrink those source disks first.

The process of making disks smaller in size depends on the operating system. If the source server runs on Hyper-V or VMware vSphere, you need to shrink the virtual disk file. The last step is to install the Process Server on-premises.

Using Migration Accelerator

When you are done installing the components, you can configure replication. At sign up for the Migration Accelerator server, you'll receive an e-mail with a URL for the MA portal. Access this portal using that URL.

In the **Cloud Services** tab, select the on-premises servers you want to migrate or protect. Select **Mobility Services** to install the agent on the source server. Once the agent has been installed successfully, click on the **Protect** button and configure the replication settings.

Once replication is configured and the source and target disk are synchronized, you can start migrating the server. Migration means Azure Migration Accelerator creates a new virtual machine on Azure, disconnects the disks from the Master Target server, and attaches the disk to the virtual machine.

Migrating with Double-Take Move

Besides the Azure Migration Accelerator, we can use third-party tools to migrate a source server to Microsoft Azure. The source server can be any Windows Server either running as a physical server or as a virtual machine on VMware vSphere or Microsoft Hyper-V.

We are going to use Double-Take Move for the migration of a Windows server to Microsoft Azure. It is necessary to have a site-to-site VPN connection between your on-premises network and Microsoft Azure. This is because Double-Take uses a dynamic range of RPC ports.

Double-Take has a server and a client component. Double-Take requires an operational Windows server as a target server. This is a difference compared to the Azure Migration Accelerator.

The steps to perform a migration are as follows:

1. Set the source and target server in Double-Take.
2. Perform a migration of data.
3. Cut over the source server to the target server.

Double-Take has the following four options for migration:

- Move data only
- Move an entire server to a new target server
- Move an entire server to a virtual machine running on Hyper-V
- Move and entire server to a virtual machine running on VMware vSphere

The need for Double-Take has reduced quite a bit since Migration Accelerator became available. Double-Take needs an additional software license plus it requires operational target virtual machines. This makes using Double-Take more expensive. To save the trouble of installing, there are multiple pre-installed Double-Take images with various licensing options available in the Azure Marketplace.

Converting an Amazon EC2 virtual machine to Microsoft Azure

Reasons for leaving Amazon EC2 for Azure can be costs, missing features, or the lack of hybrid cloud scenarios. Also, Amazon does not offer the flexibility on how to use your credits like Azure does. On Amazon, customers spend money on storage and compute credits. Compute credits that are not consumed cannot be used for paying usage of storage resources. This is unlike Azure, which has a single credit. The credit can be spent on any available Azure resource.

As Amazon is using the **Amazon Machine Image (.AMI)**, you will need to convert an Amazon virtual machine if you want to run this virtual machine on Microsoft Azure.

A couple of scenarios are possible to perform the conversion. You could use a V2V conversion tool that performs a direct conversion. You will probably need to create a direct VPN connection between Azure and Amazon.

We will focus in this paragraph on some free tools that allow a simple conversion of a virtual machine. This method is not well suited for mass conversions of virtual machines. The transfer will probably take a long time to complete depending on the WAN bandwidth available.

The steps required to migrate from Amazon to Azure are as follows:

1. Convert disks of the Windows Server instance running on AWD to `.vhd` files.
2. Download the VHD files to on-premises.
3. Convert to VHD and install Hyper-V Integrations Tools.
4. Upload the VHD files to Azure.
5. Create a new Azure virtual machine.

Migrating using Disk2VHD and PowerShell scripts

In this scenario, we are going to use the free SysInternals tool Disk2VHD to create a snapshot of a running virtual machine on Amazon. Then we are going to download the VHD to a Hyper-V host. When that is done, the VHD is uploaded to Azure and a virtual machine is created.

The following steps are performed for this scenario. (This is a high-level overview. For a complete, detailed, step-by-step description, search for a Microsoft blog post titled *Guided Hands-on Lab: Migrate VMs to Windows Azure from Amazon AWS*.)

1. RDP to the virtual machine running on Amazon that you want to migrate to Azure.

2. Download and install Disk2VHD.

3. Execute Disk2VHD. Select a local disk of the virtual machine as a destination.

4. Next we need to use the Amazon AWS PowerShell module. Using this module, the VHD disk is transferred from the Amazon virtual machine to an Amazon S3 bucket. This can be compared to Azure Storage. This step is required so we can download the VHD from Amazon to an on-premises Hyper-V server.

5. When the VHD file is located on a local server, we need to convert the disk. Azure does not support dynamic disks, so we need to covert the disk to a fixed sized VHD. PowerShell has a `Convert-VHD` cmdlet that allows us to perform such a conversion.

6. Next we need to add the Hyper-V Integration Services into the VHD. This can be done using PowerShell.

7. The next step is to upload the VHD to Azure. This can be done using PowerShell.

8. When the VHD is uploaded, we can create a new virtual machine using the VHD again using PowerShell or manually via the Azure Management Portal.

Using Windows Azure Migrator

Windows Azure Migrator is a free tool that assists in a migration from Amazon to Azure. The steps are very easy:

1. You connect using RDP to the source server running in Amazon.

2. Then you start a browser and enter the URL `http://www.azuremigrator.net`.

3. Select the drives you would like to migrate. Currently only the system disk `C:` is supported.

4. Fill in the subscription ID of Azure.

5. A certificate will be created. Upload the certificate to Azure.

6. Select the storage account or create a new account.

7. Select the virtual machine size and the cloud service.

As you can see, in a few simple steps, a virtual machine can be migrated to Azure. A detailed instruction can be found at `http://miteshc.wordpress.com/2014/03/20/migratevm-fromaws-toazure/`.

Migrating Azure deployments between data centers and subscriptions

It is very well possible you would like to either move a set of virtual machines to another Azure data center or duplicate a set of virtual machines from a data center and deploy those in a different data center. Think about these scenarios:

- Deploy to multiple data centers. You have built a set of virtual machines that serve an application in a single Azure data center. For high availability or disaster recovery reasons, you may want to duplicate this deployment to a different Azure data center.

- Avoid downtime because of maintenance. You have an application running on a single VM in a single Azure data center. You want to avoid the downtime when Microsoft performs maintenance. So the application needs to be deployed in a different Azure data center as well.

- Moving between subscriptions. Suppose you created virtual machines under a single Azure subscription and want to move those virtual machines to a different Azure subscription, or want to move virtual machines from a test environment to a production environment.

- Move to a different Azure data center. Suppose Microsoft opens a new data center that better fits your needs, for example, because it is located closer to your location.

Microsoft Azure at the moment does not offer a built-in feature to execute these scenarios.

However, in January 2015, Microsoft and Persistent Systems have rolled out an Azure Data Center Migration Solution 1.0 tool. This is an open source and free to use tool for migrations of Azure IaaS deployments.

You can migrate all of the following resources in the source data center:

- Affinity groups
- Networks
- Cloud services
- Storage accounts
- Virtual machines (VMs)

Basically, the tool automates the export and import of the preceding Azure services.

The big advantage of this tool is the automation. It will do all the work for you to move or duplicate deployments. Copying virtual disks is done in a parallel way. However, the source virtual machines are switched off before the copy process starts.

If you cannot accept downtime, you will have to use an agent-based tool like Migration Accelerator or Double-Take.

The Azure Data Center Migration Solution Tool can run on either an on-premises virtual machine or an Azure virtual machine. Supported operating systems are Windows 7 Service Pack 1 or higher and Windows Server 2008 R2 SP1 and higher.

The tool is based on PowerShell, so to use it successfully you need PowerShell skills. However, a key advantage of this solution is the flexibility and extensibility provided by the template-based and open source approach.

Azure Data Center Migration Solution Tool can be downloaded here:

```
https://github.com/persistentsystems/adcms
```

Summary

In this chapter, we discussed several tools that allow us to migrate servers to Microsoft Azure. The Azure Migration Accelerator is a very promising tool that allows multiple orchestrated migrations with hardly any downtime.

This chapter is the final technical chapter of this book. *Chapter 9, Summary and a Look into the Near Future*, will give a preview of what possible new features Azure will may bring in the future.

9
Summary and a Look into the Near Future

Congratulations! You made it to the last chapter of this book. I really hope you enjoyed reading the information and hope you learned from it. It would be great if it enables you to feel comfortable about using Microsoft Azure in your environment.

This book took you on a trip that started in the 18th century. We looked at the development of electrical power; the development of cloud computing could go the same direction. However, some major hurdles need to be overcome. The breakthrough for electricity as a utility was the discovery of alternate current. A hurdle for adoption of cloud computing in many countries is security of data. The Patriot Act and other US laws certainly make some organizations reserved about using the cloud. These issues are likely to be solved in the near future by technologies such as encryption or by adjustments of US laws. This industry is just starting on the journey of discovering the amazing possibilities of the cloud, and cost reductions and agility will surely convince many to start using cloud computing.

Then, we had a look at Microsoft Cloud OS, which is not a product but a vision of Microsoft to create a connected infrastructure using on-premises, Azure, and service provider resources that are managed as one big resource pool. Hybrid cloud is seen by many, including Gartner, as the next big thing. First, there was private cloud, and now hybrid cloud will start to march towards maturity.

As Azure is being developed, more and more features and services are being added. It started as a PaaS platform and now offers IaaS as well. However, remember that Azure offers a less rich feature set than on-premises Hyper-V. Microsoft still needs to make improvements in the availability of single instance virtual machines, clustering support, and remote console support.

As this book was printed at least a couple of weeks before you are reading this, it is likely that Azure has changed quite a bit. The challenge of writing a book on cloud computing is to keep it as current as possible for when it is going to be published.

This book explained how to create a virtual machine and how to connect Azure Virtual Networks to your on-premises environment. You also learned how to migrate from Hyper-V, VMware, and Amazon to Azure. You even looked at what is happening under the hood of Azure data centers.

The road ahead

Challenging and exciting times are ahead. I am sure what we see developing today is only the beginning. Microsoft is releasing new Azure features about once every three weeks. This is an incredible pace. Massive amounts of resources are spent on making sure the cloud is the next phase in IT. The shift has already started. Sales of servers manufactured by established vendors like IBM and HP are going down. Applications are offered on the Internet as Software as a Service and consumed by using a browser. Microsoft releases new features in its cloud-based software first before releasing them for on-premises solutions. Traditional fat desktops are swapped for thin, lightweight clients with just enough software to connect to the Internet and offer a browser and lightweight office tools.

Oracle and Citrix were amongst the first major software vendors supporting Azure. SAP joined later in 2014. Many more will follow soon.

How will Microsoft Azure develop in the next few years? What features and services will be making their way onto their roadmap? These are questions that are hard to answer, as nobody outside Microsoft really knows. A few guesses of features that are likely to come and are maybe even offered when you are reading this are as follows:

- Support for VHDX
- More granular access control for Azure Management Portal administrators
- Support for multiple IP addresses on a network interface
- Support for multiple 10 Gbps network interfaces
- Support for audit trails
- A limited or no downtime at all for single instance virtual machines during Microsoft maintenance
- A service-level agreement for single instance virtual machines
- Reduction of costs for storage and compute
- Many more new data centers

- Live migration from Hyper-V to Microsoft Azure
- Replication of VMware virtual machines and physical servers using Azure Site Recovery
- More features for billing
- Backup of virtual machine data stored in Azure
- Azure hosts with dedicated graphical cards to support high performance graphics applications for Desktop as a Service
- Support for Generation 2 VM's by Azure Site Recovery

If you would like to request a feature from Microsoft, you can use this forum: http://feedback.azure.com/forums/216843-virtual-machines.

Here you will find many requests of customers using Azure for new features. For the Virtual Machine service, the most requested feature at the moment is console access.

Many improvements are to be made on the storage level. In the near future, customers will probably be able to have a minimum guaranteed number of IOPS per disk or per virtual machine. This will make sure your application will perform as expected with controls at a more granular level.

Currently, backup storage is stored on either production storage or Azure Vault, which is much more expensive. It is likely that an offline tier such as Amazon Glacier will become available, which allows cheap archiving of data.

Software solutions that use Azure raw storage and turn this into software-based network attached storage with features such as on-premises NAS and SAN are another likely enhancement. SoftNAS is such an example currently available for Amazon.

Azure already supports serving applications by RemoteApp. The alliance with Citrix opened up many new avenues such as running XenDesktop and XenApp on Azure. Citrix Workspace Services is an interesting new concept enabling a central management console for apps and desktop publishing.

For disaster recovery, I expect some additional features to be added soon. Currently, when there is an issue with storage affecting virtual machine availability, customers have to wait for Microsoft to failover to the paired region. The decision to failover is difficult, as this will mean customers will lose data. Also, virtual machines will need to be recreated at the alternate region after a failover, which is unacceptable for larger deployments. I expect many improvements in regards to the protection of virtual machines.

Amazon Web Services is considered by Gartner as the leader in the Magic Quadrant for Cloud Infrastructure as a Service. Amazon has many features at the moment and has much more compute and storage capacity. However, Amazon is lacking a hybrid cloud strategy. While Amazon is good for hosting greenfield, newly developed, and scalable cloud applications, it lacks features to connect on-premises applications to services running in the cloud. Microsoft has a big advantage in having many customers using Microsoft products in their on-premises environment. These Microsoft solutions are increasingly able to use Azure resources. We have to wait and see how this advantage pays off in the end.

While technically still a bit immature, there are more important possible showstoppers to adopt the cloud besides lack of features. Especially in Europe and South America, many organizations are not very willing to store data in clouds owned by US companies. There is a lot of fear that the NSA, FBI, or other US authorities might be looking at their data—not to search for evidence of threats to US safety, but more often to have a look at information that might be beneficial for the US economy or politics.

Microsoft and other cloud service providers are working hard to solve this major issue, at least for Europe. Encryption of all the data being transferred into the cloud is a possible solution that will, however, present some new challenges in data management. How will enterprises make sure encryption keys are available when required? If keys are lost, the data is lost as well. Microsoft will not be able to assist in recovery of encryption keys, nor the NSA (I assume).

To enable customers to dip their toes into cloud computing, Microsoft started Azure Site Recovery. Site Recovery allows Azure to be used as a replication target for on-premises Hyper-V environments. A customer owned second datacenter for disaster recovery reasons is not required anymore, offering large cost reductions as a result.

Another tool to make the transition to Azure easier is Azure Migration Accelerator.

Once customers are used to the benefits of the cloud by using Azure Site Recovery, it is expected they will slowly start to deploy virtual machines for test and development purposes. After all, the virtual machines are already stored in the cloud, so deploying production applications in the cloud will be the next logical step.

Third-party vendors will offer a number of solutions to enhance Azure. We will see the same as what happened to Hyper-V a few years ago. Initially, just a few vendors offered solutions that supported Hyper-V. Over the years, many vendors started supporting Hyper-V. Now, Hyper-V has a fast growing ecosystem of solutions.

Zerto, which offers disaster recovery software for vSphere infrastructures, now has software that is able to perform cross-hypervisor replication. So, a vSphere virtual machine can be replicated to a Hyper-V virtual machine. In the near future, it is likely that Zerto or other companies will support the same for replication to Microsoft Azure data centers.

Amazon already has a large ecosystem of such vendors.

Additional tools will benefit from enhanced APIs such as the ones Amazon already offers. Amazon has APIs that allow a detailed monitoring of health and capacity. Also, APIs for billing are very mature.

Currently, just a few appliances are supported to run on Azure. Kemp and Barracuda Networks are about the only vendors supporting Azure. Citrix will probably soon add Azure support to their NetScaler solutions as well as for App Controller.

There are many more possible enhancements to think of. The ones above are just some educated guesses of mine.

To keep abreast of the developments on Microsoft Azure, please check out my blog on http://up2v.nl or follow me on Twitter at @marcelvandenber.

Many thanks for taking the time to read this book. Hope you liked it!

Configuration Maximums

This appendix provides an overview of the configuration maximums of Microsoft Azure. The information in this appendix is useful for designing and managing an infrastructure running on Azure.

For some parts of the Azure subscription, soft limits are effective. If you want to increase a soft limit, contact Microsoft Azure support.

The limits are adjusted by Microsoft on a regular basis. Check this Microsoft article for the most up-to-date limits: `http://azure.microsoft.com/en-us/documentation/articles/azure-subscription-service-limits/`.

Subscription limits

The following table shows the subscription limits:

Resource	Soft limit	Hard limit
Total number of cores assigned to virtual machines	20	10,000
Co-administrators per subscription	200	200
Storage accounts per subscription	100	100
Cloud services per subscription	20	200
Virtual networks per subscription	10	100
Local networks per subscription	10	100
DNS servers per subscription	9	100
Reserved IP per subscription	5	100
Hosted service certificates per subscription	400	400
Affinity groups per subscription	256	256
Hosted service certificates per subscription	400	400

Virtual machine limits

The following table shows the virtual machine limits:

Resource	Soft limit	Hard limit
Virtual machines per cloud service	50	50
Input endpoints per cloud service	150	150

Storage limits

This table shows the storage limits for Microsoft Azure. There are no soft limits for storage:

Resource	Hard limit
TB per storage account	500
Max IOPS for persistent disk for standard tier	500
Max IOPS for persistent disk for basic tier	300
Max IOPS per storage account	20,000
Maximum size of VHD	1 TB
Maximum number of disks per virtual machine	16

Networking limits

This table shows the limits for networking items in Microsoft Azure. There are no soft limits for networking:

Resource	Hard limit
Access control lists per endpoint	50
Concurrent TCP connections for a virtual machine or role instance	500K
Total number of virtual machines part of a virtual network	2048
Local network sites per virtual network	10
Number of site to site connections for a single Azure virtual network (default)	10
ExpressRoute maximum throughput for Azure Virtual Network Gateway	500 Mbps

Resource	Hard limit
Site to Site VPN maximum throughput for Azure Virtual Network Gateway	80 Mbps
Number of site to site connections for a single Azure virtual network High Performance Gateway	30
ExpressRoute maximum throughput for Azure Virtual Network High Performance Gateway	1000 Mbps
Site to Site VPN maximum throughput for Azure Virtual Network High Performance Gateway	200 Mbps
Number of Public IP (PIP) addresses per subscription	5
Number of reserved IP addresses per subscription	20 (hard limit of 100)

Index

A

Access control list (ACL)
  about 122
  enabling 122
affinity group
  about 62, 63
  creating 101
agility 8
alternate current (AC) 2
Amazon Web Services (AWS) 3
App Controller 25
architecture, Microsoft Azure Storage
  Front End (FE) layer 65
  partition layer 65
  stream layer 66
availability sets 59, 60
Azure Academic Pass
  URL 50
Azure Cross-Platform Command-line
    Interface (X-Plat CLI) 57
Azure Directory
  about 97
  additional administrators, adding to
    subscription 99
  Azure subscription, determining 98, 99
  global administrator role 97
  roles 98
  user role 97
  WAAD Premium 98
Azure ExpressRoute 81
Azure Management Portal
  about 88
  demo page 89
  features 89

  URL 88
  used, for deploying VM Depot images 114
Azure networks
  creating 103
  custom DNS server, creating 106
  custom DNS server, using 105
  DNS servers 103
  local network, creating 105
  local networks 103
  virtual network, creating 103, 104
  virtual network, deleting 106
  virtual network gateways 105
  virtual networks 103
Azure Preview
  about 34, 35
  URL 35
Azure region
  compliance 100
  deciding, for placement 100
  performance 100
Azure solutions
  categories 30
Azure subscription
  about 94
  Resource Groups 95, 96
  subscription name, adjusting 96
Azure use cases
  Big Data 31
  Dev/test 31
  identity and access management 31
  Media 31
  Mobile Apps services 30
  storage, backup, and recovery 31
  Websites 30
Azure Virtual Network 33

B

barriers for adoption, public cloud
  loss of control 10
  security 10
  vendor lock-in 11
best effort cloud
  about 54
  Microsoft Azure 36
  versus reliable clouds 35
broad network access 4

C

caching modes
  None 71
  ReadOnly 71
  ReadWrite 71
cattle type application
  versus, pet type application 13, 14
Cerebrata Azure Explorer 75
Chaos Monkey tool 14
cloud
  about 3
  essential characteristics 4
  exit plan 15, 16
  history 22
  using 14
cloud computing
  benefits 9
cloud deployment models
  about 6
  community cloud 7
  hybrid cloud 7
  private cloud 6
  public cloud 6
cloud exit strategy 15
cloud services
  about 58, 79
  creating 106-108
  deleting 109
  purpose 107
cloud washing 3
CloudXplorer 75
Communication as a Service (CaaS) 6
community cloud 7
configuration extensions 112

Content Delivery Networks (CDN) 53
custom DNS servers
  creating 105, 106

D

data centers 51
data disks 69, 70
Data Protection Manager 26
dedicated cloud
  versus private virtual cloud 36, 37
Desktop as a Service 6
Disaster Recovery as a Service 6
disk caching
  about 71
  modes 71
disks, Azure
  about 69
  data disks 69
  operating system disks 69
  temporary disks 69
distributed and replicated file system
  (DFS) layer 66
DNS server configuration
  setting 124
Dynamic IP (DIP) 117

E

elasticity 8
electricity, as utility 2, 3
endpoints
  about 82, 83
  creating 122
  virtual machine endpoints, testing 123
essential characteristics, cloud
  about 4
  broad network access 4
  on-demand self-service 4
  rapid elasticity 4
  resource pooling 4

F

Fabric Agent (FA) 55
Fabric Controller (FC) 56, 57
fault domains 58
Forefront Identity Manager (FIM) 98

Application Programming
    Interface (API) 26
  services 26
Windows Server 2012 22, 23

Z

zones 53

[PACKT] PUBLISHING enterprise 器
professional expertise distilled

Thank you for buying
Managing Microsoft Hybrid Clouds

About Packt Publishing

Packt, pronounced 'packed', published its first book, *Mastering phpMyAdmin for Effective MySQL Management*, in April 2004, and subsequently continued to specialize in publishing highly focused books on specific technologies and solutions.

Our books and publications share the experiences of your fellow IT professionals in adapting and customizing today's systems, applications, and frameworks. Our solution-based books give you the knowledge and power to customize the software and technologies you're using to get the job done. Packt books are more specific and less general than the IT books you have seen in the past. Our unique business model allows us to bring you more focused information, giving you more of what you need to know, and less of what you don't.

Packt is a modern yet unique publishing company that focuses on producing quality, cutting-edge books for communities of developers, administrators, and newbies alike. For more information, please visit our website at www.packtpub.com.

About Packt Enterprise

In 2010, Packt launched two new brands, Packt Enterprise and Packt Open Source, in order to continue its focus on specialization. This book is part of the Packt Enterprise brand, home to books published on enterprise software – software created by major vendors, including (but not limited to) IBM, Microsoft, and Oracle, often for use in other corporations. Its titles will offer information relevant to a range of users of this software, including administrators, developers, architects, and end users.

Writing for Packt

We welcome all inquiries from people who are interested in authoring. Book proposals should be sent to author@packtpub.com. If your book idea is still at an early stage and you would like to discuss it first before writing a formal book proposal, then please contact us; one of our commissioning editors will get in touch with you.

We're not just looking for published authors; if you have strong technical skills but no writing experience, our experienced editors can help you develop a writing career, or simply get some additional reward for your expertise.

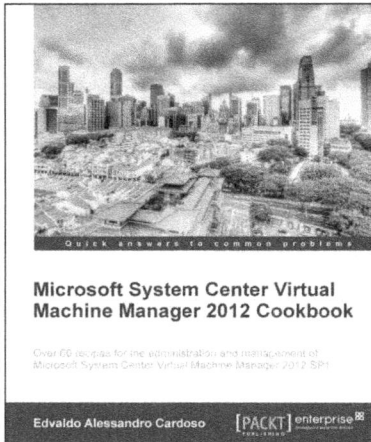

Microsoft System Center Virtual Machine Manager 2012 Cookbook

ISBN: 978-1-84968-632-7   Paperback: 342 pages

Over 60 recipes for the administration and management of Microsoft System Center Virtual Machine Manager 2012 SP1

1. Create, deploy, and manage datacentres, private and hybrid clouds with hybrid hypervisors by using VMM 2012 SP1, App Controller, and Operations Manager.

2. Integrate and manage fabric (compute, storages, gateways, networking) services and resources. Deploy Clusters from bare metal servers.

3. Learn how to use VMM 2012 SP1 features such as Windows 2012 and SQL 2012 support, Network Virtualization, Live Migration, Linux VMs, Resource Throttling, and Availability

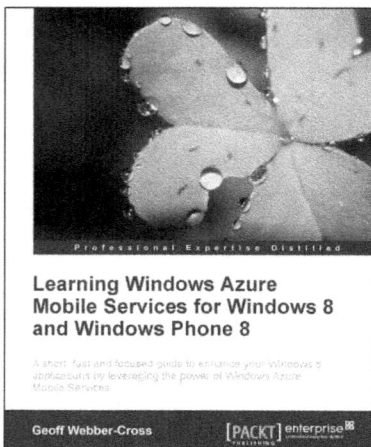

Microsoft System Center Virtual Machine Manager 2012 Cookbook

Over 60 recipes for the administration and management of Microsoft System Center Virtual Machine Manager 2012 SP1

Edvaldo Alessandro Cardoso

Learning Windows Azure Mobile Services for Windows 8 and Windows Phone 8

ISBN: 978-1-78217-192-8   Paperback: 124 pages

A short, fast and focused guide to enhance your Windows 8 applications by leveraging the power of Windows Azure Mobile Services

1. Dive deep into Azure Mobile Services with a practical XAML-based case study game.

2. Enhance your applications with Push Notifications and Notifications Hub.

3. Follow step-by-step instructions for result-oriented examples.

Learning Windows Azure Mobile Services for Windows 8 and Windows Phone 8

A short, fast and focused guide to enhance your Windows 8 applications by leveraging the power of Windows Azure Mobile Services

Geoff Webber-Cross

Please check **www.PacktPub.com** for information on our titles

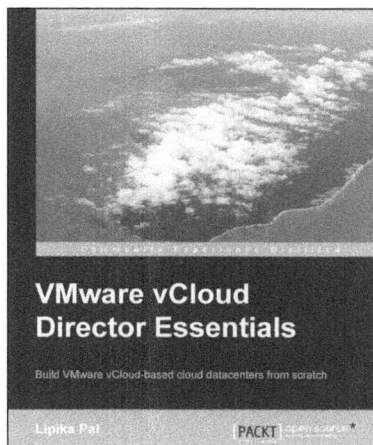

VMware vCloud Director Essentials

ISBN: 978-1-78398-652-1   Paperback: 198 pages

Build VMware vCloud-based cloud datacenters from scratch

1. Learn about DHCP, NAT, and VPN services to successfully implement a private cloud.

2. Configure different networks such as Direct connect, Routed, or Isolated.

3. Configure and manage vCloud Director's access control.

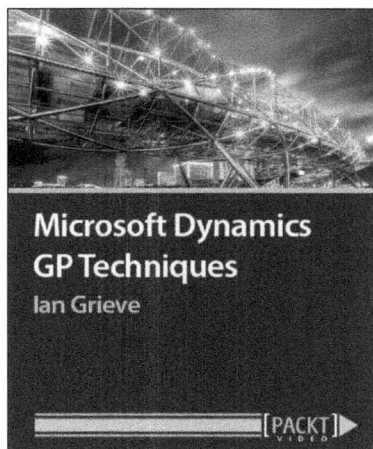

Microsoft Dynamics GP Techniques [Video]

ISBN: 978-1-84968-932-8   Duration: 02:08 hrs

Watch and learn techniques to master Microsoft Dynamics GP; improve know-how and maximize your performance

1. Learn how to keep data tidy while speeding up data entry and reducing entry errors.

2. Follow carefully organized sequences of instructions as they're performed in an easy to follow step-by-step video guide.

3. Learn advanced methods of enquiring, reporting, and system maintenance.

4. Clear, concise, self-contained videos each covering a technique, tip or feature.

www.ingramcontent.com/pod-product-compliance
Lightning Source LLC
Chambersburg PA
CBHW080936220326
41598CB00034B/5806